BY THE EDITORS OF CONSUMER GUIDE®

WHOLE BATHROOM CATALOG

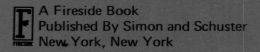
A Fireside Book
Published By Simon and Schuster
New York, New York

CONTENTS

Manufactured in the United States of America
1 2 3 4 5 6 7 8 9 10

A Fireside Book
Published by Simon and Schuster
A Division of Gulf & Western Corporation
New York, New York 10020

Library of Congress Catalog Card Number: 79-8045
ISBN: 0-671-25200-3 (cloth)
       0-671-24768-9 (quality paper)

CREDITS

Lifestyle Design—Photos

Amerec Corp., page 8
American Olean Tile Co., pages 7, 10, 11
Artesian Industries, page 6
Crane Co., page 9
Kohler Co., page 5

Dream Bathrooms

Photographer: Kurt Brabbée

Remodeling Home Is Her Labor Of Love
Designer: Arlene Semel
Architect: Ronald Handler

Landmark Home Looks Glorious
Designer: Arlene Semel

Tiny Room Looks Bigger Than It Is
Architect: Ronald Zriny
Owner: Bruce Ross

Elegance Is Architect's Custom
Architect: Joel Scheckerman
Owners: Mr. & Mrs. Robert Wislow

Taking Charge Has Headaches And Rewards
Owners: Mr. & Mrs. David Liddell

Wide-Open Spaces Suit City Clan
Owners: Mr. & Mrs. Jerry Barrad

Promise Fulfilled: Home Is Perfect
Designer: Arlene Semel

Sometimes It's Best To Break A Few Rules
Architect: Ronald Zriny
Owners: Mr. & Mrs. Michael Murphy

Bachelor Creates An Opulent Condo
Owner: Lowell Wohlfiel

Couple Finds Just The Right Angle
Designer: William Ishmael
Owners: Mr. & Mrs. Bruce Powell

Design Matches The Address Of Success
Designer: Shelly Barrad

House Grows To Fit Family, Move Avoided
Designer/Contractor: Nick Barba

There Was Nowhere To Go But Up
Designer: William Ishmael
Owners: Mr. & Mrs. Jerry Reinsdorf

Townhouse Is Black And White And Beautiful
Owners: Mr. & Mrs. William Nellis

Eminent Victorian Has Charm
Architect: Ronald Zriny
Owners: Mr. & Mrs. Stanley Pillman

Floor plans and illustrations: Clarence Moberg
Cover Design: Frank Peiler
Cover Photographs: Kurt Brabbée

There is no rule requiring that a bathroom be merely utilitarian. Every household has different needs. Your bathroom should be suited to the lifestyle of the people who use it daily.

Lifestyle Design

We all know that a home bathroom is a good deal more than just a room containing a lavatory basin, toilet, and bathtub. Every bathroom is different, and every person or family has different basic requirements for a bathroom, as well as different notions as to just what constitutes an ideal arrangement.

If you are planning to remodel existing facilities, the first step is to analyze thoroughly all of the needs and requirements of the occupants of the house, evaluate in depth the existing facilities, and then relate the two. This will point up both the shortcomings and the assets of the existing bathroom. If you are planning to build a new bathroom, begin by analyzing your needs and requirements, then work out the ideal general bathroom arrangement to suit. In both cases, the next step is to decide exactly and in detail what you can do to reach your goal. All of this requires a good deal of

pondering, soul-searching, research, thought and, probably, a good deal of head-scratching.

The following is set forth with the remodeling of an existing bathroom in mind. However, the ingredients are much the same for considering the addition of an entirely new bathroom.

EVALUATION

Analyzing the needs and requirements of the occupants of the household, considering their desires and evaluating the existing facilities, requires asking a good many questions and conferring with other members of the household. Making notes is a good idea so that you can later refine all the information into a set of specifications and a working plan.

Family Size

Although a single person or a couple might get by quite nicely with a lavatory basin, toilet, and stall shower in a small room, the convenience of this kind of an arrangement diminishes rapidly as the number of users increases. The larger the family, the larger the bathroom should be, not only in terms of square footage, but also with respect to storage space of all kinds, bathroom accessories and perhaps plumbing fixtures as well. In many circumstances, auxiliary bathrooms are the only good solution to a crowding problem. If family growth is anticipated, take this into consideration, too.

Ages Of Family Members

The ages of the various members of the family also will have a bearing upon bathroom design. Toddlers have one set of requirements, youngsters another, and teenagers often have still another. Adults in good health generally carry the same set of needs and requirements (as far as bathrooms are concerned) for a good many years. Elderly persons are frequently less able to cope than others, and may need special aids for convenience and safety in the bathroom. There are no blanket rules; this is a matter of tailoring the bathroom to the requirements dictated by the various ages of the family members.

Family Schedule

When there is one bathroom available and six persons who must use it—often all at the same time—the inevitable result is chaos, confusion, and perhaps short tempers. Multiple bathrooms can alleviate this situation and so can a compartmented bathroom. Even just two washbasins in a well-arranged master bathroom will allow a working couple to simultaneously prepare themselves each morning with minimum mutual interference. Bathroom facilities should be extensive enough and so arranged as to eliminate or at least minimize conflicts in bathroom use.

Bathroom Size

Comfort, convenience, and general usability are dependent to a great extent upon the size of the bathroom. There has to be a certain minimum amount of room around, and spacing between, plumbing fixtures and storage facilities, but minimum spacing or small rooms should only be employed where overall house space is at a high premium. For best results, plumbing fixtures should be comfortably spaced, storage facilities and furnishings well-arranged, and plenty of free space included for maneuvering room. Spaciousness aids in cleaning, and layout is important, too.

Arrange everything to eliminate nooks and crannies, awkward placements and interfering elements.

Although a small and compact house is well-served by a single central bathroom, a large and sprawling ranch house may not be. For convenience, a two-story house might best have two bathrooms, one up and one down. A spread-out design might call for a substantial master bathroom plus one or two smaller auxiliary bathrooms. The positioning of a bathroom in the floor plan is important, too; the room should be easily accessible with no awkward traffic patterns and a minimum of inconvenience or long trips for the users.

Plumbing Fixtures

The minimum fixtures for a full bath consist of toilet, lavatory basin, and bathing unit—bathtub, tub/shower, or stall shower. Old fixtures can be replaced or refinished and their mechanical and plumbing parts rebuilt or replaced.

Storage

A single medicine cabinet is by no means sufficient storage space for even a tiny bathroom. Plans for either remodeling or a new bathroom should include ample storage for medicines and bathroom supplies, health aids, sickroom apparatus, toweling, make-up articles and similar gear. Within reason, the more storage space that a bathroom has, the more convenient and workable it will be.

Electrical

A dark and gloomy bathroom is dreary, inefficient, and potentially dangerous. Old and worn lighting fixtures, wall switches, and wiring are also dangerous, particularly in a bathroom. There should be enough lighting fixtures to give a high level of general illumination, plus more intense lighting at lavatory mirrors and make-up areas. Switch control should be convenient, and the entire bathroom electrical system in top repair and well-grounded.

Heating

To avoid drafts, bathroom heat should be distributed as evenly as possible; it is preferable that heat in the bathroom be controlled by an individual thermostat. Heat capacity should be sufficient to maintain a temperature of as high as 80°F, if necessary, for maximum comfort. The room should be draft-free, including cold air falls from windows and skylights. Bathing fixtures are best not installed against an outside wall in cold climates.

Extra Facilities

Current lifestyles often demand that a bathroom have extra facilities beyond a purely functional arrangement. The specifics vary greatly but include multiple and perhaps compartmented plumbing fixtures, the presence of both bathtub and shower, dressing space with

Good lighting can be decorative as well as functional. In the bathroom at left, general ceiling lighting reflects off sleek surfaces to create an atmosphere of cool efficiency. At right, localized lighting from the soffit over the counters creates a welcoming coziness when combined with the warm, earthy tones of tile and wood.

Some people like to refresh themselves in a sauna at the end of a hard day. To others, a whirlpool tub is the ideal way to relax. Is your bathroom too small for such features? Consider stealing space from an adjacent room or taking over completely a seldom-used room.

attendant closet storage, make-up table or counter, exercising equipment, or health-care equipment such as whirlpool bath or sauna. In many cases the extras extend to furnishings for quiet relaxation, planters, sunbathing equipment, stereo music gear, and similar somewhat luxurious items.

Bathroom Beauty

Attractiveness has little to do with the proper functioning of bathroom facilities, but for most people it is an important factor in livability. It also plays a part in the overall value of the property.

Is your bathroom ceiling showing its age? Is the wall covering faded, dismal-looking, and beginning to lift off its backing? How about the floor; is it worn and lifeless, perhaps uneven, or the covering beginning to curl in spots? And the fixtures; are they scratched and stained, finish worn off the faucets, styles long outmoded? If any of this is so, your bathroom is below par, and work needs to be done. And that's true not only from the standpoint of beauty, but also because a shabby, run-down bathroom can be unhygienic and unhealthy, both physically and psychologically.

WHAT TO DO?

Analysis and evaluation points up needs, wants, shortcomings, and strong points in existing or planned bathroom facilities. Next you must decide what to do to make those facilities fully effective and compatible with your goals. This is not an easy chore, because the choices seem endless and compromise is inevitable. The budget is one big restraint—few of us can afford everything we'd like to have. Practicality also is a big factor, closely allied to cost. There might be other limiting factors, too, such as building codes, what materials are locally available, and structural problems or space considerations. The choices must be weighed and balanced against the constraints to arrive at an ultimate plan workable for you.

Apart from building an entirely new bathroom from scratch, either by addition to, or construction within, an existing house, there are four basic approaches to upgrading bathroom facilities: adding extras, redecorating, redesigning, or complete remodeling.

Adding Extras

Adding a few extra pieces of equipment is sometimes all that is needed to make a bathroom satisfactorily functional, livable, and/or attractive. For instance, you might replace a single lavatory with a double, convert a bathtub to a tub/shower, add a bidet or even build in a sauna. If a lack of storage space is a principal cause for dissatisfaction, the situation can be remedied by adding cabinetry; even where space is at a premium there is nearly always some way to expand storage facilities. Consider above-toilet shelves, vanity and hamper cabinets, medicine cabinets, shelving sections and the like. Space-saving devices, such as small racks and swing-out shelves, can be installed in existing shelving or cabinetry to increase effective storage space.

Inadequate lighting can be corrected by devising a new lighting plan and adding lighting fixtures. Unsatisfactory heating or ventilating can be improved by installing new comfort heater units or vent fans, or combination units. Comfort and convenience might be improved by adding new furnishings. Beauty might be enhanced by building planters, sprucing up window-shade treatment or putting in a bathroom carpet ensemble. The addition of simple bathroom accessories can simultaneously enhance decor, increase con-

venience, and improve safety and functionalism. Installing more or larger mirrors, for instance, is a step both decorative and practical.

A judicious selection of added extras can improve the bathroom sufficiently that no further work is needed. Costs are largely confined to the prices of the articles themselves, since in most (though not all) cases they can be installed by the buyer. Even if professional installation is required, a large outlay is seldom involved. And, since extras can be added slowly over a period of time, even the total costs are relatively painless. The charge per added unit might run from as little as $5 for a new towel bar to $250 or so for new lighting.

Plumbing fixtures are available in an enormous range of styles. If you are replacing a worn old faucet, a new faucet of a different style can lead to an entirely new character for your bathroom.

When the wall-to-wall vanity was built, above, the basin was located to fit over the existing plumbing.

At left, a new radiator cover was built, tile was added to walls and floor, and lighting was redesigned, but no plumbing fixtures were changed.

Redecorating

If the bathroom itself and the fixtures and equipment in it are in basically good condition, redecorating may be a good choice. The job could be done partially depending upon need, piecemeal over a period of time, or all at once. A complete redecoration is not terribly difficult, even if the plumbing and lighting fixtures are included. Nor is the cost especially high, and often much or all of the job can be done by a competent do-it-yourselfer. Do-it-yourself costs might range anywhere from $25 for paint to $1000 or so for a complete facelift. For a complete, professional redecoration, figure on spending around $2000.

Redecorating involves repainting and/or recovering the floor, walls and ceiling with fresh new finish materials. Finish hardware can be refinished or replaced, and switch and outlet covers can be replaced to match a new decor. Mirrors and other accessories might be refurbished, relocated, and/or added to. Cabinetry and built-ins might be refinished. Even the plumbing fixtures, including the toilet, can be touched up or completely reglazed. During the redecoration process minor repairs or replacement of mechanical parts (faucet stems, light switches, etc.) can be made as necessary. The end result is a fresh, attractive and properly operational bathroom.

Redesigning

In a redesigning job, the plumbing fixtures can be replaced, but their original locations stay the same. The remaining elements of the bathroom—cabinetry, equipment, and accessories—can be dispensed with entirely or in part and another bathroom designed and built into the existing room without disturbing any of the original basic structure.

All new elements, or a mix of new and old, can be introduced in the same or different locations. The plumbing system, for instance, might remain basically intact, while the electrical system is completely redone. New flooring, wall covering, and ceiling finish can be installed in conjunction with new cabinetry to effect a completely new decor. Windows might be changed or added, perhaps a skylight installed. In short, though the plumbing fixture locations and the room structure are the same, and though some of the old bathroom equipment may be reused, the end result is essentially a new bathroom.

This situation allows excellent flexibility of design. Although no new space is gained, that which exists can often be made far more useful at less cost than remodeling or building a new bathroom. A do-it-yourself redesigning job can cost upward from as little as $750 to $1000. A professional job, though, including design work, would likely be in the $2500 to $4000 range, and up.

Complete Remodeling

If a satisfactory bathroom arrangement cannot be gained by any of the previous methods, the only recourse is to remodel completely. The minimum-size bathroom for the three standard plumbing fixtures is approximately 5 feet by 7 feet, or 35-40 square feet, although this requirement is variable to some extent, depending upon the configuration of the room and whether standard plumbing fixtures are used. Bathrooms of this size can be successfully remodeled if no plumbing fixture and very little else is added, although only in limited fashion. However, an expansion of square footage is necessary for anything ·beyond minimum bathroom requirements.

There are numerous ways to gain additional space; the specifics depend entirely upon the structure and design of the house and the relationship of the bathroom area to surrounding rooms. Some of the possibilities are to incorporate an adjacent closet; expand into an adjacent room; repartition one or more existing rooms and modify or dispense with one or more abutting bathroom walls; incorporate an adjacent unused space, such as high under-eave areas; or expand into a little-used adjacent hallway by rearranging doors and partitions. A bathroom positioned on an outside wall can be expanded by making an addition to the house.

A complete remodeling involves actually making a partly or entirely new room by virtue of rearranging part of the house structure and revamping the whole bathroom area. At the same time, considerable changing of electrical circuits must be done, and that portion of the plumbing system involving the bathroom generally has to be completely rebuilt. The job should be approached with some degree of caution and with ample investigation, because there are occasions when building code, structural, architectural, or plumbing complications arise that can make bathroom remodeling difficult or perhaps even prohibitive from a practical standpoint.

A complete remodeling job is expensive; the costs depend entirely upon the extent and complexity of the work involved. All-new fixtures, equipment, accessories and finish materials must be added to the costs for design, structural materials, and a considerable amount of labor. Total costs of between $4000 and $5000 for a small and relatively simple job are likely. An "average" project for a bathroom of 150 square feet or so could reach the $10,000 level, and a large and complete luxury bathroom might top $20,000.

COST ESTIMATING

No matter how much or how little you do in the way of bathroom building or renovation, there will be costs. Obviously, total cost is dependent entirely upon exactly what is done and how it is accomplished. There are several factors that should be considered.

Materials

One of the most substantial costs is for materials. This includes all of the items that will be needed to put the job together—lumber, finish coverings, trim stock, plumbing fixtures, lighting fixtures, and so on. The first step in determining costs is to work up a complete set of plans and specifications covering the entire job. From this you can derive a bill of materials that lists everything needed, along with quantities. Find the unit price of each individual item and tally up the numbers. Add about 10 percent for waste and contingencies, and the result is a total materials cost estimate.

For sunning or soaking, a garden spa was created by extending the bathroom beyond the original wall of the house. The sunken tub was custom built in place to keep the overall design sleek and simple.

Labor

The labor cost for a complete professionally-done job is likely to make up the bulk of the total job cost. If you do all the work yourself, there will be no labor cost in terms of cash outlay. If you oversee the job but hire casual labor, estimate as best you can the hours of labor that you will probably need, add a factor of 10 percent, and multiply by the going hourly rate for casual labor. Do the same when hiring individual skilled helpers or tradesmen. If work will be done by subcontractors you can get either an estimate or a firm bid price for each job phase. In some jobs there are combinations of casual, skilled, and subcontracted labor; adding them all together results in a total labor cost.

Incidentals

Overlooking the incidentals sometimes causes a slight trauma, because in many jobs the total amount of cash involved can be substantial. For instance, the issuance of building permits frequently involves an attendant fee. There may even be three—one each for construction, electrical, and plumbing. You might have to hire the services of an architect, engineer, or interior decorator. And, of course, there are the miscellaneous supplies to be considered, such as glue, caulk, screws and nails, sandpaper, and so on.

Time

In a minor redecorating job, the cost to you in time spent may not amount to much, but in a big remodeling project it can be substantial. You will already have spent some time thinking and planning; you'll spend more in searching out materials, fixtures, furnishings, and accessories. If you plan to do all or some of the work yourself, you will spend large chunks of time actually on the job. Even if you do none of the work yourself, you will have to spend time conferring with an architect, interior decorator, and/or contractor.

Inconvenience

The cost in terms of inconvenience is also to be reckoned with. One such "cost" can be the time cost just discussed. Another can lie in having a gang of tradesmen banging around the house. The normal family schedule and lifestyle may well be disrupted. If there are delays and holdups in the work, that inconvenience may turn into frustration and black thoughts. But inconvenience is likely to occur, and should be counted upon.

Taxes And Assessments

Depending upon the nature and expense of the job being done, the assessed valuation and property taxes on the house may be increased by virtue of the improvements. Bathroom remodeling or adding a new bath may also involve increased assessments. This occurs where taxing districts make calculations for periodic water consumption or waste disposal assessments in terms of the number of plumbing fixture units installed in a given building.

Property Values

Improvements in bathroom facilities increase property value tangibly and intangibly. A tangible value increase is brought about by making a major improvement that elevates the potential selling price of the home. An intangible increase occurs when the bathroom improvements actually add little, if any, dollar value to the house but do result in additional convenience, comfort, and workability for the occupants.

Note that in both cases, bathroom improvement costs should be considered either wholly or partly as an expenditure, not as an investment in dollar terms. Where property value is not tangibly increased, the cash outlay for improvements is simply a direct expense or an "investment" in comfort and convenience. Where property value is tangibly raised, a certain portion, but almost never the entire amount, of the bathroom improvement cost may eventually be returned when you sell the property. A $5000 expenditure for bathroom improvements seldom results in a $5000 increase in selling price, but rather some relatively small fraction thereof.

GETTING THE JOB DONE

One way to get the job done is to do it yourself. This saves money (usually) but the do-it-yourselfer should recognize before he or she begins exactly what the job entails in the way of time, skill, knowledge, experience, and equipment. There is a common tendency among home mechanics to dive into a project headfirst to the eventual detriment of the finished job.

Another possibility is to oversee and also do part of the work yourself, hiring either casual labor or skilled tradesmen to assist with or complete certain portions of the job. This situation works particularly well with the relatively smaller projects and where competent help is readily available.

A third method is to act as your own general contractor, hiring out all the various phases of the job to a series of skilled craftsmen or subcontractors. The homeowner thus does all the coordinating, planning, scheduling, and general "bossing." This arrangement requires that the homeowner have some knowledge of, and experience in, management, supervision, and the building trades.

And finally, you can place the whole project in the hands of an architect, who will do the planning and arrange for a general contractor to do the work. This is the most expensive method of getting the job done. But, for most people, it is also the most satisfactory and the least problematic in the long run.

Your Dream Bathroom

The bathroom probably is the only room in the house to which it is possible to escape. Once the door is closed, the room is magically transformed into a very private space, off limits to all but the occupant. It offers a brief refuge for a harried mother, a sanctuary in which a businessman can gather strength to face the day, a place where a child can be out of range (for a little while, anyway) of his or her parents' seemingly prying eyes. How nice it would be if the bathroom itself enhanced the illusion of welcome seclusion.

Whether the bathroom actually will be used only by one person, or whether a couple or children must share the facilities, the inclusion of special this-is-just-for-me features should not be overlooked. In fact, they are high on the list of components people desire for their dream bathrooms.

A hard-driving businessman pictures himself getting ready for work in a wood-paneled bathroom, showering in a glass-doored, quarry-tile-lined enclosure, reaching for a hot towel encased in a warmed compartment, shaving over a marble basin sunk into the top of an antique wood dresser. An exhausted mother of four fantasizes about emerging from her pristine chamber serene and beautiful after exercising in a plant-filled alcove and relaxing in a whirlpool bath. A working couple conjures a streamlined layout that offers fixtures for simultaneous showering and bathing, dual vanities, and a compartmented toilet for privacy. Even children have their fantasies. A five-year-old imagines a place near the tub for storing bath toys. An eight-year-old wishes for a showerhead positioned for his or her height. Thirteen-year-olds picture a well-lighted mirror for experimenting with makeup or razor.

What Makes A Dream Bathroom?

There is no single answer to the question, "What makes a dream bathroom?" A necessity to one person is an extravagance to another. So, the only person who can answer the question for you is you. A bachelor's marble tub and wood-paneled walls easily could be all wrong for your family bathroom. And the bachelor probably would not appreciate the finer points of a twin-bowl, plastic laminate-topped vanity, something without which your family might not make it through bedtime.

The question really is, "What would make your personal dream bathroom?" Although ten people reading this book certainly would arrive at ten very different solutions, the ten bathrooms all would have one thing in common: each would fit the lifestyle of the person or persons using it. As the following portfolio of dream bathrooms will show you, there are many ways to arrange the standard bathroom elements, and the only criterion of right or wrong is whether the bathroom fulfills the owner's highly personal dream.

Of course you will want to apply your money where you will enjoy it most—perhaps to a whirlpool, to special-color fixtures, or to additional lighting. But as you read about the dream bathrooms in the coming pages you will learn how to save money and probably still get the bath of your dreams. For example, one owner got the same vintage effect by reglazing the interior of an old tub-on-legs and reusing it as he would have by replacing it with a similar but costlier new tub. Many dramatic and effective light fixtures wear price tags that are just a fraction of those on similar models by other manufacturers, and mirrors and vanities bought in standard sizes cost far less than others that may be just a few inches larger or smaller. If your budget truly is budget, concentrate on key pieces or accessories to set the style; use a large print to take the decorative place of an expensive stained glass window, or team an impressive marble vanity with a standard toilet and tub.

Necessary Compromises

Unless you have the best of all possible situations—and plenty of money, too—your dreams probably won't materialize exactly as you hope. You might have to work around your home's structural limitations or those of local building codes. The fixture model or color you have dreamed about might be discontinued by the time you are ready to start your make-over. You might have to make compromises in function and decor with others who will use the bathroom, and you certainly won't escape your share of surprises once construction begins, particularly if you are tearing out an existing bathroom. Costs might get so out of hand that you end up doing some of the work yourself, whether that means setting tile or hanging wallpaper. We won't go on—you will have your own particular compromises to make soon enough. Just remember that the owners of each of the bathrooms you are about to see all had problems, too.

Remodeling Home Is Her Labor Of Love

"Pretend you are Jacqueline Kennedy and can have anything you want," the architect had said. With those words, visions of dream bathrooms began to fill the imagination of the woman who lives in the house containing the bathrooms shown here. For herself she wanted an extra-long vanity, complete with lavatory, plus a dressing area and a luxurious sunken tub. She wanted her husband's lavatory positioned so that they could talk while each prepared for the day or for an evening out. And she wanted a separate shower stall with the dual heads her husband said he would like. For the children's bathroom, the woman wanted a low-budget, cleaned-up look with the addition of much-needed storage, and for the new powder room, she said "make it classy and sparkly and special."

The family may not be the Kennedys, but eight years ago when they decided to redo the six-bedroom house they already had lived in for awhile, they were fortunate to be able to draw on as much expertise as money could buy. The interior designer, who since has established a successful business, was just starting out and had hours to spend for consultation and shopping trips. "One day a week was set aside just to go antiquing with me for furnishings for the house," the woman recalls. "She never would be able to put in those hours today." Also, because the job was to be done over the winter, both the contractor and the architect were less busy with other jobs and could be more giving of their time and expertise. The owners remember long sessions with all three, going over plans, bouncing ideas off each other, encouraging each other's creativity. At these sessions, the group mapped out a master plan for remodeling the home a piece at a time, and though the ongoing project still is not quite complete, the family has, as the designer commented, "always known where they were going with the house."

The three-story house is situated on a large corner lot, and that fact played a large role in both the purchase and remodeling of the structure. "I liked the location of the house from the beginning," said the woman, the mother of three children now aged 18, 15, and 12. "It is directly across from the school and near transportation, and we liked the character of the house; it was a home, not just a bunch of square rooms. The kitchen was new, too. But more than that, the yard was all wilds and left a lot of room for expanding the house and adding patios. Though we didn't tear the house

The one-piece shower stall, above, is so large that it had to be brought in through the oversized window beside where it now stands.

The woman's vanity was custom-crafted of oak. Two medicine cabinets are recessed into the walls to the sides.

The walls around the sunken tub, right, are covered with oak flooring and inset with antique tiles. The ledge was built to display antique ironstone.

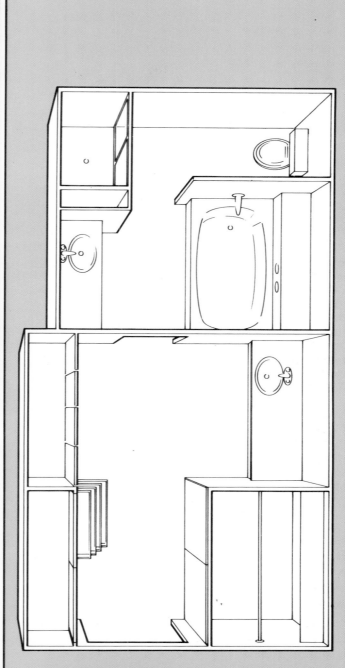

The 10-foot-wide bathroom has two sections, one 12½ feet long and the other 9 feet long. The woman's vanity and the storage areas were placed in the first compartment to isolate them from steam.

apart the minute we bought it, we always knew it would lend itself to a lot of possibilities."

Much of the expansion was planned to make the couple's frequent entertaining easier, although some of the family areas, specifically the two full baths, also needed improvement. Phase One of the changes included enlarging the dining room about 75 percent and adding a huge foyer with new front door, which made the old front door a secondary entrance. A new powder room (shown on these pages) was included in this addition on the advice of the architect and contractor, who told the owners it would cost as much to expand and update the existing half bathroom off the kitchen as it would to start afresh, and with better results. The old half bathroom has been maintained and serves the family, while the new one is closer to the living room and dining room and is off-limits to all but guests.

Upstairs, this phase-one addition encompassed a remodeling of the master bathroom into a room more fitting for the oversized master bedroom. That phase completed, the family started work on other sections of the house. Over the years, outdoor entertaining areas have been added, as well as a new driveway and landscaping, and recently attention turned again to the interior, where the children's bathroom finally has had its turn at beautification.

The master bathroom that greeted the architect, contractor, and designer eight years ago possibly was original to the house. With doors from both the master bedroom and the son's bedroom, it was a sparse room that contained nothing more than a pedestal lavatory, toilet, and tub with shower. The designer remembers it as "a very cramped, tiny bathroom tucked under the eaves; going into it was like stepping into a garret."

With "Jacqueline Kennedy's" requests in mind, the team fashioned a new bathroom that would encompass the previous room's space in an addition. The new area is divided into two sections, the first measuring 10 by 12½ feet, the second measuring 10 by 9 feet.

The woman had asked that the bedroom be as free of furniture as possible. That meant that the bathroom should offer storage space—and it does, in the form of a 4½-by-6½-foot walk-in closet, 6-foot-wide built-in drawers, and another 6-foot expanse of double-rod hanging space, hidden by mirrored bi-fold doors. Also in this first area is a 5¾-foot long lavatory/dressing table for the woman. Custom-crafted of oak, the vanity is topped by a one-piece counter. Above, an antique picture frame surrounds a mirror, and two medicine cabinets and a tissue dispenser are recessed into the walls at either side.

Since the woman asked that she be able to converse with her husband while each was at his and her own lavatory, but also that each lavatory be able to be closed off if one or the other person rose earlier in the morning, the design group decided to place the two lavatories on opposite walls, one in each compartment. In this way, they are within view of each other when the pocket door is open.

The materials in the husband's 4¾-foot-wide vanity match those in his wife's, but a mirror fills the wall behind. His medicine cabinet is recessed into the wall at left, while at right, eight shelves hold linens behind matching oak doors. The remainder of this side of the room is taken up by a fiberglass shower stall with dual heads, as the man requested. The one-piece stall is so large that it had to be brought in through the window, something other would-be remodelers perhaps should plan for.

Along the other side of this room lie the toilet (at the end of the room in its own 33-inch-wide niche) and a nearly 6-foot-long tub, sunken into the floor so that it shows only 8 inches above. The construction of the entire tub area is typical of the precision involved throughout the bathroom. For example, to make sure that the side-mounted handles would be in just the right

A pair of stained glass windows, left, are the focal point of the master bathroom. They actually are hand-painted door panels that had been intended for use elsewhere during remodeling of the house.

The focal point of the 5-by-10-foot guest powder room is the marble-topped vanity made from an antique French oak dresser. Crystal fittings, an antique-framed mirror, and custom-colored foil wallcovering add to the glamour.

place in the over-sized tub, the contractor had the woman sit in the tub and stretch her arms. Also, in their antiquing forays, the designer and the woman had turned up two sets of Italian tiles and pieces of brown and white ironstone for which they had no specific plans. When this bathroom was in the design stage, they remembered these pieces and decided to include them. The ledge behind the tub was built especially to hold the ironstone, while the tiles were inset into the wood walls.

The use of the wood throughout this compartment (the dressing area walls are painted gray) gives the room a rich shell that adds to the look and feel of opulence. Composed of oak flooring laid horizontally, the walls are coated with spar varnish, a finish so effective that no further treatment has been necessary, even though the couple "shower and steam up the

place like crazy." Particularly in the tub area, however, the walls haven't gotten the abuse they were treated for. Although husband and wife had planned to use the tub for luxurious soaking, neither has found it comfortable after all. "The pitch of the slope doesn't fit either of us," the woman explained, "and it is difficult to negotiate getting in and out and also hard to stoop down to clean the tub. We haven't enjoyed it nearly as much as we thought we would."

One thing they are happy about, however, is the use of two magnificent stained glass windows as the focal point of the room. Actually hand-painted door panels, the two are from a set of four made in Paris in the mid-1800s and bought by the designer to use as sidelights for the new front door entry system downstairs. Parts of each were cracked and her original intention was to use two of the doors to repair the other

Redoing the children's bathroom consisted mainly of reglazing the tub and installing a new toilet, stock vanity, and medicine cabinet. The decor was intended to be neither masculine nor feminine.

a mirror. The silvery foil wallcovering in the room was custom colored in grays and bright pinks especially to counteract the darkness of the home's Tudor styling and of the stone flooring that continues into this room from the foyer. The vanity is jam-packed with accessories that include pink porcelain, pink hand towels, a gold-and-crystal double towel rack, and a gold mirror set. Indeed, the owners asked that the room be furnished with special pieces, and the only readily available item to be found there is the American Standard toilet that has its own 3-foot-wide cubicle.

While the children's bathroom upstairs equally fulfills the family's requirements, it does so after much less expense. Described by the designer as having been "a sloppy kids' bath with no storage," the 5½-by-10-foot room today is a contemporary remake of a vintage bathroom. The children's mother decided to tackle the bathroom recently after attending a home improvement show and learning that the surface of old, worn fixtures could be made to look like new with an electroglazing process. It was just the impetus she needed to start.

"Actually, this bathroom evolved a little at a time," the woman said. "At first we were just going to turn the green tub white, but after that was finished, we decided to replace the green toilet with white, too. And then the children were getting older and needed room to put cosmetics and hair dryers; and pretty soon, the pedestal sink was on its way out and the whole bathroom was done over."

Although the woman did most of the leg work and supervision of the installation of the new toilet and vanity (a stock cabinet ordered at a plumbing supply house), she did turn to the designer and contractor for advice. The interior designer, for example, recommended that the room would look cleaner with a glass shower door instead of a shower curtain. She also suggested and ordered the thin-slat white blind for the window and the crisp, primary-colored geometric wallcovering, basically white, that was purposely neither masculine nor feminine, since the couple's son and daughters share this bathroom. At the suggestion of the contractor, the woman found a wall-hung medicine cabinet that allowed the wall behind to be left intact. "We didn't know what problems we would run into if we cut into the wall," the woman explained. "So we decided not to chance it."

As with this bathroom, the woman played an active role in the remodeling of her entire house. From the beginning, she was prepared with pictures cut from magazines or page references in decorating books so that she could more easily communicate her likes and dislikes to the designer, architect, and contractor. Her files are so good, she says, that many friends borrowed them when it came time to redo their houses. But even with a whole design and contracting team on hire, "Jackie Kennedy" never simply turned the project over to them. "I looked for faucets and tile and fixtures, to save everyone extra steps; but also I know it saved us money," she said. "I did a lot of running around, but mostly this has been a labor of love. I've enjoyed being involved."

two. It turned out, though, that all four could be saved, so she made plans to install the "extra" two at the large window in this bathroom. "That is why the rest of the room is fairly quiet," the designer explained. "These panels are visible from the first compartment and from the bedroom, so I wanted the surroundings to be subdued."

The powder room downstairs that was part of this same addition has a totally different look. Meant to make guests feel glamorous, it got the star treatment, too. The focal point of this 5-by-10-foot bathroom is another French antique—an oak dresser with marble top that was drilled to receive the white sink that turned it into a vanity. The contractor found the crystal fittings that are positioned at the side for easy access, and the crystal is repeated in two sconces that flank the dresser and the antique picture frame that now houses

Landmark Home Looks Glorious

Often, when people move into a house that needs work, they will first concentrate their efforts on finishing those areas their guests will see—the living room, dining room, and downstairs bathroom. Next they might turn their attentions to the master bedroom and bathroom and, if the resources aren't depleted, a child's room.

Not so in the family whose bathroom appears here. Upon moving into their spacious city home, they were less concerned with pretense than with practicality. Their first thought was to have a comfortable master bedroom suite for themselves and more-than-just-habitable rooms for their three sons. So, these rooms were the first to be modernized and freshly decorated.

"The house had been neglected and needed to be brought up to date," recalls the interior designer who was called in for her expert assistance. "In its day, the

house must have been extraordinary. In fact, it is located in an historic landmark area. But over the years it had been tampered with and badly."

Still boasting rich paneling, oak flooring, a workable layout, and plenty of light, the house, nevertheless, needed a new kitchen and bathrooms and a general sprucing up. Previous attempts at updating the three-level home had consisted of painting the woodwork, adding layer upon layer of bathroom tile, and replacing outmoded fixtures. Basic deficiencies remained untouched. One such flaw was the master bathroom positioned between the bedroom and the dressing room and closets.

"The whole thing was just nonsense, having to go through the bathroom to get at your clothes," the designer said. The 11½-by-13-foot bathroom, while accommodating a dressing table, lavatory, toilet, bidet, tub, and separate shower stall, still was a single room that offered no personal privacy. And beyond it, the 9-by-11½-foot dressing room clearly could be put to more imaginative and efficient use.

Although the makeover of these facilities was just part of a complete refurbishing dictated by the structure's run-down condition, the couple was thrilled at the chance to buy the house. Once confirmed apartment

Reflected in mirrored doors are custom-made "his" and "her" vanities and tub deck, all of Dupont Corian. Her vanity is for seated use, his is for standing.

dwellers, they lived in a condominium until the appearance of their second dog and third child, at which time they moved to a rented house down the street from their current home.

"As soon as we moved in, I liked the idea of a house," the woman said. "The privacy you have in a house is much different from that of an apartment, and this particular street has an interesting quality about it since it is historic."

The fact that their new house is located in a recognized and designated historic area gave the couple and the designer the confidence to invest in its modernization. As the woman said, "We plan to live here for a long, long time, and the value of what we put into the house is what we will get out of it for a long, long time, even beyond the real estate value, in sheer enjoyment."

With so much work to be done on the house over several years' time—from total cleaning and redecorating to structural changes—the couple zeroed in on the bedrooms as their primary target. With themselves and the boys settled comfortably in their own quarters, they figured the family could more happily endure inconveniences in the rest of the home. As former apartment dwellers, whose bedrooms had doubled as dens, they could be comfortable using the new ones as TV and game rooms until more specialized areas were developed.

The bedroom remodeling required little structural work, but the master bathroom was another story. First to go was the wall separating the dressing room from the bathroom. Then all the fixtures, cabinets, flooring, and tile were scrapped, too. With the resulting 11½-by-22-foot space to work with, the designer easily met the couple's requirements for a "really beautiful, luxury bathroom."

"When we first discussed plans for a new bathroom, we told the designer we wanted something beautiful, but simple," the woman said. "We didn't want anything exotic, like a mirrored ceiling or marble, because we are practical. We wanted beautiful, but practical, materials."

The couple asked the designer for "something new and pretty." This translated as "contemporary, but not too slick." On the practical side, the designer knew they would need closet and storage space, especially since the dressing area, which had served as storage for the closetless 16½-by-17½-foot master bedroom, was being eliminated. Instead of simply building a closet into the generously-sized bedroom, the designer maintained that gracious space by keeping storage in the bathroom but making it much more accessible than it had been originally.

The couple asked that the shower stall be separated from the grooming areas so steam would not cloud the mirrors, and they wanted some semblance of privacy while still being able to talk to each other during the morning pre-work rush. Since husband and wife—a commodities broker and a psychiatric social worker, respectively—both have schedules to meet, the shared moments in the bathroom form an important part of their daily communication.

Putting aside the former layout, the designer set about revamping the newly opened space by dividing it once again—this time along more logical lines. The room was split into two sections measuring 11 by 15 feet and 5½ by 11 feet. For maximum privacy, the toilet, bidet, and steam-producing shower were

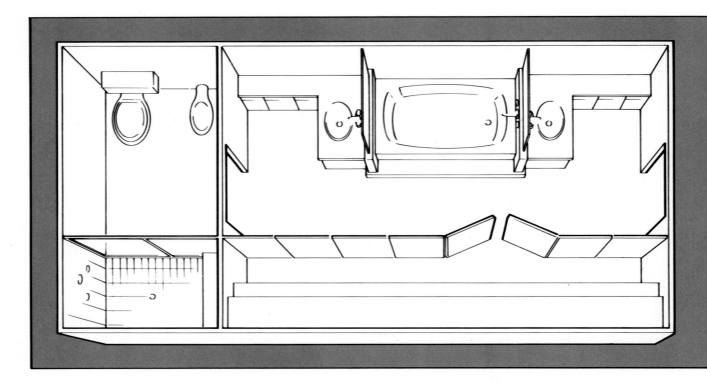

grouped in the smaller room, beyond the combined dressing/grooming area.

To replace the ripped-out storage, a five-section, floor-to-ceiling, mirrored closet was installed along the length of the larger room. On the other side, two vanities were set to flank a large soaking tub.

"The lady told me she and her husband wanted to have everything in one place and to be able to completely prepare for the day from this bathroom," the designer said. Consequently, each end closet provides double hanging space for clothing directly across from their respective vanities. The next two inside closets contain single rods and shelving, and the center closet has six drawers, 2½ feet deep, which the couple share. Opposite the mirrored wall, the 6-foot-long Kohler tub separates the vanity areas, each an ample 4½ feet square. The Kohler lavatories match, but the remainder of the vanity areas were planned specifically with the user in mind. Her side features a dressing table with a drawer for sit-down makeup application. His includes three drawers and cabinets and standing room only. Concealed in the wall behind each vanity is a 14-by-30-inch medicine cabinet.

DuPont's Corian synthetic marble was selected as the primary construction material. It is a practical yet luxurious-looking alternative to marble. Off-white Corian forms the vanity countertops, the steps and ledges surrounding the tub, and even the radiator covers. The designer still marvels that the contractor was able to support the mirrors with it. Cabinets are constructed of white plastic laminate.

To continue the subdued yet glamorous feeling, the bathroom walls were covered with 1½-inch-wide strips of pine wainscoting which had been given a wash of white and then spar varnished for protection (a treatment that will need to be repeated every three years). The wainscoting continues across the doors of the medicine cabinets, so there is minimum visual disruption, and is used in the shower room as well.

Natural light pours through clear plastic rods woven with natural fibers, materials that complement the wood color and acrylic accessories. The combination admits light but offers enough distortion to maintain privacy. Artificial lighting takes the form of recessed spotlights teamed with strip makeup lighting at the sides of the mirrors. Heat lamps near both the shower and the tub provide warmth.

For color, the couple selected an 8-inch-square Italian tile, which is white with a border line of blue. The blue is repeated in towels and other accessories and also ties the bathroom to the adjoining master bedroom, which is decorated in light tans and navy.

This beautiful bathroom was eight months in the making, but much of that time was spent waiting for fixtures or tile to arrive. Everything in the room was either custom-made or special ordered. Standard bathtub fittings, for example, were sent to Guerin, the manufacturer of the lavatory fittings and other hardware, to be plated to match the pewter finish.

Now that they can comfortably use their bedroom and bathroom, the couple have turned their attentions to the kitchen and family room and are well on their way to having a "glorious, really fabulous" house. They will strive, as they have in this bathroom, for a quiet, not garish elegance, throughout the other rooms. "The bathroom looks kind of fancy, but it is extremely practical," the woman said. "We want the rest of the house to be that way, too."

The floor plan, left, is in two sections measuring 15 by 11 feet and 5½ by 11 feet. For privacy and to help contain mirror-fogging steam, the toilet, bidet, and shower were placed in the smaller room.

Floor-to-ceiling mirrored doors, right, give an open feeling to the corridor-like layout. The walls are covered with vertical pine strips colored antique white.

Tiny Room Looks Bigger Than It Is

It is difficult to remodel a standard 6-by-8-foot bathroom and come up with something dramatically different from the one you started with. Although you can update the toilet, tub, and vanity, there are not many ways to arrange them in such a small space. But as the architect of the bathroom shown here said: "That doesn't mean the room can't LOOK bigger than it is. This might look like a big bathroom, for example, but it is tiny. What gives it the illusion of more space is the variety of textures and lighting; there is enough going on to make it look theatrical and keep your mind off its size."

Five years ago, when the single man who lives here was planning the renovation of his Victorian duplex, he saw no reason to change the layout drastically. Situated over a rental apartment, the second and third floors of the building formed a house with living room, dining room, and kitchen on the main floor (a half bathroom has since been added), and three bedrooms and this full bathroom upstairs.

Aside from repairing the ravages of time, little reconstruction was needed. Working with the architect and contractor, the owner decided he could have a magnificent city house just by stripping woodwork, mending damaged ornamental plaster, making minor changes in layout, and modernizing the kitchen and bathroom. Even the home's mechanical systems were in relatively good repair, and although supply plumbing was replaced, the bath's soil stack was retained.

According to the architect, the major objective, aside from modernization, was "to get as much light as possible to the center of the house. In a rowhouse, you are stuck with light from the front and the back, except for the top floor, where skylights can be used. This bathroom is in the center of the house, between the one large room at the front of the house and the two others at the rear, and we wanted to introduce natural light to the bathroom, as well as improve the situation in the bedrooms, which have windows along only one wall."

The solution turned out to be the economical installation of a single skylight to illuminate both the bathroom and the bedrooms. According to the owner, "like all good ideas, the source of that one probably is untraceable, and I don't mean to detract from the architect by saying that." A real estate developer with his own firm, the owner worked closely with both the architect and the contractor. The contractor, the owner said, "is a person with many creative ideas who had a tremendous amount of input." By the time the job was finished, it was hard to pinpoint who thought of what. The spectacular results here illustrate what continued refinements of an idea can yield.

Previously, the bathroom had ended with a wall behind the tub. On the other side of that wall were two 3½-foot-wide by 3-foot-deep, back-to-back closets that served the bedrooms at the front and rear of the house. The architect decided that if closet space could be developed elsewhere, the 3½-by-6-foot area could be annexed to the bathroom. The bedrooms were reworked to gain additional footage, and the bathroom fixtures remained in their original spots. This new space became a plant showcase. Beyond the decorative effect of the lush greenery and the textural appeal of the exterior brick wall, the most dramatic change was the addition of a skylight to allow natural light to flood both the bathroom and the adjacent bedrooms. Two fixed-pane windows—one on either side of the tiled plant deck—now light parts of the bedrooms that had never seen daylight before.

But what about privacy? "I designed this house with myself in mind," the owner responds. "We combined two of the three bedrooms, for example, to make a large master bedroom, and the other bedroom on this floor is set up like a den. I never really thought the windows would cause any problems because I live here alone."

Still, the owner has had to reconsider the situation now that his two children, who visit him every weekend, are growing older. Both the boy, 10, and girl, 13, have been known to draw the shower curtain before using the toilet! Even for ultra-shy guests, however, such precautions are really unnecessary. To peer through a window into the bathroom, one would have to stand in the corner of either bedroom; furniture arrangement also inhibits accidental glimpses of a bather. Future owners may insure privacy, however, with the simple installation of decorative, adjustable blinds.

In the functional part of the bathroom, a sense of compartmentalization was created by semi-dividing the tub/shower from the rest of the room with a 2-foot-wide, floor-to-ceiling wall. The wall conceals the tub fittings and shower curtain (when it's not in use), thereby giving a sleeker look to the plant area. A soffit further frames the tub/plant ledge and hides the shower curtain rod, ceiling lights, and a speaker hooked up to the stereo downstairs.

In the toilet/vanity portion of the room, a reverse soffit, or partial dropped ceiling, contains venting ducts and conceals the lights above the sink. Although the owner is not a tall man, he specified that the lavatory/vanity be kitchen-counter height since he "never could understand why most vanities make you bend down at a 90-degree angle to wash your face." Storage is provided below and behind a portion of the mirror. The mirror at the lavatory is a fixed glass, but the one over the toilet is on a touch latch and opens on a four-shelf medicine cabinet.

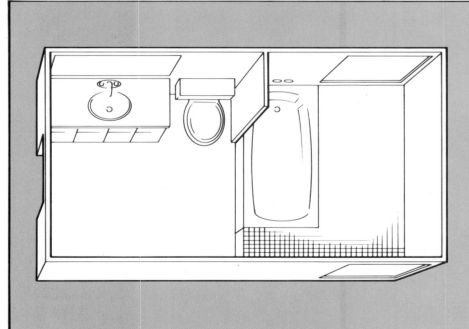

A wall section, above left, conceals tub fittings and shower rod for a sleek appearance.

The windows, above right, are not to the outdoors but to adjacent bedrooms. The skylight over the plant deck therefore helps light the bedrooms.

The original bathroom was 6 by 8 feet. The plant deck behind the tub was built after annexing 3½ feet from adjacent closet space, bringing the new dimensions to 6 by 11½ feet.

The owner selected white plastic laminate for the vanity and all-white fixtures. He introduced color with 1¾-inch-square terra cotta-toned quarry tiles that reinforce the aged clay brick wall. Oak towel bars are almost oriental in their simplicity, and the green plants and towels provide the only other color.

Along with the plants, the owner has thrived in his remodeled bathroom. Beginning the day at 6:15 with a regular run, he returns home to shower and dress for his pressure-packed day. He turns on the stereo, brings up a cup of coffee, steps into the soothing shower, and then, he says, "I'm in heaven."

Elegance Is Architect's Custom

When the couple that now owns the house containing these two bathrooms first found it five years ago, the vintage, two-story, frame building had just been given a superficial makeover after having been boarded up for three years. The contractor who did the facelift had only made the house livable again. He had skipped the amenities that were being added to neighboring homes undergoing modernization in this rejuvenated area north of Chicago—but it turned out to be just as well that he had. Not having to pay for frills they didn't want meant that the couple could afford to move in immediately and live comfortably, if not elegantly, until they arranged their own plans and financing for a tailor-made renovation.

"Though the contractor had upgraded the heating plant, he had left the kitchen the way it was and kept the fixtures in the baths," the woman remembers. "When we bought it, the house was basically one floor with a second story that had one bedroom, some closets, and a small bath. There were no dormers to make more room under the pitched roof."

The couple lived in the house the way it was for six months, getting a feel for the house before turning over their ideas to the woman's brother, a Florida architect, for refinement. Not quite ready to decide what to do with the kitchen and the two bathrooms, the couple went ahead with work on the rest of the house. By adding onto the back of the structure, they were able to have an interior stairway to the basement, which today is part adult recreation room and part children's playroom. Walls were removed on the main floor to make gracious spaces where there once were several tiny rooms. And, on the second floor, one entire side of the house was given a dormer, which allowed room for two large bedrooms separated by a combination hall/den/TV room. Three years after they moved in, all work was finished except the remodeling of the kitchen and the bathrooms.

The couple still was up in the air about the design of those spaces when they met a local architect who later became a friend—and who came up with a plan for the kitchen. Shortly after the kitchen project was completed, the architect was visiting one day and suddenly started sketching possibilities for the first floor guest bathroom. Soon, that job was his, too.

The existing 4½-by-7-foot dimensions of this half bathroom were pretty firmly established, because the room is hemmed in by a dining room wall and staircase on one side, and the plumbing backs up to the kitchen wall on the other. But the architect thought a more open feeling could be achieved with mirrors and gentle curves that would counteract the rigidity of the room. The architect says the curves were a reaction, in part, to the angularity of the rest of the house. The hardwood flooring throughout the first floor is laid on the diagonal, and the entrance to the powder room is on an angle, too, but at a right angle to the flooring. As a counterpoint to all this angularity, the architect specified a half-cylindrical vanity. This rounded shape also allows maximum room for maneuvering inside the powder room.

Since this room is just off the dining room, and because the angled doorway only gives a better view of the bathroom, placing the toilet beyond the vanity makes the scene more palatable. Two other design features distinctly improved the situation, too. First, the designer reversed the door, which opens inward, so that when it is left open, anyone seated at the dining table sees a plain, suede-covered wall, instead of the door. The impression is that the tiny room might be a

small den or study. Second, the materials used are so elegant that the room hardly could seem offensive.

The materials used in the room all were heartily selected or approved by the husband, a confessed bathroom aficionado. A washable vinyl suede cloaks the walls, the vanity and soffits are wrapped in anodized brushed aluminum, and the counter surfaces are topped with richly veined marble. Needless to say, the husband is extremely pleased with the new guest bathroom. Surprisingly perhaps, the materials also please the woman; she says that although this bathroom is not at all off limits to the children and gets constant daily use, signs of wear and tear are yet to appear.

Though the bathroom gets more use from the family than from guests, when party time comes this room performs like a jewel. Incandescent light filtering through silvery grids over the sink and along the outside wall gives soft down-lighting that makes everyone look glamorous. The softly textured walls and plush gray nylon carpet add to the elegance, while the

gleam of the mirrors and silver vanity add sparkle. Silver Mylar film blinds and clear Lucite acrylic accessories create interesting distortions of light, further enlarging the visual space.

It is hard for the couple to remember today what this room looked like when they moved in, except to say that "it could have been ordered straight out of a mass merchandiser's catalog and installed the same day." The new bath, on the other hand, is strictly custom and took three months to order, build, and install. Part of this was due to the precise workmanship that was necessary, particularly on the vanity and matching light soffit; part was due the unexpected mistakes and shipment delays that are an aspect of any construction. Neither the existing behind-the-walls supplies nor the waste or vent stacks were moved, so plumbing was confined to hooking up new fixtures and was not a major time factor.

Custom work for the bathroom included creating the light soffits and vanity from ⅛-inch-thick plywood, forming the necessary curves, and then glueing on the

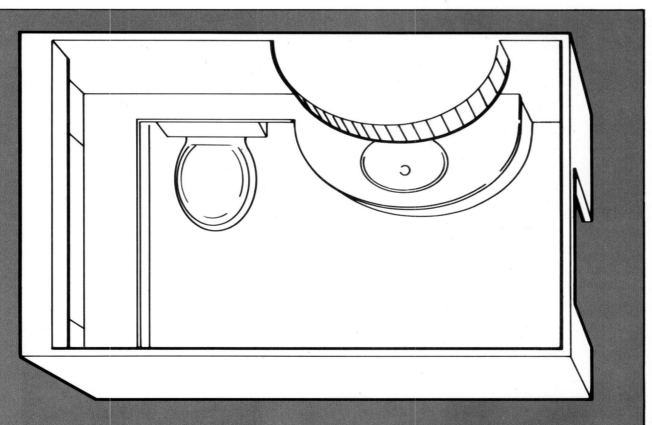

The angularity of this small half bathroom is offset by a semi-cylindrical vanity. The mirrors over the vanity and the side shelf make the room look more spacious. The walls are covered with vinyl suede, and the marble-topped vanity, as well as the soffits, are wrapped in brushed aluminum.

The 4½-by-7-foot dimensions of this bathroom could not be changed because of its location in the house. The room was cosmetically changed by the addition of the half-cylindrical vanity. No plumbing needed to be changed.

An 11-inch-deep medicine cabinet is recessed adjacent to the counter-to-ceiling mirror and under the pitched ceiling. Sliding doors conceal storage space beneath the vanity.

Other delays were more common. There was a wait for the delicately scaled, white Sherle Wagner bowl and chrome fittings. And the small window in the corner went bare for a time while the vertical blinds were made to take the place of chrome thin-slat horizontal blinds that had been ordered but had turned out to be a discontinued style. Since the two generous mirrors are frameless, held in place behind counter and soffit, their rolled and polished edges took extra time, too, as did the fact that they came in the wrong size the first time.

When the room finally was complete, right down to the white, fingertip towels hung on rectangular chrome loops and to the ceramic artwork on the walls, the family was ecstatic, declaring it their pet project in the house. "It has all the elements I like," enthused the man. "There's chrome, ceramic, marble, mirror, all of which really couldn't be used in the rest of the house; and it all makes the room seem so much larger than it did when we started."

The remodeling of the family bathroom upstairs is another success story, although for different reasons. There, the major stipulation was that the remodeling be low in cost. Again, none of the behind-the-walls plumbing was to be changed, and it turned out that both the tub and toilet could be retained, too, although the ongoing plan is to upgrade the tub and replace the surrounding tile someday. Tucked under a pitched roof and without a window, the bath presented problems that easily could have been solved by constructing a dormer or cutting in a skylight. But the budget precluded those solutions. Instead, the 5-by-9-foot bathroom was updated cosmetically, not structurally.

The same architect who had worked on the downstairs bathroom concentrated his attention here on revamping the vanity, adding storage and decorative interest above the toilet, and giving the room more light. Where a tiny sink on chrome legs once stood, there now is a 5½-foot-long vanity set with a Kohler men's lavatory with shampoo spray, a useful attachment for washing children's hair as well as adults. Storage space beneath the vanity is concealed with sliding doors that take up no room when opened. Since a counter-to-ceiling mirror covers the wall behind the vanity (an addition that instantly "enlarged" the room), the 11-inch-deep medicine cabinet is built in at the end of the counter under the pitched roof. The entire vanity, medicine cabinet, and shelf over the toilet are constructed of an easy-care, off-white, plastic laminate.

Although all the plastic laminate sufaces were custom made, the family felt that the expense of such custom work was worth getting the room out of the ho-hum category. Having already foregone a skylight and dormer, they further compensated for the custom costs by installing inexpensive vinyl floor tiles and selecting a standard chrome lighting strip for the lavatory area and a stock vent fan/light for the ceiling. Now that they have used this "new" bathroom for a time, the couple says they are happy with their compromises. "We were looking for a relatively clean-looking, budget solution, and I think we got that," the husband says.

aluminum sheeting. The same sheeting was applied to two under-the-counter drawers near the toilet. Meticulous workmanship also went into the marble counters—three times. The first marble arrived on the site with the sink hole cut slightly off-center. The second showed up in pieces. The third is the beautifully veined marble that is in the bathroom today. The man of the house, who says he is a "marble freak—I have a marble-topped desk in my office too," takes some of the blame by saying he selected an extremely fragile marble. Unfortunately, the marble that broke could not be duplicated, and the counters in the bathroom now have a black background rather than the hoped-for gray. The presence of orange-toned striations that repeat the rich color of the vinyl suede wallcovering, however, subtly links the marble to the color scheme. The counters are in three sections—the rounded vanity, the counter over the toilet, and the counter over the drawers—so that the piece over the toilet can be removed when that fixture needs servicing.

Taking Charge Has Headaches And Rewards

The young couple that now lives in this three-story city rowhouse knew, even before completing its purchase, that they would have to revamp at least one of the bathrooms. The 85-year-old dwelling had five bedrooms. The bathroom that served the three second-floor bedrooms, including the master bedroom, could be entered only from the hall. Since the people are both employed full time and have a sitter who cares for their two-year-old son in the home, they needed more privacy than the existing arrangement would allow. The sitter arrives a full hour before they leave for work, and they preferred not to have to continually encounter her during the early-morning rush to get ready for work. Also, since both husband and wife often must use the bathroom simultaneously, the existing bathroom, with its single vanity and cramped fixture arrangement, simply would not do.

As they proceeded with buying the house, the couple agonized over how to redesign the second-floor bathroom to meet their specific needs. The rooms on that floor were laid out along a hall; from front to rear, there were the master bedroom, a second bedroom, the bathroom, and a small third bedroom. The obvious solution to the problem would be to steal space from the 10-by-14-foot middle bedroom. But the couple resisted losing the extra room.

"Even though we knew right off we never could live with the original bathroom, we didn't know how to change it," the husband said. "We talked for a long time about whether we could afford to give up that middle bedroom, and the problem was more than just the square footage. Unfortunately, of the five bedrooms, that was maybe the prettiest. It was very sunny and was a good size."

Amid discussions of financing and paint colors, the couple kept coming back to the question of what to do about the second-floor bathroom. Finally, shortly after moving day, they settled on a plan.

"We decided that, eventually, after minor repairs were made and the two bedrooms and bathroom on the third floor were redecorated, that would be the kids' floor, and the second floor would be adult space," the woman explained. "The room our son now uses on the second floor then would become a TV room or den; and we wouldn't want another bedroom on that floor as much as we would a larger, more private bath."

Although they summoned an architect for consultation on plumbing and electrical locations and require-ments, the couple planned the basic layout themselves. To economize, they retained the tub/shower and the toilet from the existing bathroom, as well as the hall entry to that area. But the vanity, which backed up to the middle bedroom wall, had to go if those spaces were to be combined. The plan called for most of this entire bedroom/vanity wall to be removed, the doorway to the middle bedroom to be blocked up, and a private entrance to be installed from the master bedroom. Where the middle bedroom stood, there would be a shower flanked by matching vanities, as well as a triple closet and a dressing area.

The layout was decided upon only after several discussions with the architect, who said he could construct a plan with a shower or a triple-rod closet, but not both. "We were firm that we wanted both in the final design," the woman remembers. "Finally, after dragging out a wardrobe carton—remember, we had just moved in!—and using it to simulate a shower, we discovered that by making one of the vanities three feet wide instead of four (to duplicate the other), the pieces fell into place."

After the architect had drawn the blueprints, the couple decided to save on further architect's fees by contacting tradesmen directly. They learned, however, that this arrangement can have severe drawbacks. "It was extremely frustrating, especially since neither of us really had the time," the man said. "Our phone calls

Earth tones complement the sleek, contemporary feeling that is created by the continuity of materials and the crisp, uncluttered spaces.

were not returned, and even after I'd make initial contact and drop off plans, people wouldn't get around to giving us a bid. The people who finally did the work actually were the only ones we could find who were seriously interested."

A contracting division of a retail plumbing supply store was hired to begin work nearly nine months after the couple had moved into the house. The job was to be done for a flat fee of just under $10,000. The couple feel fortunate about the flat-fee arrangement, because the many surprises encountered and occasional mistakes surely would have added to the bill had the price not been set beforehand.

Previous remodelings in the 85-year-old house had long since removed any logic from plumbing, heating, and electrical layouts. Right away, workmen ran into trouble when they broke through the wall between the old bathroom and the middle bedroom. The wall contained water supply and waste pipes for the old vanity, which they had expected; but it also concealed heating ducts for the forced air system and a gas pipe that supplied fuel to a kitchenette on the third floor. When the wall had been completely removed, and the situation could be assessed, it was obvious that the new doorway could not be as wide as had been planned (it was narrowed to 25 inches) and a pocket door could not be used. This proved to be a major disappointment, since the couple already knew there was no room for a swinging door, and now the opening would be too narrow for even an accordian-type closure. Since leaving the two bathroom areas (old and new) open to each other cuts down considerably on privacy, especially since the old portion of the bath-

room still serves their son, the couple still is seeking a solution to the problem.

Other difficulties presented themselves as work progressed. The carpenters' electric saws, plugged into the bathroom's outlets, kept tripping the circuit breakers. The electrician on the job finally announced that, unless a separate circuit were arranged to serve just the bathroom, the family would continue to have similar problems when using the lights and vent fans at the same time as such electric grooming aids as hair dryers and curling irons. Fortunately, there was room on the circuit breaker panel, and the new bathroom now has a circuit of its own.

Work on the bathroom was done during the day, by tradesmen, so the couple soon got used to finding "surprises" upon arriving home at the end of the day. One night they were thrilled to find that the shower base had been installed—until they realized that it was in the wrong place. To save the expense of having a custom shower constructed on the site using a lead pan, the couple had selected a standard 36-inch-square terrazzo base. The couple had planned for the base to be installed 6 inches from the walls in a corner. They had designed a cultured marble ledge to cover the gap between the walls and the edges of the shower base. This design would allow greater elbow room within the shower than there would be if the walls were built straight up from the base. However, the first time the terrazo base was installed, complete with drain connection, it was placed snug against the walls. So, the base had to be repositioned and reconnected to the plumbing.

Sometimes, the headaches were minor. After the job

The owners gained elbow room and saved money by building a 40-inch-square shower stall over a standard 36-inch-square base. The vanities are 4 inches higher than standard—a convenience for the tall owners.

The bathroom is accessible from both the hall and the master bedroom. The vanity/shower area of the room measures 8 by 10 feet, and the tub/toilet area is 6½ by 7½ feet. The smaller area is the original bathroom.

already had stretched from the promised three weeks to two months, the tile setter was prepared to grout. "He asked me what color grout we wanted," the woman said, explaining that this was a detail they had overlooked in the planning stage. "The choice was white, champagne, and brown, and I decided champagne would be nice. The man said fine, he'd be back in two weeks when it came in. Something made me ask how soon we could get brown, and when he told me he had that on the truck; I said, 'Brown will be terrific.' "

With those headaches and others behind them, the couple today enjoys the spaciousness and privacy of their new master bathroom, as well as the increased storage space of the new closet. From the master bedroom, a door opens on a 9-foot-long dressing corridor that leads past the two louvered doors of the 6-by-9-foot master closet. At the end of this corridor is the new 8-by-10-foot bathroom, and beyond that lies the old bathroom, which measures 6½ by 7½ feet.

In the larger of the two bath compartments, the layout was determined to a great extent by the entrance from the dressing area and by the location of a large window. The two vanities flank the new shower stall. One of the vanities is 4 feet long, and the other is 3 feet long, but aside from that, the vanity areas appear identical. Each has a Kohler self-rimming lavatory with Moen faucet, a white plastic-laminate countertop, wall-mounted medicine cabinet on a side wall, and two adjustable lights reflected in a counter-to-soffit mirror. Because both husband and wife are tall—he is 6'5", she is 5'8"—the vanities are kitchen-counter height, 4 inches higher than standard for a bathroom. But below, the husband has two doors that open on two shelves,

while the wife has four doors and two drawers, since her vanity is longer. Plumbing for the shower and both vanities connects to supply and waste lines that served the old vanity in the other room.

For decorative continuity, walls in both bath sections are painted white, and the same 2¾-inch-square tan Summitville tile was used in both compartments for flooring, baseboards, and tub and shower enclosures. Although the tub and toilet were retained in the old section, the cracked plaster walls around them were taken down to the studs and replaced with wallboard.

In addition to the lighting provided above the vanities, the shower has its own light, there is a ceiling fixture near the tub, and each of the two bathroom areas has a combination ceiling light/vent fan. During the day, there is plenty of light through narrow-slat blinds on the window in the main area and on two smaller windows in the toilet/tub room. These two smaller windows, formerly composed of small panes of frosted glass, were replaced, not only because they did not fit with the overall design, but also because their frames were rotten. One of the new windows is a fixed pane, while the other is double-hung; both are treated with matching narrow-slat blinds.

The sleek, clean, contemporary feeling, created by continuity of materials and crisp uncluttered spaces, is maintained in the accessories. Towels are suspended from simple, modern, white plastic hooks, and artwork consists of framed contemporary prints and a geometric hooked rug hung on the wall. Warmth comes from the rich tones in the tile, a nubby earth-toned area rug, and an antique washbowl and pitcher set on a Victorian dresser, a link with the stately home's origins.

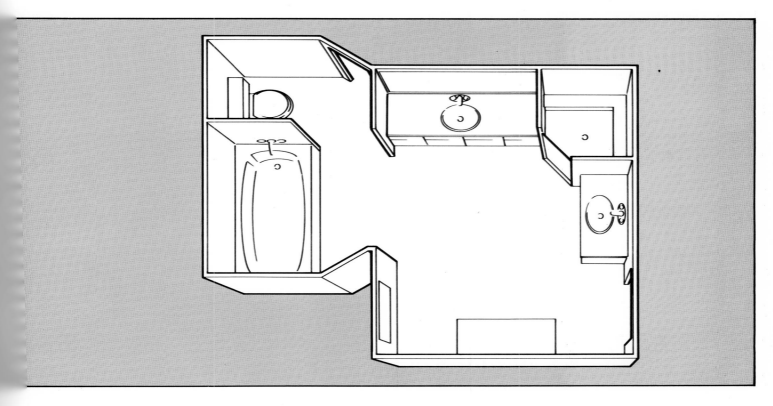

Wide~Open Spaces Suit City Clan

Although this pleasant bathroom is home to two parakeets—lime-green Pretty Bird and peppy yellow Ruby—one hardly could say it is for the birds. In fact, it is a contractor's own master bathroom, and he and his wife brought to the project not only the technical skills needed to solve unique problems, but a sense of proportion and design that makes this bathroom the focal point of the master bedroom suite.

One of the three full bathrooms in the three-story home that the couple crafted from a dilapidated brick apartment building, this room reveals the knowledge the contractor gleaned during the several years he spent renovating turn-of-the-century buildings in the same neighborhood. Since the surrounding homes had been built originally in a subdivision, many of them shared characteristics, much as subdivision houses do today. This meant that the contractor was familiar with the common space problems caused by steeply pitched roofs, stress situations created when modern fixtures are substituted for old, and layout limitations imposed by the narrowness of most city houses. This familiarity proved invaluable when he and his wife

decided to take the plunge and trade carefree apartment living for designing and moving to a renovated dwelling of their very own.

Though now parents of an infant son, the couple felt free to create an open plan when they sat down to design their house four years ago. After living in what the woman calls "a typical cramped apartment," they were ready to tear down walls and create rooms that could be considered vast by city standards. Their living room would be a sweeping 32 feet long (by 22 feet wide); their kitchen, complete with greenhouse-style eating area, a wide-open area of 458 square feet; their family room, 22 by 18 feet. And only three generous bedrooms plus the bathroom pictured on these pages, rather than numerous smaller rooms, would divide the space on the 900-square-foot third floor.

All this, of course, meant retaining little of the structure as it stood when they bought it, but, like many urban pioneers, this couple found little that they felt would be worth salvaging. If the Victorians had not built tiny rooms to begin with (a member of the working class typically slept in a bedroom measuring 7½ by 11 feet), the ravages of the Depression would have left the dwelling with warren-like rooms anyway. The building long since had been divided to serve as a boarding house, and the new owners felt justified in starting afresh, gutting the house to the brick walls and joists and then rebuilding.

With remnants of the past dismissed, the couple planned a wide, cantilevered stairway to run from the front door on ground level all the way to the third floor. Today, visitors climbing to the top find themselves

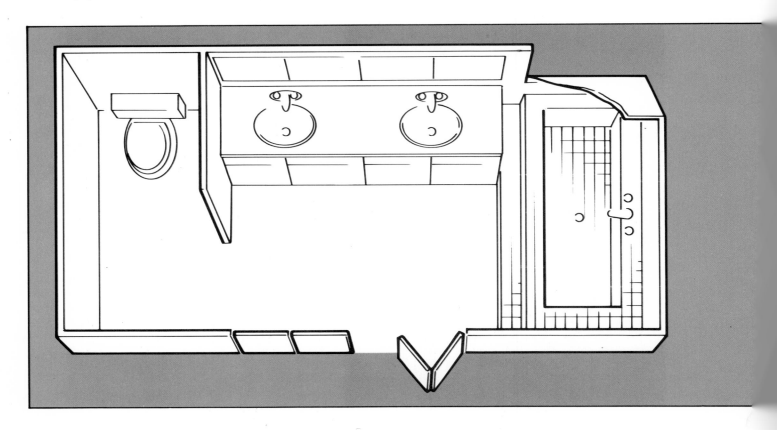

standing before two magnificent antique wood doors, 10 feet tall, that open on the master bedroom suite that includes this bathroom.

The approximately 5-by-15 foot grooming chamber runs along an open, skylighted area that leads to the master bedroom, which features a platformed area for the king-sized bed. The skylight, therefore, illuminates not only the hallway, but the bedroom and bathroom, too, when the doors are left open. Coupled with another, six-foot-long skylight over the tub/shower area, there is enough light all day long to make this a luxurious haven for plants as well as a well-lighted place for grooming.

For privacy, there are two bi-fold doors to close off the bathroom; these are mirrored both as a functional aid to grooming and to reflect the decorative accomplishments within and without. On the bath's side, the focal point is the 5-by-8-foot shower/tub area, custom-built on the site to the contractor's specifications and surrounded today by lush greenery, decorative artifacts, and plush towels. The space, itself larger than many complete bathrooms, is highlighted by two stained glass windows the couple retrieved from a jaded mansion just before its demolition, restored to lustrous beauty, and then installed in the tiled shower wall.

The couple overlooked nothing when they were planning this end of the room. After carefully measuring the possible space, they decided to include the area under the eaves to allow room for a tubside planter and also visually to extend the large feeling of the pool-like tub they had in mind. Because the oversized tub would contain a greater volume of water than any standard tub, the contractor/owner next calculated the maximum possible water weight. His calculations showed that it would be necessary to reinforce the floor in this portion of the house; therefore, each of the original 2-by-12-inch joists was doubled.

After the area had been beefed up and all new plumbing had been installed, carpenters constructed a frame of 2x4s and plywood, building the planter area, two approximately 10-inch-wide steps, and the tub itself, the interior dimensions of which are 3 feet wide, 5 feet long, and 22 inches deep. Lead sheeting was laid over the plywood, all seams and corners were soldered, and finally, 2-inch-square unglazed natural quarry tiles were set in concrete. A champagne-colored, mildew-resistant grout formulated for swimming pools finished the project. Although the Summitville tile originally was planned only for the tub, steps, planter, and two walls, matching tile later had to be added on the sloping ceiling over the tub when condensation from the skylight and shower began to damage the painted wallboard.

The tub can be filled from a faucet located along a ledge under the stained glass windows and/or from two Speakman self-cleaning shower heads. These heads, which can be operated together or separately, are installed 4½ and 7 feet from the floor to accommodate the disparate heights of the couple—she is 5'3" and he is 6'2"; because the tub is extra wide, all water falls into the tub, so no shower curtain is necessary.

The bathroom contains two lavatories, one for him

This 8-by-17-foot bathroom is divided into three sections: the tub/shower, vanity, and toilet areas. Over the tub is a 6-foot long skylight. The lavatory area is lighted by fluorescent tubing, and the toilet area has its own recessed lighting.

The entrance to the bathroom is closed off by two bi-fold doors at the left. The "his" and "her" lavatories are dark brown, and the countertop is palomino tan.

Two stained glass windows highlight the tub/shower area. Two shower heads, which can be operated together or separately, are installed 4½ and 7 feet from the floor.

The skylight over the tub/shower makes this area excellent for growing plants. These plants, the rug, and other accessories are all in keeping with the natural theme of the bathroom.

and one for her, both tucked into a generous 7 foot-long vanity that allows plenty of elbow room when the lavatories are used simultaneously. The Kohler lavatories are a dark brown color that Kohler calls "Expresso," and the Formica laminate countertop is a palomino tan color in keeping with the natural theme of the bathroom. Under the countertop, oak wood cabinets house four 20-inch-wide drawers and two double-doored storage compartments. These provide ample space for all the couple's grooming aids and towels and eliminate the need for a linen closet. The only auxiliary storage space necessary was four shelves concealed behind sliding mirrors above the basins. Here are kept small items such as cologne, makeup, bath oils, and powder. Because the wall follows the slope of the roof, the shelves decrease in depth from 14 inches at the bottom to 5 inches at the top.

Lighting in the shower area consists of two low-voltage adjustable can lights, which spotlight the planter, and, of course, the skylight. The light over the lavatories is fluorescent tubing shielded by a white Formica valance. For general illumination, there are two incandescent recessed cans in the ceiling. The 32-inch-by-5-foot toilet compartment to the left of the lavatories has its own recessed light and vent fan.

To strengthen the feeling that the bathroom is a part of a larger master bedroom suite, the flooring used in the bathroom is the same as that in the bedroom—new, 4-inch-wide, beveled planks stained with a mixture of equal parts coffee color and ebony, sealed with DuraSeal varnish, and finished with a coat of wax. The wood floor and cabinets team with white walls to form a subtle background for myriad plants that include grape ivy, a ponytail palm, trailing philodendron, and ficus. If the tub is great for the couple (and, occasionally, their son), it is terrific for the plants, too. When it is time for watering, the plants all go in the tub for a communal soaking.

The natural theme is continued in accessories such as a wicker waste basket, cotton rug, brass toilet paper holder, and giant seashells, to which have been added such personal touches as a camel blanket the couple purchased in San Francisco, an inherited soapstone vase (which now holds cotton balls and Q-Tip swabs), and an Eastlake-era magazine/newspaper rack that doubles as a guest towel holder during large parties. Well-planned accessories that add the ultimate convenience to the comfortable room, however, are a laundry chute (in the toilet compartment) and a telephone jack, positioned so that even the most leisurely bather need not miss a single call.

Promise Fulfilled: Home Is Perfect

The saying that one thing leads to another was never more true than in the case of the house that contains the lovely bathroom shown on these pages. What began as the simple addition of a dining room eventually became a project that encompassed the whole house—an enlarged bedroom, a new den, a new back entry/mud room, a remodeled kitchen, and a refurbished family room. Hardly an area of the 10-room house escaped reconstruction.

The woman who now lives here had been hunting for a new home for her family of five for 1½ years. She was afraid she never would be satisfied when a realtor showed her this house. For someone so selective, it seemed an unlikely candidate; the home had been used, hard, for 12 years by a family of eight, and although the house had been new when the previous owners moved in, it had been sadly neglected.

But there was something appealing about the home. The lot and location were desirable, and the home itself showed promise of being bright and cheerful. But above all, the size offered more breathing space to the woman, her husband and their three rapidly growing and ever-active sons, then aged 12, 10, and 6. Life in their present three-bedroom, one-bathroom dwelling made it obvious that they couldn't go on searching for a dream home forever.

One thing bothered the woman about the house, however—the traffic pattern from the garage through the family room into the kitchen. She wanted a back door area for coats and boots rather than have everyone enter directly into the family room with muddy feet. She took her husband through that same day. The house appealed to him, too, so she went home and drew and redrew possible layouts for remodeling.

"The house had been so neglected that the price was under market," the woman recalled, "and I knew if we could get the house at a reasonable price, we could afford to make some major changes in it to suit ourselves. I did little else the rest of the day after seeing it except sketch plan after plan of changes that would make it into a house I would like to live in."

That same day, she called a contractor she knew to determine any limitations that might be imposed by lot size, the structure itself, or by local building codes. Given the green light by the contractor, the couple put in a bid that night and barely slept, their heads swimming with ideas. By the next morning, the house—and its problems—were theirs.

At an only slightly more leisurely pace, the couple met with the contractor and a designer whom he suggested and carefully went over the dozens of sketches and layouts the woman had put on paper. The couple's hopes were refined by the experts to mesh with the realities of the house, and a beautiful, comfortable, and more workable arrangement of rooms began to emerge.

It was decided that a better entrance from the garage could be made into the dining room area. A wall was added and a hall created from the garage. The smaller dining room eventually was turned into a den, which meant a new dining room had to be created; so it was decided to add onto the living room at the other end of the kitchen.

From there, it was just another step to adding a second story. Upstairs, this had the effect of enlarging the 13½-by-15-foot master bedroom significantly, an idea the couple hardly opposed. Since everything was to be torn up, they went ahead with plans to reconstruct the bathroom, annexing a dressing closet to the prosaic 5-by-8-foot rectangle and giving the newly enlarged master bedroom a private bathroom.

"In the end, it was like building a new house," the woman said. "Practically all the walls were down and there was construction going on everywhere. Everyone moved quickly, though—some days there were as many as 18 workmen here—and we moved in in three months, and they were finished three months later."

The job went quickly because the couple was fairly certain of their needs and desires and were able to make decisions quickly. When they sat down to discuss changes in the master bedroom/bathroom, for example, their requirements were clear. They wanted plenty of light, two vanities, a shower separated from the tub and from the woman's vanity, and lots of shelving, hanging, and storage space. They also wanted the bedroom to contain as little furniture as possible, particularly no dresser; they preferred that type of storage be built into closets.

The original bedroom/bathroom area was set up with an entrance in the middle of the combined space. To the left of the doorway was an 11-by-12-foot dressing area—filled with hanging rods, shelving, and a vanity/dressing table, and was dimly lit with a pull-chain light—that opened into the 13½-by-15-foot bedroom. Arranging furniture in the two spaces was awkward since the first area was nothing more than an enlarged passageway, and the bedroom beyond was relatively small by comparison. To the right of the entrance was a 9-by-10-foot dressing room/closet, and, through it, the bathroom, containing nothing more than a conventional toilet, tub/shower, and vanity. There was nothing special there.

Considering both the bedroom and the intended dining room downstairs, the couple planned an addition of 15 by 18½ feet. The resulting bedroom area was a magnifient 15-by-32-foot chamber. To bring the room down to earth a little and to replace the storage space to be lost with the dressing room, the designer planned his and her closets for one end of the new bedroom. Measuring 7½ by 7 feet each, the closets

Above left, reflected in the 9-foot expanse of mirrored doors, a skylight illuminates the vanity.

The same wallpaper is used both on the walls and the ceiling. When reflected in the doors, this has the visual effect of increasing the dimensions of the bathroom.

The 5-by-8-foot tub/toilet/bidet compartment was the original bathroom, and the remainder of the present room was originally a dressing area. The bidet replaced the original lavatory. The present dimensions are 8 by 14 feet.

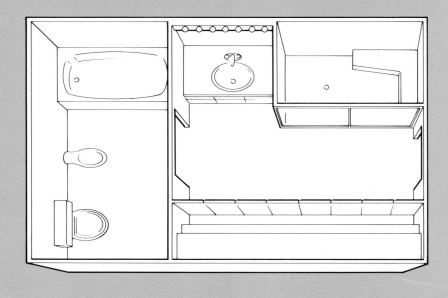

contain a combination of hanging space and drawer storage tailored for the users. The remaining 15-by-25 foot space is the new bedroom.

With storage more than adequately provided for, the new bathroom was planned to incorporate the former dressing room. Because the house wasn't very old and the existing bathroom was in good shape, both the tub and toilet were retained in place, but the old vanity was scrapped and easily replaced with a bidet.

Light was the first priority in the old, dark dressing area. A 3-foot-square skylight was positioned to illuminate a new, 4-foot-wide vanity. Alongside the vanity, a 5-foot-wide fiberglass shower module, complete with both stationary and hand-held shower heads and a seat, was installed. Glass doors let in outside light. Across the room, where the dressing table/counter had been, a 9-foot expanse of shelving was constructed and concealed behind three mirrored sliding doors.

During the planning stage, it was decided that the woman's vanity would be placed in the anteroom to the bedroom, away from the steam of the tub/shower and showerstall. (In the anteroom a large window provides natural light, and the bedroom beyond makes the area good for little else.) Since only 7½ feet of the old dressing room's 10-foot width was needed, there was a 2½-by-9-foot slice left over—the perfect size for a laundry area accessible from the hall outside the bedroom.

"Everything just seemed to fall in place for us," the woman admitted. "Not only was that a perfect location for the laundry—upstairs where the laundry is generated—but the plumbing already was there from the new vanity and shower, so there was hardly any additional expense.

"This whole bathroom is right over the kitchen, and we already had decided to put a bar sink in one corner," the woman said. "We just ran the water from that straight upstairs!"

Because the vanity would be on display at the entrance to the bedroom, the woman wanted something that would look more like a piece of furniture than a bathroom fixture. She and the designer found it in two antique armoire doors.

"That's all we found—just the doors," said the designer. "But I knew we could get a cabinetmaker to construct a system around them, and that turned out to be better than trying to fit a sink into an existing armoire."

From the 6½-foot-tall-by-4½-foot-wide doors, a 2-foot-deep-by-7-foot-wide unit was constructed to fulfill the woman's unique needs. The door widths determined how wide the lavatory counter would be inside. Drawer and cabinet storage and a 4½-foot mirror were custom-built to fill the interior. Recessed lighting was built into the newly constructed bonnet. On either side, a column of clear plastic drawers now holds small clothing items and accessories. Finally, fulfilling its decorative function, when closed the unit looks like a beautiful piece of antique furniture.

"If I'd wanted to design the perfect house for us, this

Starting with only two antique armoire doors, a cabinet maker crafted this unique vanity cupboard, complete with marble lavatory, mirror, and recessed lighting. The cupboard is located outside the bathroom.

would have been it," the woman said, "but I never could have come up with it from scratch. I knew what I didn't like about this house and found it was easier to change those things than it would have been to start fresh. Now, there's not a thing I would change!"

Sometimes It's Best To Break A Few Rules

For both economic and practical reasons, most architects and contractors will recommend to the bathroom remodeler that plumbing be concentrated in as compact an area as possible. Bathrooms cost less and the piping causes fewer problems if the bathrooms (and kitchen or laundry) are stacked or laid out back to back, because the length of the piping is at a minimum and there are few bends and curves in the piping to cause future maintenance or replacement headaches.

Fully aware of such rules of thumb, however, one couple disregarded them on the advice of their architect. The architect believed that a better overall layout could be achieved for the seven-room, two-story home if the two full bathrooms, one on each floor, were located on opposite sides of the structure. Since every inch of the plumbing needed to be replaced anyway in this conversion of a century-old two-flat into a single family home, the architect reasoned that design considerations rated higher than economic or functional arguments for keeping both bathrooms in their previous locations, one atop the other.

"Paramount to any remodeling is a good layout," the architect commented, adding that his concept of remodeling includes more than simply replacing one thing with another in the same place. "If you have a poor layout and you remodel your home but don't change the layout, you still will have a constant annoyance. That's why I think sometimes it is not worth 'remodeling' a bathroom. But if you have to put in a whole new waste stack and plumbing, and are not just replacing fixtures, that is the time to also seriously consider relocating the bathroom altogether. Though the two bathrooms in this house are not one above the other, they do share the same new stack and plumbing, angled from one side of the house to the other. While this cost more and there are some functional risks involved, if we hadn't taken them, the layout would have suffered tremendously."

The long, narrow building used to contain two apartments with three bedrooms each. Each apart-

ment was laid out with the tiny bedrooms and the bathroom lined up along one side of the apartment and with the larger living room, dining room, and kitchen along the other. In trying to maintain as much of the original Victorian woodwork and accoutrements as possible, the couple wanted to rearrange the two apartments into a home without destroying the building's past glory. On the first floor this was relatively simple. Both the dining room and kitchen were widened to the full 20-foot width of the rowhouse simply by removing the walls of the bedrooms adjoining those two rooms. The bathroom on this floor was reconstructed virtually in the same location. Upstairs, however, the bedrooms were too small by contemporary standards, so it was decided to shift the traffic pattern from the main rooms of this floor to a new hall in the area where the bedrooms had been. This left the former living room, dining room, and kitchen on this floor as graciously sized bedrooms. But, since the new hall would destroy the old bathroom on this floor, the bathroom had to be moved across the "hall" and be tucked into a new area carved between the former dining room and kitchen.

"When we bought the house two and a half years ago, it had been abandoned and was unlivable," the woman remembers. "The heating system had been ripped out, and pipes had frozen and burst. And there wasn't a functioning toilet in the place. Each room was worse than the last. But the original fireplaces still were intact and the woodwork was nice enough to save; so we knew it could make a nice home."

By tying their builder to a contract that specified monetary penalties if the work was not completed on schedule, the couple ensured that the entire renovation, including the bathrooms shown here, would take only four months. In that way, they could count on all the work being finished before they moved in.

Before a single hammer was lifted, though, they carefully worked out a plan with an architect familiar with the peculiarities of old houses. The couple presented him with basic ideas on how to salvage as much as possible, and he refined their ideas. They also credit him with finding creative ways to introduce light into each of the bathrooms, as well as into other areas of the home, and with keeping the resale value of the home in mind so that the remodeling would not result in an over-individualized white elephant. In the upstairs bathroom, for example, this meant compartmentalizing so that more than one person could use the bathroom at a time, even though this couple has no children and their schedules don't really overlap.

For this second floor bathroom, which serves all three bedrooms and is entered from the new hall, the couple asked for a room that had the feel of a

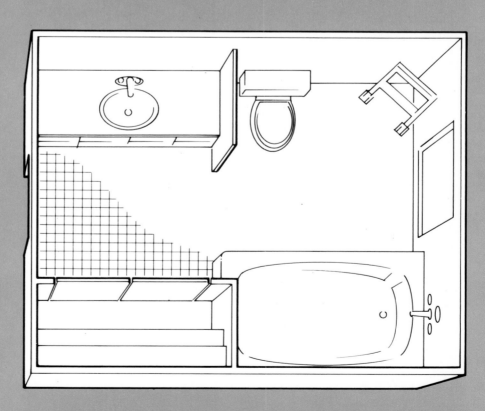

Although building a sunken tub proved impractical, the impression of one is created by an oversized fiberglass tub unit. The antique wringer is useful as well as decorative.

As part of their overall scheme for turning a two-flat into a single-family home, the owners designed this 10-by-13-foot bathroom in space formerly occupied by parts of a dining room and kitchen.

throughout this bathroom. A single row of the tiles forms a backsplash and baseboards, and the tile throughout is grouted with a taupe-colored mix.

If the sheer size of this bathroom (10 by 13 feet overall) were not enough, the spatial excitement was further heightened by piercing the walls above door height with windows to admit light from a hall skylight. The ceilings are 9¾ feet high, so they left plenty of room for the 10-foot-long horizontal wall openings both between the hall and the vanity compartment and between the vanity compartment and the bathing area. (The first opening is glassed in for accoustical privacy but the second is left free for air circulation.) The 5-foot-wide mirror behind the vanity extends upward to a point where the windows begin, which increases the actual light and the feeling of space within the room.

The hall skylight also provides light to adjacent bedrooms through transom windows. But its most ingenious function is to help illuminate the downstairs bathroom!

Although the downstairs bathroom is on the other end of the house from the skylight, its ceiling is directly beneath the hall floor. A section of this ceiling/floor was cut out, and two antique stained glass panels were set into the opening. In effect, the downstairs bathroom was given its own skylight, the light source for which is the second-floor skylight. A handrail was placed around the opening in the hall floor.

The stained glass windows in the ceiling of the downstairs bathroom sparkle by day with natural light; at night, they glow with artificial light from the hall above. Other links with the past, besides the antique windows, are suggested by the mirror, which is surrounded by an antique picture frame that was purchased at a church auction, and by a new light fixture patterned after a Victorian gas lamp with fluted shades.

This room, which measures 5½ by 9 feet, features irregularly toned blue tile that picks up the shades in the windows above. The floor is laid with 3½-inch-square tiles, while the 3-foot-wide vanity and the entire shower are tiled with 1-inch squares; gray grout was used throughout. The use of tile for the shower, including a 21-inch-deep seat, and for the floor and the vanity countertop makes this bathroom one that is extremely easy to keep clean, according to the woman. Another feature in both bathrooms that she recommends is slideout trays in the storage compartments of the vanities. "There is no fishing for anything," she says.

After having used these bathrooms now for nearly three years, the couple has found that their original desires haven't meshed exactly with their needs. The man has pretty much taken over the downstairs bath for his morning showers, while the woman, who plays racquetball three or four times a week, now showers more often than not away from home at her club. The vanity upstairs has seen plenty of use, but the wonderful, huge tub there is reserved for infrequent days when there is a wonderful, huge chunk of time just to sit and soak.

Japanese bath—natural colors and a sunken tub. Though the latter turned out to be impractical to construct, the impression of it is created by American Standard's Ultra Bath, an oversized fiberglass unit that fills a 3⅔ foot by 5¾ foot area in one of the bath's two compartments. The overall measurements of this compartment are 7¾ feet by 10 feet, and it contains only the toilet and an antique wringer that the woman has waited years to be able to display properly. Although the relatively empty floor space might seem wasteful, the design fulfills the couple's request for a spacious and luxurious bathroom; there is no doubt that one is "bathing" here, rather than merely "taking a bath." It is wonderful to fill the tub in the summertime and just submerge yourself," the woman reports.

The room through which one enters this bathing chamber meaures 5¼ feet, by 10 feet and contains a vanity with storage on one side and closets and a laundry behind bi-fold doors on the other. The vanity, which holds a white self-rimming lavatory, is topped with a counter made of the same 2¾-inch square, mottled sand-colored tiles that form the flooring

Antique stained-glass windows in the ceiling of the first-floor bathroom admit light from a skylight in the second-floor hall.

Below left, an antique picture frame around the mirror and a Victorian-pattern light fixture are links with the past.

The use of gray-grouted tile for the shower, the floor, and the vanity top makes this bathroom extremely easy to keep clean.

Bachelor Creates An Opulent Condo

Resale value was uppermost in the mind of the bachelor who created these two sumptuous bathrooms in a three-story, glass-and-steel penthouse he planned to occupy himself—for a while, anyway. A real estate investor/speculator, he was excited about the possibilities for a 50-year-old building he found on Chicago's near north side; he planned to convert the former factory to a luxury, 11-unit condominium, including a penthouse for himself. He had lived in many of his previous projects, however, and knew that ultimately he would be selling this unit, too. In fact, a year and a half after he started this conversion, he was ready to move to a Frank Lloyd Wright landmark home, and this spectacular 5400-square-foot penthouse was on the market for a cool $685,000.

"For that price, people expect some extraordinary and elegant touches," the man explained. "I wanted this to be a luxurious apartment, so while I included many features for myself, much also was done for resale. For example, I use the shower area in the master bathroom only infrequently, and I don't use the spray attachment on the men's lavatory. But I still think an apartment as grand as this should include them."

And the apartment is grand. Perched atop the sixth floor of the massive 60-by-60-foot brick building, it features a central 41-foot-tall glass-enclosed atrium. From the steel cantilevered stairs that thread their way up the atrium, visitors can step off to any of the three levels. The first level is the main living area, which includes a living room, a dining room, and a kitchen.

The same earth-tone tile was used for the floor, the shower walls, the top of the custom-built oak vanity, and both the inside and outside of the whirlpool tub. The tub was custom built on the site by covering a plywood form with lead sheeting and then tile. Bronze-tinted windows allow shower-users a spectacular view without being seen.

Each of these spaces has a 17-foot ceiling and measures 20 feet square to conform to the 20-foot modules created by the window bays and supporting columns. A library/guest room is located on this level, too, as well as a full bathroom and the ultra-chic, white-tiled guest bathroom shown here. All walls on this level are white, and furnishings are kept to a sleek, bare minimum.

Although furnishings on the second level, which was added to the top of the factory, also are intentionally sparse in keeping with the architecture's purity, the mood here shifts, and all interior walls are painted a glossy chocolate brown. Outside walls are floor-to-ceiling glass that is shielded with thin-slat blinds, and the flooring is handsome glazed Mexican brick. These elements are used throughout this level, which houses two bedrooms, two sitting rooms, the master bathroom, and a small but complete kitchen. The third level is an all-glass greenhouse that opens onto two 20-by-40-foot terraces. A double gas grill and oven outdoors and a wet bar at the top of the stairs provide for convenient and comfortable entertaining.

In planning the unique home, the bachelor used top-of-the-line equipment and appliances, and the bathrooms reveal no exceptions. In the master bathroom, the tub has a Jacuzzi whirlpool, and the large stall shower features a steam attachment. Both full bathrooms are equipped with Kohler's men's lavatory and Rochelle model toilet.

The 10-by-12-foot master bathroom is a natural extension of surrounding rooms. The same Mexican brick continues into the bathroom, but here it is not limited to flooring. In the first of the two compartments, which houses the tub and vanity as well as a linen closet, the 4-by-8-inch tiles enclose the tub and also cover the countertop. In the second compartment, the medium-toned, natural-colored tile climbs the walls in the shower stall and are set in the same two-on-one pattern.

When planning this bathroom, the owner wanted to keep it to a functional minimum. There would not be a lot of plants, pictures, and other accessories used, so

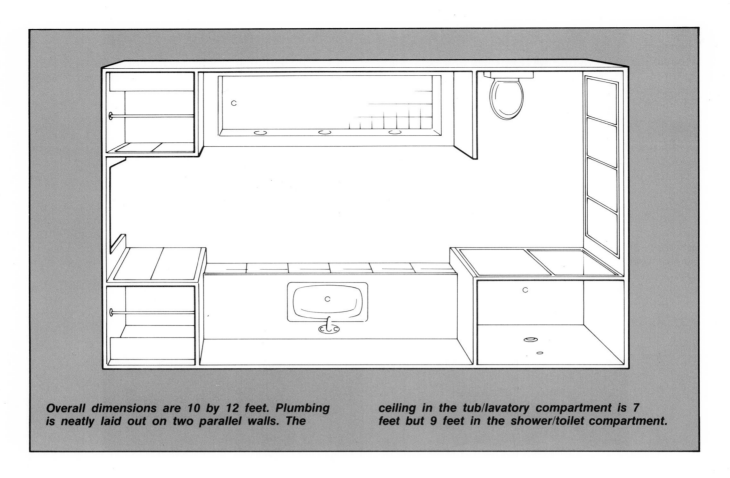

Overall dimensions are 10 by 12 feet. Plumbing is neatly laid out on two parallel walls. The ceiling in the tub/lavatory compartment is 7 feet but 9 feet in the shower/toilet compartment.

the materials had to provide the decor. Consequently, in the 7-by-10-foot first compartment, the major pattern and "color" come from the neutral tiles. These were used to cover the whirlpool bath that was custom-constructed on the site to fit a 3-by-5½-foot niche. The Jacuzzi motor and whirlpool jets were built into a plywood frame that subsequently was covered with lead sheeting and then the tiles. On the other side of this compartment, the tile tops a custom-built oak vanity set with an Expresso brown lavatory by Kohler. The vanity was built a few inches higher than standard to accommodate the owner's 6-foot-2-inch height. The generous 3-by-5½-foot top is banded in oak to match the wood on the three drawers and three doors below. Two of the vanity doors open for storage, and the third actually is a slide-out hamper. To the right of the vanity is a full-size linen closet.

Lighting in this area consists of two recessed incandescent spotlights over the vanity and a row of bare bulbs over the tub-to-ceiling mirror that backs the tub niche. All the lighting is controlled by rheostats so that it can be subdued when the bachelor entertains and can be made brightly functional at other times. And, although the walls in the area are painted a light-absorbing brown, the illumination is multiplied many times over by the infinity effect created with a second mirror, vanity-to-ceiling, that faces the one behind the tub.

Stepping from the first compartment into the second gives a feeling of emerging from a tunnel (indeed, the ceiling in the first compartment is a relatively low 7 feet, both for mechanical and aesthetic reasons). The ceiling in the second compartment is 9 feet high, and the 5-by-10-foot area is flooded with light from the 10-foot expanse of floor-to-ceiling glass along the exterior wall. (At night, a recessed spotlight over the toilet and another row of bare bulbs along the outer wall provide illumination in this compartment.) To the right, as you face this spectacular window, is the 3-by-5-foot shower enclosure with ceiling-height glass doors. The shower is so positioned that a bather is allowed an unencumbered view of the surrounding neighborhood and downtown Chicago. Outsiders cannot see in, however, because bronze-tinted Thermo-pane windows are used throughout the condominium.

Opposite the shower, light-toned prefinished flooring covers the wall behind the Expresso brown Kohler Rochelle toilet and continues up over the ceiling. The wall, from which a pocket door emerges to shut the room off, is painted the same glossy chocolate brown found in the first compartment.

Downstairs, the ambience in the 5-by-10-foot guest bath is decidedly different. Pure white, glistening 4-inch-square tiles are found everywhere except on the white-painted front and back walls and on the mirrored wall behind the vanity. The tile covers the floor and completely enwraps the bathing area and the custom-built vanity.

The ceiling in this bathroom is 14 feet high. The owner not only did not lower it, as many people might have; he accentuated it by mirroring it. The room was brought back to human scale, however, with the use of two canopies, both fully tiled in white, over the vanity and shower areas. Only the center of the bathroom was left full-height.

The vanity, which is attached only to the two side walls, "floats" above the floor and also is free from the mirrored wall behind it. Measuring 5 feet long, 22 inches wide, and 16 inches high, it is completely wrapped in white tiles and is set with a pure white Kohler men's lavatory. A soap dispenser in the unit eliminates the need for a separate soap dish. Above, a

matching 22-inch-wide canopy holds two recessed spotlights, which are controlled by a rheostat.

A Kohler white Rochelle toilet is in the center of the room, and opposite the vanity is the shower. This 2½-foot-wide by 5-foot-long area does not include a tub. Instead, a tub was created by sinking the shower floor 16 inches and building an 8-inch-high lip up from the floor to provide an edge. The clean lines also are not interrupted by a shower curtain; water can be contained in the bathing area, and if any does escape, it will not harm the tiled floor. The luxury of a heat lamp is tucked alongside the vent fan in the canopy over the shower. As a final touch, a single spray of eucalyptus graces the vanity in this otherwise pristine chamber.

The vanity in the guest bathroom "floats," attached only to the two side walls. The 14-foot ceiling over the vanity was lowered by "floating" a canopy-like soffit in the same manner as the vanity.

A half bathroom, above, is concealed behind inconspicuous closet-like doors.

Couple Finds Just The Right Angle

Long before the owners of this ultra-sophisticated bathroom had even decided to build their home, they had resolved that someday they would have a bathroom with a whirlpool in it. They had first marveled at a whirlpool's comforting effects while indulging in a poolside unit at a resort hotel. Subsequent encounters had strengthened their resolve to have a whirlpool of their own. "We decided that if we ever had the chance, we would have a whirlpool in our home, even if it meant skimping on something else," the woman said recently. "As it turns out, it isn't really a luxury at all. It's extremely therapeutic, and my husband relies on it to help him unwind."

It also turned out that the couple didn't have to skimp on anything else, in order to include a Jacuzzi whirlpool bath in their house plans. Since the 3-by-6-foot unit also serves as a tub, it eats up no extra floor space. And, because the house was not yet built when the bathroom was planned, the installation cost of the whirlpool was not significantly higher than it would have been for a conventional tub.

Even if the whirlpool had been huge and outrageously expensive, the ingenious couple would have found a way to have one. The woman, a former model and accomplished musician, spends the majority of her time at home mothering the couple's two young daughters. So, she says, her home and its comforts are "extremely important" to her. And, although her husband is away from home for long periods working as a cameraman for CBS network news, when he does come home, the whirlpool and its serene surroundings are crucial to the transition from the hectic pace of his job to the tranquility of home.

This definite desire for a comfortable home, which would specifically include a whirlpool bath, is typical of

the clear-cut requirements and goals that guided the couple throughout the years of their search for a house that ideally suited their tastes and lifestyle. Once city-dwellers who truly enjoyed the liveliness of the downtown scene, they found themselves seeking a different environment after having children. "I was getting tired of struggling with carriages in the apartment elevator," the woman explained. Her husband was under more stress, too. Away from home as much as 300 days a year, he was traveling abroad regularly and arriving home at hours that bore no relation to his family's routine. It became clear that quieter surroundings were in order.

After a long and disappointing search for suburban housing, the couple decided that the only way they were going to get what they wanted at a price they could afford would be to build their own house. An exploration of undeveloped property turned up an ideal setting—a two-acre lot in a heavily wooded community on the Fox River in Illinois. If the acreage would not separate them from hustle and bustle, the foliage would. The plot was so densely dotted with oak and maple trees that, in summer, other houses barely would be visible.

Although homes constructed on neighboring lots easily could be listed in the luxury price category, this couple's four-bedroom, three-bathroom dwelling was kept within their budget by a number of money-saving methods. Just as they knew there had to be a way for them to have a whirlpool, they knew that if they cut corners where it mattered least, they still could have what they considered essentials. For example, the pair rejected as too costly the idea of hiring an architect to design their dream home. Instead, they began perusing home decorating and building magazines for a house plan that would equally suit their dreams and their pocketbook. Their diligence paid off when they received a packet of plans they had seen offered in a small back-of-the-magazine ad. Among the dozen or so plans was one for a nine-room, two-story house that featured an attractive kitchen/family room arrangement, a spacious master bedroom suite, a den on the first floor, and enough bedrooms and baths for the children to have privacy then and in the future.

"The only trouble was that while the floor plan was to our liking, the Colonial style wasn't," the woman recalled. "We had something more contemporary in mind." So, the couple sought the advice of the interior

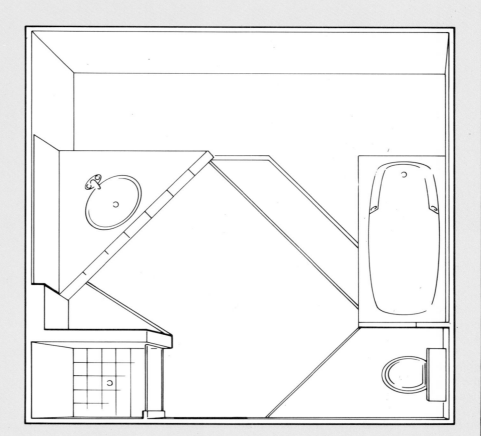

Lotions and scents are displayed on open shelves, while less decorative items are stored behind vanity doors that open at a touch. The shower is a fiberglass module fitted into a constructed alcove.

A generously proportioned 12-by-12½-foot bathroom was created by capturing space from an adjacent closet and by building outward under the house eave.

designer they were planning to hire for assistance in furnishing their future home. While the house was still in the blueprint stage, the couple and the designer worked together and "tore the house apart" so completely that the couple now believe the original architect wouldn't recognize it.

After carefully studying the basic structure and determining which walls could be moved or eliminated, the couple and the designer set about customizing the house. Skylights were added. The fourth bedroom was turned into a playroom with a laundry area. The front entry hall was expanded to incorporate space that formerly had been part of the front porch. And, the master bathroom and closet were so thoroughly revamped—in virtually the same space alotted by the

original blueprint—that these results alone dramatize the possibilities for turning a builder's model into a one-of-a-kind, dream-come-true dwelling.

In a 9-by-18-foot space along one end of the master bedroom, the original house plans called for a walk-in closet and a tub and toilet room. The closet was approximately 9 feet square, and the tub and toilet room, which included a linen closet, measured 5 by 9 feet. These two areas were separated by and entered from a 4-by-9-foot open space that housed a single-bowl vanity and ceiling-height mirror. Though the bathroom was along an outside wall, it had no windows; that, plus the layout, left the bathroom dark and resembling a motel's grooming set-up.

"The plan was claustrophobic, especially in comparison with the openness of the rest of the house," remarked the designer. "Also, there was no privacy at all with the sink out in the open—and no good lighting for grooming, either. Since the husband has erratic hours, the bathroom had to be completely separated from the bedroom. And besides, no one wants to watch his or her mate brush their teeth."

The owners stipulated only that the new bathroom design include a whirlpool tub and sufficient privacy. They left the rest of the bathroom planning to the designer. The designer's first step was to make a new drawing of the original floor plan. From the drawing, he erased the nonsupporting walls of the entire 9-by-18-foot area so that he could make a fresh approach to this design problem.

To make the bathroom a separate, more private room, the designer decided to put the entry to the walk-in closet in the master bedroom and, at the same time, decrease the giant closet's square footage by a third, making it 6 by 9 feet. The extra space could be put to much better use in the bathroom, he reasoned, and shaving the closet's proportions resulted in a negligible loss of hanging space.

Reworking the closet left a generous 9-by-12-foot space for the bathroom. But the designer still did not feel that the area was satisfactory. "I drew many plans, all incorporating a whirlpool, of course," he said. "But they all involved conventional runs of counters, and that made for a lot of wasted floor space."

The designer hit on a new angle when he rough-sketched a skylight for illumination. The addition required opening the space under the roof eave to allow the skylight to be installed on the sloping roof. A happy by-product of expanding beneath the eave was the gain of 3½ feet of room length, bringing the room's total dimensions to 12 by 12½ feet.

With those decisions made, the designer said, the angled placement of fixtures, tile, and a half wall "just seemed to fit." Coupled with a raised platform in the eave area, they also give the room its unusual and smashing good looks.

In placing the fixtures, the designer was guided to some extent by the original floor plan. The toilet and tub are maintained near the first plan's locations so that they still can share a plumbing wall with the children's bathroom to utilize common water and waste lines. Similarly, although the lavatory now is located a few feet to the left of the position called for in the original blueprint, the plumbing extends through the raised platform to the old location. Plumbing for a separate shower, an amenity the original plan lacked, runs under the floor to join the lavatory plumbing.

Once he started playing with angles, the designer had a field day. He followed the pitch of the roof in a tiled wall next to the whirlpool tub, which is Jacuzzi's Premier Roman Bath model. The slant is suggested again on the opposite wall, behind the angled vanity, in a custom-cut mirror bordered by a strip of Hollywood-type lighting. Even the two-inch-square floor tiles (American Olean's Crystalline in antique white) are set on the diagonal, as are steps to the tub and exercise/sunning platform. In fact, the only right-angled areas in the room are the 32-by-36-inch shower enclosure (Kohler's Trinidad fiberglass bathing module) and the area for the toilet (Kohler's Rochelle model in Parchment). Even the half-wall separating the toilet from the tub is angled downward to echo the wedge of tiled surface behind the tub.

As for decoration, the owners asked only that the room be "serene, rather pure, with no wallcovering," said the designer. Parchment and antique whites form a shell that is gently punctuated with peach and sand colored towels, which are stacked or gathered in baskets, rather than hung on rods. Lush greenery springs from a galvanized metal plant pit at the end of the tub, and a collection of shells and baskets adds to the tropical feeling.

For a touch of class, the triangular vanity (set with a Kohler lavatory and Unilever faucet) was constructed to the designer's own specifications from brushed metal and plastic laminate. The vanity's metal top can be scratched, the designer admits, but since this is a bathroom for adults, maintenance problems should be minimal. The vanity doors open when pressed, revealing storage space for grooming aids. Four recessed shelves on the vanity side of the shower wall hold additional lotions and scents.

Construction of the house took seven months. The entire project was supervised by the woman. Not only was this high level of participation personally satisfying, it also avoided the cost of hiring a general contractor.

The master bedroom and bathroom were among the first rooms to be livably furnished, and now this adult bathing sanctuary (the children still don't know that mom and dad have a whirlpool) has been put to use at virtually every hour of the day. The woman, who starts every morning with coffee and a quick shower, saves the whirlpool as an end-of-the-day treat: "for after the kids are fed and put to bed and I can tell myself I deserve it," she said. "It's terrific when my back hurts, and when I use bath salts, the fragrance stays in the room for days." For the future, she plans to add a sun lamp to take advantage of the platform, which is covered with a low-maintenance, mildew-resistant wool and acrylic carpet by Urotex.

When her husband is home in the morning, the couple share coffee in the master bathroom and find it "a nice, relaxing, soothing place to be before the breakfast circus with the girls." If the man arrives home exhausted, he often grabs a book, turns on the whirlpool, and in 20 minutes "is a new person, willing to tell all about his latest trip," said his wife. "That was the whole idea for this house, to give my husband as much serenity as possible. That bathroom can stimulate him or relax him, depending on his frame of mind."

And that's just what this bathroom is for. As the woman explained. "Our home is important to us and we want it to be nice. We are not doing this for anyone else, to impress anyone; it's for us. It's especially important to me because we don't go out a great deal or entertain often, so I spend all my time at home, and I want it the way I want it. Your home can be your prison or your castle. I'm trying to make this a castle."

Design Matches
The Address
Of Success

When you are buying a 2500-square-foot apartment in a newly constructed condominium at one of the most prestigious addresses in town, you expect the latest in appointments. The bathroom in particular might be expected to offer a bidet, sauna, and separate shower and bathing facilities, and spaciousness would be taken for granted.

All of these features were included in the three-bedroom, three-bathroom unit that a newly divorced man purchased as his first real apartment for himself. But even all those amenities couldn't make up for a certain blandness, and his experience suggests that it isn't just a bathroom's layout or fixtures that make it something special; decoration plays a role in comfort, too.

When the man, the father of two young sons and the head of his own company, purchased his city apartment, it already had been constructed but had not been lived in. The developer offered some selection in bathroom cabinetry and fixture models, but basically the room was to be delivered with a prime coat of paint on the walls, a cement floor, a single lavatory, and a marble-walled shower stall. A sauna was an option, that the builder would install, and the management also would cooperate in putting in any other custom items, such as flooring, additional lighting, or mirrors—for an extra charge, of course. The man, who travels a great deal and didn't have time to concern himself with

overseeing the installation, turned the bathroom, as well as his entire apartment, over to an interior designer to complete.

"In order to design the apartment to fit this man's lifestyle, I had to spend a lot of time up front discussing what he expected, whether he entertained, what colors and styles he preferred," the interior designer said. "But then he pretty much turned the job over to me, and I had access to the apartment at any time."

With the exception of the bedrooms used by the boys when they visit, rooms are decorated in grays and burgundy throughout the apartment for continuity, and furnishings run to an eclectic mix with an emphasis on Art Deco. Most of the rooms are clad in gray flannel walls with wool carpet dyed to match and feature burgundy upholstery or accessories. Antiques mix freely with plastic and chrome, and mirrors are used extensively. These same colors and materials show up in the master bathroom and link it with the adjoining 16-by-17-foot master bedroom and the rest of the unit.

When the designer first approached the decoration of the approximately 14-foot-square bathroom shown here, she was hampered somewhat by her client's decision to select from the builder's cabinet and fixture offerings. For example, although the vanity's interior contains such niceties as a pull-out hamper, the designer would have preferred flush doors that could be mirrored. Selecting white as the color was one way of minimizing the impact on the overall room.

Such limitations aside, the designer prescribed two lavatories instead of one, allowing for the possibility of remarriage. She specified that the same marble that was to be used for the shower stall be continued throughout the bathroom (as flooring, as a vanity countertop and backsplash, and to encase the Kohler tub that in other apartments is tiled). The mirrored medicine cabinets above the lavatory basins were included, but the mirror around the tub is a decorative extra. "Mirror is a dramatic and sensuous element, especially in a bathroom," the designer explained. "I

The countertop of the double lavatory is made of the same marble that was used in the shower stall and around the tub. The mirrors above the lavatories were included in the original bathroom. The television to the left can be viewed easily from the tub.

The cloisonné vase and horse-head figures give the bathroom a dash of the antique. The burgundy towels were specially dyed to match the burgundy used in other parts of the apartment.

wanted to mirror the ceiling above the tub, too, but the builder convinced me that moisture in the room might bring it crashing down."

The mirrored look is continued on all other walls via a silvery foil wallcovering that was custom colored with the same grays and burgundy used elsewhere in the apartment. For a perfect match, the lush towels were dyed to order, and these are hung on chrome rings and clear plastic bars the designer installed to replace standard chrome racks.

Accessories fit both the decor and the man's lifestyle. Repeating the mirror and clear plastic are a crystal ashtray, mirrored tissue box and waste basket, and Lucite plastic soap dish. A dash of the antique is evident as a cloisonné vase and two horse head figures whose bits hold hand towels. Because the man is both a shower and a bath person and must have access to a telephone at all times, a white phone is perched atop a mirrored cube within easy reach of either the 3½-by-8-foot tub or the 4-by-6-foot shower. An extension also can be found in the 5-by-6½-foot toilet/bidet room.

This bath also is equipped with a television (positioned on the 8½-foot-long vanity so the man also can watch from the tub) and with dimmer switches for both the fluorescent lights over the basin and the incandescent spotlights in the ceiling. Arriving home late at night, the man can fill the tub, switch on the television, turn down the lights, and settle in for a relaxing soak during the midnight movie.

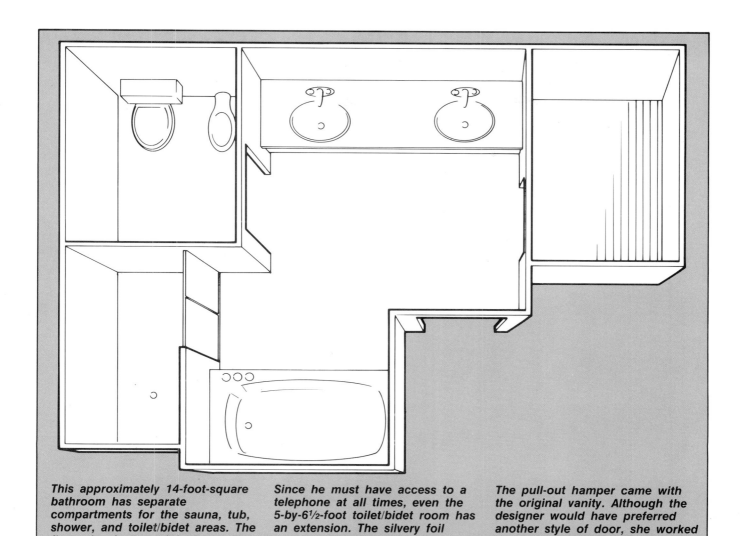

This approximately 14-foot-square bathroom has separate compartments for the sauna, tub, shower, and toilet/bidet areas. The floor plan is the original one that came with the condominium.

Since he must have access to a telephone at all times, even the 5-by-6½-foot toilet/bidet room has an extension. The silvery foil wallcovering adds to the bathroom's mirrored look.

The pull-out hamper came with the original vanity. Although the designer would have preferred another style of door, she worked around it in creating this bathroom.

House Grows
To Fit Family,
Move Avoided

Many families today are undertaking home remodeling projects as a way of avoiding a move. Perhaps family size has grown or the children have become teenagers, and suddenly the house that functioned so well for so many years seems cramped and no longer offers much privacy for either parents or children. One solution is to move to another home that better meets changed needs. But with the cost of housing rising so rapidly throughout the country, more families have found it more economical to rethink their current dwellings. Basements and attics are being finished to provide more space. Garages are being converted into family rooms. Room additions are sprouting in all directions and for myriad purposes. Restructuring a family's long-time home has added benefits, too. Children don't have to change school systems, and family friendships and civic affiliations need not be disrupted either.

Such considerations entered into the thinking of the owners of the master bathroom shown here when they were assessing their situation nearly three years ago. They had moved into the two-story suburban house, which had four bedrooms and three bathrooms, just after their son was born in 1970. They already had a three-year-old daughter and thought the house would satisfy their needs for space for many years to come. The location also was ideal, and there was no reason to think they would not live in the house a long time.

But, as their daughter was approaching her tenth birthday, it became obvious that quarters were becoming close. "Our bedroom was on top of the kids'," said their mother, "and we needed lots more privacy, both for us and for them. We didn't need a larger house or more bedrooms, and we didn't want to move, but the space needed to be arranged differently."

After asking friends for recommendations for designers, architects, or contractors, the couple chose a man who could both design a better plan and oversee its construction. He surveyed the existing space and then proposed a 500-square-foot addition to the second floor, over the garage. Although the son's bedroom would be lost to future closet and hall space, the number of bedrooms still would be four, because the addition would contain a new master bedroom and this grand bathroom. The son could have the room previously occupied by his sister, and she could move into the former master bedroom suite, complete with private bathroom. Best of all, the parents' bedroom and bathroom would be secluded, lying beyond the new hall and closets, over the garage. It was ideal.

As requirements for the master bedroom, the couple stipulated that it be "white, clean-looking, and shiney. We wanted it bright and open, with plenty of light both in the day and at night," the woman recalled. They also asked the contractor to include twin vanities facing each other, a deep sunken tub, and a separate shower, and to use materials that were easy to clean. The woman additionally requested that her lavatory basin be as large as possible because she likes to wash her hair in the basin.

Of the 500 square feet added, 175 would be devoted to the bathroom, compartmented into a 5-by-10-foot toilet/shower room and a 10-by-12½-foot main room with tub and vanities. The roofline slopes from a high point of 10½ feet along the vanity side. In the planning stage, the contractor advised the couple that vanities placed perfectly back to back would waste too much floor space and that a sunken tub was an impossibility

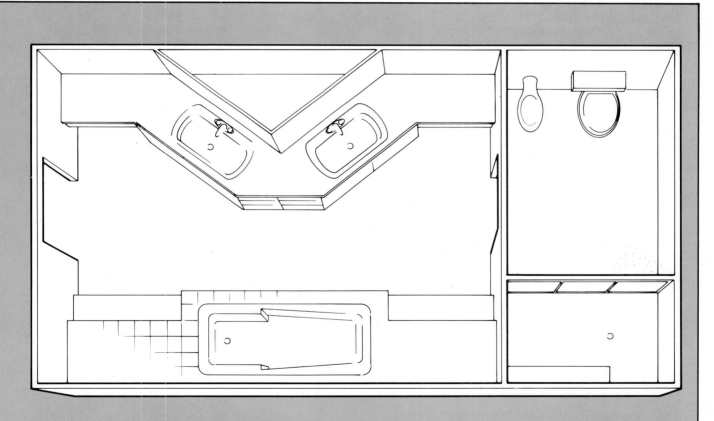

This new bathroom is clean-looking, shiny, bright, and open. The built-up floor area gives the tub a sunken look. The skylight above the tub provides the room with a great deal of natural light. The door in the back leads into the toilet and shower area of this modern bathroom.

By extending the original bedroom and bathroom over the garage, the designer created a spacious 10-by-17½-foot bathroom. This design provides a roomy bath area and privacy for the toilet/bidet and shower areas. The tub has a "sunken" effect and the positioning of the vanities saves floor space.

The two vanity areas are separated visually by a central protrusion of the counter and mirrors. They are identical except for the lavatories and a side-mounted medicine cabinet for the woman. The woman's lavatory also has a hand-held spray for washing her hair.

because it would interfere with garage space below. Instead, the two vanities would be positioned at an angle to suggest a division and give a sense of facing each other, and the impression of a sunken tub could be created by building up the floor around an extra-deep soaking tub. Since a wonderful, 8-foot-long skylight, easy-care white Italian tiles and DuPont Corian synthetic marble countertops, as well as a separate shower room, also were part of the plan, the couple agreed to these minor variations. Completion of the bathroom took five and a half months.

The new bathroom is entered first into the vanity/tub room. At left, four 7½-foot-tall mirrors stretch to the ceiling above a counter that undulates along the 12½-foot-length of the room. The two vanity areas, separated visually by the central protrusion of counter and mirrors, are identical except for the lavatories and a side-wall-mounted medicine cabinet for the woman. As requested, the woman has a lavatory with hand-held spray to make washing her hair a breeze. Both sides feature drawer and conventional storage, and the squared-off protrusion is outfitted with four more shared drawers. The custom cabinets are constructed of white plastic laminate and fitted with Lucite hardware, and the countertop is DuPont's Corian synthetic marble, a material that looks like marble but is much easier to maintain. Rows of six makeup bulbs seam the mirror panels in the vanity areas.

At the right, a 1½-foot-high, completely tiled platform stretches all the way to the toilet/shower room. The 6-foot-long "sunken" tub is nestled in the center and can be reached from either end of the room via two 3-foot-wide steps tiled in the same 7¾-inch-square white import used for the flooring in both compartments. The gray grout never looks dirty, as white would have, and the white and gray combination echoes the colors of the pebble-patterned vinyl wallcovering.

A pocket door separates this room from the shower room beyond, an arrangement that helps contain mirror-fogging steam until the vent fan clears the air. A 34-inch-by-5-foot fiberglass shower stall spans one side of this room, and the toilet and bidet sit side-by-side on the other.

Both compartments are sparked with red accents, including towels, pictures, rugs, and even flowering plants, such as a deep pink cyclamen. A magnificent staghorn fern that takes advantage of the abundant natural light is doubled in the mirror. Lucite accessories that seem to multiply the light include decorative obelisks, a soap dish, a tissue box, and a makeup tray.

Since construction of the addition didn't disrupt the rest of the house, the family experienced little inconvenience. When winter came, however, water froze in the pipes because the garage below the bathroom was unheated. Happily, before any damage occurred, the problem was solved by insulating the garage.

Other than that scare, the couple has been totally pleased with the outcome of their decision to remodel. "The bath is the easiest thing in the world to take care of, and my husband and I easily can use it at the same time," the woman said. "I adore the bath...and our bedroom... and I'm thrilled to death we put them on."

There Was Nowhere To Go But Up

When the couple that now lives in this large suburban house first saw it four years ago, they immediately knew they wanted to buy it. The sprawling, two-story brick house had enough bedrooms to provide privacy for each of their four active children, and the schools in the area were first-rate. The house also had a spacious master bedroom, a well-equipped kitchen, a sunny family room, and a lovely yard overlooking a magnificent golf course. As a bonus, the location was just minutes away from the office of the husband, who is a tax attorney. Everything was perfect—except the master bathroom.

Although the bathroom was conveniently located for privacy as part of the master bedroom suite, it was skimpy compared with the lavish scale of the rest of the house. Off the 16-by-18-foot bedroom was a dark hall arranged as a dressing area with closets along one side and a twin-bowl vanity and mirrors on the other. The hall ended at a 4-by-7-foot room that housed a conventional toilet and shower. Not only wasn't there a tub for the lady of the house, who enjoys soaking, but

"Her" side of this oriental-motif bathroom has a Jacuzzi whirlpool tub, a shallow-countered makeup area, good makeup lighting, complete swing-out mirrors, and many electrical conveniences, such as an intercom, telephone, television, and radio.

the dressing hall was so narrow that open closet doors would be more than just a nuisance; they would be dangerous. The couple could foresee that when both of them were in the area at the same time, the scene would be nothing less than chaotic.

"It was a joke that that bathroom was in that house," said the couple's interior designer, who had accompanied them in their house hunting. "Even the people who lived there before had talked about adding a sauna to make the bath less mundane."

A quick survey of the home's layout showed that a room addition for an entirely new and expanded bathroom would be possible, adjacent to the existing toilet-shower room, over a one-story library on the first floor. The placement was so natural that no one could figure out why the 10-year-old house had not been planned that way in the beginning. Though the construction would not be minor—involving everything from new plumbing to new exterior walls and roofing—

the couple had no reservations about giving the master chamber·the bathroom it deserved. They closed the deal on the house, and the designer began planning the spectacular bathroom shown here.

During the planning stage, the designer collaborated primarily with the woman, since she had been more displeased with the arrangement than her husband. With his on-the-go schedule, he was concerned only that he have a well-lighted place for shaving and a roomy shower; he had no time to spend enjoying the pleasures of the bath.

The woman, on the other hand, felt an acute need for a special room that would allow her to pamper herself. As the mother of three sons and a daughter, aged five to twelve when this bathroom was designed, she felt she needed a sanctuary, a room in which she could calmly prepare for her day and in which she could unwind at night. An organized person who juggles her own school schedule with those of her children, she

The "his" and "her" vanities are positioned back-to-back. The wall that separates the two areas provides privacy and helps prevent steam in one area from fogging the mirror in the other.

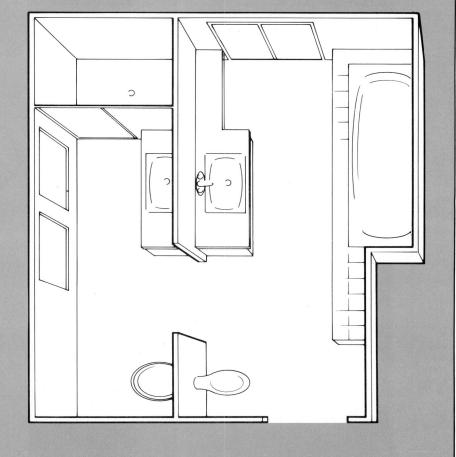

The original 4-by-7-foot room was extended to make this 14-by-14½-foot custom-designed "his and her" bathroom. The area at the left provides him with a place to shave and shower on-the-go. Her section is spacious, luxurious, and gives her a place to unwind in privacy.

was well-prepared when the designer asked for her specific requirements.

"My major request was for my own area with tub and mirror," she said recently. "In our last house, the master bath had only a shower and a single vanity, all in the same room. Though we had the house built for us, we didn't think about compartmenting. Whenever we got ready to go out, my husband would shower while I made up; only pretty soon the mirror would fog up and he would be asking me to move over. After a while, I just used the children's bath, which had twin vanities. But after living there for 10 years and having more children, that became a problem, too. There always were toys around and the lighting wasn't very good, and eventually my sons were too old to have to share a bathroom with their mother. It seemed as though everyone had a bathroom but me."

Although, in her new home, she left the actual placement of the bathroom fixtures to the designer, the

woman specifically wanted the following:

● A bathroom divided so that the husband's shower and vanity would be separated from the wife's vanity, mirror, and tub. The couple could share a toilet and bidet.

● A large tub for soaking and relaxing on the woman's side and a generously sized shower on the man's.

● Fixtures arranged on the woman's side to accommodate her left-handedness. "All my life I've had to work to the right," she said. "And I wanted the sink to the left of my make-up area."

● A shallow counter in the make-up area. This would allow the woman to sit closer to the mirror than a standard-depth counter would.

● Good makeup lighting.

● Movable mirrors that would allow the woman to see the sides and back of her head while grooming.

● An earth-tone color scheme.

Keeping these requirements in mind, the designer went to work planning the new bathroom. He started by determining the 14-by-14½-foot space possible for the addition. The construction of the new room began with the demolition of the old roof over the downstairs library and the removal of the previous bathroom's fixtures, both in the toilet-shower room and in the dressing hall. The new second-story room was then constructed of common brick to match the exterior of the rest of the house, and windows were to be placed to comply both with local building codes and with design considerations inside the bathroom. The former toilet-shower area was turned into an anteroom to give the new bath added privacy.

After the shell of the room had been constructed, the designer divided the room into "his" and "hers" sections with a single wall. This allowed the two vanities to be positioned back-to-back. The wall also created privacy and helped contain mirror-fogging steam when the couple used the bathroom at the same time. In keeping with the man's scaled-down needs, his portion of the room measures 4½ by 14 feet, a corridor shape that allows the 32-by-36-inch shower to be placed at one end, the toilet at the other, and the 3-foot-long vanity between. The entrance to this side of the bathroom is through the woman's side, between the toilet and the vanity.

On the woman's 10-by-14-foot side, a bidet was placed back to back with the toilet located on the other side of the dividing wall. At the other end of the dividing wall, backing up to the man's shower, the woman's side features a makeup center, complete with swing-out mirrors, a recessed counter that enables her to sit close to the mirrors, and myriad lights above, below, and along one side of the mirror. The lavatory is conveniently located to the left of the makeup center so that the left-handed woman can work with ease. Opposite the vanity wall, a 3-by-6-foot Jacuzzi whirlpool tub nestles into an 8½-foot-long niche created when the chimney for the downstairs library fireplace was boxed in.

The chimney, which of course previously had gone up along the exterior of the house, was not the only construction element that determined placement of the bathroom fixtures. The existing soil stack determined the locations of the new toilet and bidet. Similarly, the necessary water and waste plumbing for this entire bathroom runs under the new floor and connects with water and drain lines from the former shower and vanities. When it came to extending the home's heating and cooling system to this room, however, the couple was less fortunate. Since this is a corner room, with exposures on two sides, a separate heating and cooling system was required; these mechanical components are housed on the roof of the new section.

With other mechanical and electrical provisions

A 3-by-6-foot Jacuzzi whirlpool tub is nestled into a 8½-foot niche created when the downstairs fireplace was boxed in. Surrounded by plants, the tub area adds to the oriental ambience.

made for an intercom, telephone, and a raft of other communications equipment, such as television and radio, the designer turned his attention to the decorative aspects of the project. The entire house had a French "feel" that extended even to such detailing as the panels on the closet doors in the dressing hall. The couple knew from the beginning that they wanted the decor changed, where possible, toward a more natural, oriental effect. In the dressing area, this was accomplished by attaching beautifully simple, rectangular, ¼-inch-thick oak panels over the newly painted black closet doors. Matching doors were fabricated for the new storage closet that was installed where the twin vanities had been.

In the new bathroom, of course, the designer was able to start fresh and combine modern technology with the natural elements that suggest oriental tranquility. For the shell of the room, he suggested American Olean's Murray quarry tile in Sand Flash color, set in brown grout and spaced at intervals with 3½-inch-wide oak strips, stained to appear weathered and then sealed with polyurethane. The same wood and tile are combined to enclose the off-white Jacuzzi Premier Roman Bath whirlpool. The wood also surrounds the door and window openings and caps a dado, or half wall, formed by continuing the tile up the wall in the tub niche. The orange wallcovering is a grasscloth-textured vinyl, and the ceiling is painted sand color.

Both vanities, which were custom-fabricated to the designer's plans, feature split bamboo and oak cabinet doors. They are topped with travertine-patterned Formica laminate counters that hold matching Kohler Rondelle lavatories, in the rich brown Expresso color, and Alterna faucets, which also are by Kohler. Flush drawers are incorporated into the face of the lavatory counter. Four-foot-high mirrors are surrounded by theatrical-type makeup lights on gold tracks, and ceiling can lights, wired to dimmer switches provide additional adjustable lighting. Natural light is admitted through a 4-by-7-foot window on the woman's side and two standard-size windows on the man's. The translucent panel treatment of these windows completes the oriental theme. Constructed like shoji screens, the custom-made sliding panels allow access to the windows behind.

During the six months that work was in progress on the master bathroom, the designer was striving for the same oriental mood in the 4½-by-8-foot guest powder room downstairs. The left-over French style of this half bathroom was sorely out of place among the oriental-style furnishings of the rest of the first floor. The designer thought the problem could be resolved, however, by some healthy redecoration, thereby avoiding a full-scale make-over. Consequently, the project did not require any behind-the-walls reconstruction of plumbing and was limited to easily changed fixtures. The existing toilet and marble floor tile were worked into the new plan.

The existing vanity was also retained, but it was painted a gold color all over to camouflage the French-style panels that had been highlighted before.

The downstairs powder room was converted from French to Oriental motif to match the oriental-style furnishings of the rest of the ground floor. The original toilet and vanity were slightly modified to fit into the new decor.

The old porcelain pulls were scrapped in favor of new, square, oriental-style hardware, and a Formica laminate countertop was replaced with real marble. The new lavatory, a platinum bowl by Sherle Wagner, is a rich detail matched in warmth by new pewter faucets with tiger's eye inserts. The pewter/tiger's eye combination is repeated in the towel bars.

An undistinguished wallcovering was removed, and in its place there now is a generously textured version of an oriental mainstay—grasscloth. Each grasscloth panel is strikingly bordered with ebony-stained wood strips that echo the thick ebony boards used in making the shadow box on the room's end wall. This box, holding an artful arrangement of dried flowers, framed oriental portraits, and two tiny dolls, is a focal point of the room, which looks far larger since the installation of a ceiling-height mirror on the wall behind the vanity.

Now that the French look has been erased, both this bathroom and the new one upstairs are in keeping with the rest of the home's oriental furnishings. But perhaps even more important, they function perfectly for the dynamic couple who for so many years dreamed of having such elegant bathrooms.

Townhouse Is Black And White And Beautiful

The three-story city townhouse was an enviable "find" for this couple. It had eight rooms, three full bathrooms, and a basement that could be made into a playroom for their growing children. Thumbnail sketches can be deceiving, however. A closer check revealed that the structure, originally designed as a single family dwelling had been converted into a rooming house in the 1940s. Every room had a lavatory in it, and each door had a big lock. Of the three full bathrooms, one was in the basement, the one off the kitchen featured a tiny tub-on-legs, and the other included a miniscule stall shower. Clearly, some restructuring would be in order if the building were to become a home again.

Before the couple moved in, eight years ago, they called in a contractor to make some sense of the previous "remodelings." Within three months, this striking black and white bathroom had been installed, and the home had been made more comfortable in other ways, too. Central air conditioning was added,

new flooring was installed throughout, the basement was finished and carpeted, and a tiny living room and dining room were combined to create one gracious space.

One in a row of 10 townhouses, this home is nearly identical to the neighboring house (described on pages 27-29). When the owners sought to improve upon the second floor bathroom, they decided, like the couple two doors away, that the only way to get enough space for a decent-sized bathroom was to expand it by incorporating an adjacent bedroom. However, unlike their neighbors, who joined their bathroom with the middle bedroom on the second floor, this couple annexed the bedroom at the rear of the house. (The front bedroom on this floor became the master bedroom, and the middle bedroom belongs to a daughter.) The entire family uses this compartmented bathroom on the second floor.

The 5-by-8-foot space that had been the original bathroom is today merely a compartment, containing the toilet and a scallop-edged lavatory that was salvaged from one of the rooming-house-era bedrooms. This room now is only 7 feet long, however; a foot was walled off to form a shallow closet for cleaning supplies. Now the only entrance to this compartment is through the bath area (the converted bedroom).

Although the stall shower was removed from the old bathroom and a new entrance had to be cut through the bedroom wall, the project involved surprisingly little construction. The new toilet occupies the same location as the old one, and the new tub and pedestal lavatory in the converted bedroom are connected to the water and waste lines that served the bedroom lavatory during rooming house days. Because the floor in the old bathroom was slightly higher than the bedroom floor, a platform was added to the bedroom section to put all the bathroom fixtures on a single level. While this allowed the contractor room to work with piping under the floor, it also created a sense of drama and suggests a division between the functional part of the bathroom and the lounging area.

The dramatic appearance of this bathroom was adapted from pictures the woman saw in decorating magazines. She selected the colors and the vinyl wallcovering, while a decorator's assistance was sought for the shower curtain and other accessories. The black-on-white scheme is built on a checkerboard floor of vinyl tiles, a black-and-white patterned fabric behind lattice shutters, a black area rug in front of the tub, and black ceramic tile in the tub enclosure. The wicker chaise, piled high with black, white, green, and yellow pillows, nestles among myriad plants and is a favorite reading spot for the two pre-teenage girls.

When the bathroom was completed several years ago, "it was a big, wonderful room," the woman remembers. But as the girls have grown older, the room always seems to be occupied, and their father has sought refuge in the basement bathroom to shower and shave each morning. He now contemplates adding a new bathroom on the third floor—one that the girls can call their own—that will return this classic bathroom to him and his wife.

The final appearance of this multi-sectioned bathroom was inspired by decorating magazines.

The plants and wicker chaise in the sunken lounging area of this spacious, dramatic bathroom make the room liveable as well as functional.

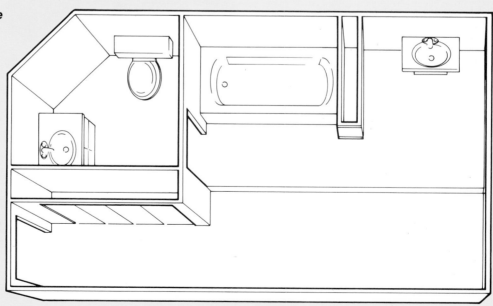

The upper left-hand compartment was the original 5-by-8-foot bathroom, which contained only a toilet and lavatory. Incorporating space from an adjacent bedroom made the new bathroom a spacious 12 by 15 feet.

Eminent Victorian Has Charm

Two years ago, the couple who own the Victorian-era house that contains the two bathrooms shown here were living in a spanking new, three-story townhouse. It had everything most people want in a home—plenty of space, new kitchen and bathrooms, a family room—but it was only temporary housing.

"I love old houses," the woman explained. "I love hissing radiators and leaky windows, and I always wanted the charm of an older building. Though we bought a new townhouse, it was always in our plans that as soon as we could afford it, we would renovate an old Victorian house."

Finally, the couple's equity built up and they found their dream house, a two-story structure with an in-law apartment in the basement. Once a gracious home, the structure had been divided into four apartments during the Depression; by the time this couple saw it, there was hardly a mechanical system that functioned properly. Only four radiators in the entire place worked, and there was water damage everywhere from leaking radiators, lavatories, and tubs. Those problems and numerous building code violations had put the place in housing court—and made it the perfect target for loving energies. The couple moved into the in-law apartment with their infant daughter and, alongside the contractor, started the painstaking work of transforming the four apartments upstairs back into a home.

Although they had turned a handsome profit on their townhouse, the couple still couldn't afford an all-out beautification. Instead, they concentrated on retaining as much as they could while adding modern conveniences. Rather than a new forced-air heating system, for example, they had the radiator system repaired. Old woodwork was stripped and refinished, and as many of the old walls and windows as possible were left intact. Mostly, the project required undoing the do-it-yourself additions made over the years and, of course, refurbishing the kitchen and bathrooms.

From the beginning, the couple knew they could salvage a few of the apartment building's more beautiful bathroom fixtures. Since the conversion to apartments had been done as cheaply as possible, the old fixtures had been kept rather than replaced and were, by now, almost antiques. Those previous economies meant that an upstairs bathroom still boasted a large tub-on-legs, a marble-topped lavatory, and an oak medicine cabinet. The cabinet's charm was disguised by layers of peeling paint and the tub and lavatory were so stained and dirty that "we wouldn't even touch them, let alone use them," the woman

related, the couple, nevertheless, realized they could be restored. They had the tub and the lavatory bowl reglazed, the marble cleaned and polished, and they applied their own elbow grease to the medicine cabinet.

Working with an architect, the couple reduced the number of bedrooms on the second floor to three and kept the two bathrooms on that floor in roughly the same back-to-back locations. Downstairs, two more bathrooms had been crammed back to back into such a small space that "you could barely stand in either one without hitting all the fixtures," said the architect. "We took most of the space of those two baths and made a single half bath out of it!"

Because of the years of neglect and the numerous leaks, all the piping for the lavatories and tubs was replaced. It was also necessary because below-zero

This stock oak unit with a self-rimming lavatory and plastic laminate countertop replaced a marble lavatory, which was moved downstairs.

The antique-style fittings for the legged tub were expensive, but no others would have created quite the same atmosphere.

Behind the tub is a tiled box, which is used to hold plants and fill in the angular end of the room.

By increasing the size of the 6-by-9-foot bathroom to 6 by 12½ feet, moving the tub to the right of the toilet, and adding a hall entrance, the architect made this room into a spacious, elegant, and practical bathroom reflecting the Victorian styling of the house.

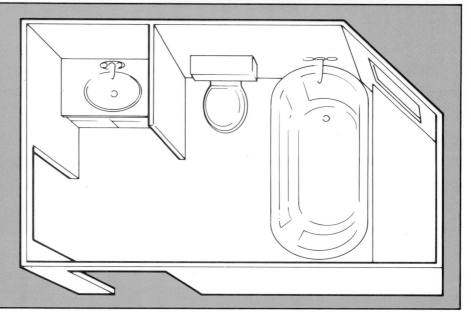

temperatures wreaked havoc with the empty, unheated house, and frozen, bursting pipes were a common nuisance as work progressed.

"After we had torn the place apart and had endured our eighth flood, I just sat down and cried," the woman remembers. "I couldn't imagine why we had left our very modern, very clean, unflooded townhouse to live in a basement under a catastrophe." The catastrophe offered one benefit however—the discovery that the waste stack for the toilets was salvagable, and the two and a half new bathrooms all tied into this single column.

"Keeping the stack setup was a situation that was kind of like the tail wagging the dog," the architect said. With the position of the toilet in each bathroom determined, the rest of the fixtures had to fit around it. "Actually, we wouldn't have gone ahead if the floor plans didn't work out decently, too. But since the stack location didn't cause a problem, and there was no other reason to replace the stack, we started the plan of each bathroom with the toilet."

The bathroom selected to become the master bathroom measured 6 by 9 feet with a corner sliced off for a window/airwell. The marble lavatory was to the right of the toilet, and the tub-on-legs ran parallel to the opposite wall. The entryway was set in the narrowest part of the room, across from the window at the foot of the tub. Although that layout was serviceable for the bedroom, there was no doorway from the hall. Such a doorway would be necessary because there was also a bedroom/den located on this floor. Working with these requirements—that the toilet be replaced where it was; that the marble lavatory be moved downstairs and replaced with a larger vanity with storage; that the

The marble lavatory and antique-styled medicine cabinet were moved from the upstairs bathroom to the 5-foot-square half bathroom downstairs.

window, the architect had a sleek, tiled box installed to hold plants and to fill in the angular end of the room. The old radiator was replaced with an electric baseboard heating unit. Overhead, a soffit hides the electrical fixture that holds the row of decorative bulbs that bathe the rear wall in soft light.

The rest of the room is decorated to highlight the 64-inch-long tub-on-legs. Walls and ceiling are painted a deep rust color to contrast with the white toilet and tub. The two-inch-square tiles on the floor and plant ledge are a red-brown color that no longer is being manufactured. A glass-block window is covered with a woven wood shade to echo the basketry, a good example of the compromises made in an effort to keep to the budget. The contractor had estimated that bricking up the window or replacing it with new glass and frame would cost about $300. The couple decided to live with the existing window and, instead, sank nearly $200 into antique-style fittings for the tub-on-legs. Specially designed to go with Kohler's Birthday Bath, a tub-on-legs being manufactured today, the faucet itself cost more than the dishwasher downstairs.

Although the tub fittings might seem an extravagance, the tub *is* the focal point of this bathroom—so much so, in fact, that a much-desired shower was omitted so that there would be room for the tub. "Whenever a newly installed bath has a tub-on-legs, the reason usually is primarily decorative, and that is spoiled if a shower curtain ring is included," the architect explained. "I try to have a separate shower; but in this room, there just wasn't enough space." Unfortunately, the resulting situation is awkward; the daughter likes to splash in the master bathroom's generous tub, and her father takes his morning shower in her bathroom.

That compromise aside, the couple is happy that the bathroom was completed within their budget. Contributing to the cost savings was the 3½-foot-long vanity, which completes the bathroom nicely but inexpensively. The cabinet, a stock oak unit that matches the kitchen cabinets, provides drawer space as well as slide-out shelving, and a self-rimming Kohler lavatory is set into a plastic laminate countertop. Because a ¼-inch plate glass mirror stretches wall-to-wall and counter to ceiling, a medicine cabinet is mounted on the wall at the left. Lighting for the vanity consists of two 8-inch incandescent fixtures by Thomas. The room also is lighted by a recessed can over the toilet/tub area.

Although the medicine cabinet and marble lavatory that once functioned in this space have been separated from the companion tub, they are equally highlighted. Now in the 5-foot-square first floor half bathroom, and joined by a new Kohler toilet, they offer guests a glimpse of the home's rich past. For the couple, though, these fixtures are a constant reminder of their reclamation efforts. "For the first three months after we moved from the basement into our 'new home' upstairs, I thought it was a figment of my imagination," said the woman. "I couldn't believe we finally were living in our four pages of plans."

tub-on-legs be retained; and that the room be accessible from both the hall and the master bedroom—the architect decided to lengthen the room to 12½ feet.

Part of the overall plan was to knock out a number of old walls, making halls and rooms as spacious as possible. Upstairs, this meant opening a tiny bedroom directly across the hall from the master bathroom and annexing this space to the hall. Now this 10-by-14-foot landing is an airy passageway and a playroom/sitting area, too. The new bathroom incorporates 3½ feet of this area, just enough space for a vanity to the left of the toilet, a new entrance from the bedroom, and one from the hall, too.

With the tub-on-legs placed perpendicular to the wall at the right of the toilet (where the old vanity had been), all the plumbing is against the same wall as the plumbing in the other full bathroom on the floor. Placing all the fixtures in the master bathroom along one wall also improved the traffic pattern and maneuverability within the room. With the old bedroom entrance blocked up, there now is a nice smooth wall for the new oak towel bars and pictures on that side of the room. The second bathroom features a vanity that is open to the room and a compartmented toilet and an oversized stall shower.

Where the clumsy radiator had sat under the

Planning And Designing Your Own Bathroom

The major problem in planning a bathroom is space. The bathroom usually is the smallest room in the house. Yet, compared with other rooms, it must accommodate a disproportionate amount of activity. Not only that, but the bathroom must necessarily contain certain immovable and relatively large fixtures. Getting the greatest possible convenience out of this small space is what planning is all about.

First, you must decide exactly how your bathroom is to function within the lifestyle—or lifestyles—of your household. Function, not size, should be the guiding factor in planning a new bathroom or remodeling an existing one. In terms of function, there are four basic types of bathrooms.

Single bathroom. A single bathroom is one that has full facilities (toilet, lavatory, tub or shower) and is designed for use by only one person at a time. Such a bathroom can be as small as 30 square feet or as large as you wish. The "standard" single bathroom is 5 by 8 feet, a size that stems from the fact that the most popular tub size is 30 inches wide and 5 feet long and that the tub usually is installed across one end of the room.

Family bathroom. Besides having at least the same facilities as a single bathroom, a family bathroom also is compartmented to allow it to be used with reasonable privacy by two or more people at a time. Although it's a great convenience to have two lavatory basins for scrubbing kids before meals or at bedtime, this is a task that doesn't require privacy. A bathroom with twin lavatories but no privacy compartmenting is still a single-function bathroom and not really a family bathroom.

Master bathroom. This type of bathroom is intended for the exclusive use of the head or heads of the household. Usually, a master bathroom is entered from the master bedroom and is an integral part of the master bedroom suite. It need not be the largest bathroom in the house, but often it is the most luxurious; if there is to be an extra-special fixture anywhere in the house—a whirlpool tub, for instance—the master bathroom is the likely place for it.

To truly fulfill its function, a master bathroom should be compartmented in the same way that a family bathroom is. However, since a house with a master bathroom will also have at least one other bathroom, this is certainly not a rigid rule.

The ultimate master bathroom is the His and Her bathroom. This kind of master bathroom is possible only where there is plenty of space. Its layout provides for full and private use by two people simultaneously. It is, in effect, two full bathrooms divided for privacy but entered from the bedroom through the same door. Each half of the bathroom contains its own toilet and lavatory, often with a bidet in Her half. The bathing facilities may be in a shared area of the room, but many couples prefer to have a bathtub in the woman's section and a shower in the man's.

Half bathroom. Also called a powder room, a half bathroom contains only lavatory and toilet facilities. A half bathroom is almost a necessity in two-story homes in which the only full bathroom is on the second floor. A half bathroom can be incorporated into any area of the house where plumbing lines are nearby. The minimum comfortable floor space is 3 by 3½ feet, although half bathrooms have been squeezed into spaces only 2 feet wide. If the room is to be used by guests, an area of at least 3 by 4½ feet is preferable.

Limitations

Before you become committed to a particular bathroom concept, you should become aware of some factors that can impose limitations on bathroom planning.

Plumbing. Changing the location of an existing toilet requires extensive plumbing work. So, it's desirable to not change toilet location. Plan to install a new toilet in the old location, if it's possible to do so without compromising your overall objectives.

If your home is built atop a concrete slab, any change in drain lines will be very expensive because the existing drains are buried in the concrete slab.

Wherever floor joists must be cut into for new drain or supply lines, the cut joists must be reinforced before the floor is closed up. This job is not particularly difficult or expensive, but it must be done to avoid seriously weakening the floor structure.

Another major consideration is whether the water supply pipes are located within one, two, or three walls of the bathroom. You can determine the plumbing layout simply by looking at the fixtures. If the toilet, and the faucets for the lavatory and for the tub and/or the shower, are all along one wall, you can be sure that the room has one-wall plumbing; if these elements are distributed on two walls, the room has two-wall plumbing; and so on.

If your bathroom has one-wall plumbing, you cannot simply plan to place a fixture on a wall that presently has no water supply pipes without also planning for what easily could be major and expensive changes in the entire plumbing layout. Changing from one-wall to two-wall plumbing, or from two-wall to three-wall, requires not only that new supply pipes be added, but that the drain lines be changed as well.

In view of these potential problems, you may decide to settle for new fixtures in all the old locations. That's not a mandatory solution, but you should be aware of the impact of major plumbing changes.

Clearances. Plumbing codes and human comfort require minimum separations between fixtures. So, clearances are definite limitations to planning. There's just so much that can be put into an existing space and be functional.

We're all aware that there's a space between our toilet and the wall beside it; and if we have twin wash basins in a vanity or countertop, we know there's a comfortable space between them. Yet, we rarely think of those clearances in terms of inches or feet. Now, you'll have to do just that—partly for physical comfort, and partly because your local building code establishes some minimum clearances.

The most important clearances usually are governed by plumbing codes. However, codes are not all in agreement, so you'll have to determine what's required in your locality. In addition, even the clearances required by most codes are minimums; you'll surely want greater separation between fixtures wherever it's possible. For example, some codes require 15 inches between the center line of a toilet and a wall or tub, while other codes

Above, and on the facing page, are some minimum fixture clearances.

set this minimum at 18 inches. Yet, for cleaning you'll appreciate having at least 6 inches between the side of a toilet tank and any object alongside. The center line of a lavatory bowl must be 14 to 18 inches from an adjacent wall, but convenience demands at least 6 inches between the side of a lavatory and an adjacent wall. To enter and leave a shower stall, you'll need a minimum of 18 inches between the shower door and a facing wall. But, if you want to avoid walking sideways to get into that shower, allow at least a 28-inch-wide space. For knee room, you'll want at least 18 inches between the front of a toilet and a facing wall, although codes often require a 30-inch separation if the toilet faces the side of a bathtub. When you plan for twin lavatory basins, be sure to allow space for elbow room. The minimums are 30 inches between bowl centers and at least 14 inches between the center of a bowl and the adjacent wall. And remember: those are minimums, and comfort requires more room. Also, try to make counters at least

20 inches deep with at least 6 inches between the edge of the bowl and the end of the counter to minimize splashing on the floor.

Fixtures And Floor Space

There is more to consider when selecting fixtures than aesthetic appeal. Tubs, toilets, lavatories, and showers are all available in a variety of sizes and styles. These differences can be significant when you are attempting to design the greatest efficiency into a small space. In some cases, they can also have an impact on the structure and plumbing of your house.

If a standard tub exists, it is rectangular, 5 feet long and 30 inches wide. It is not essential to plan your bathroom around a standard tub, however. As an alternative to a rectangular tub, a receptor tub can be a good space saver. Even the so-called standard rectangular tub is available in 29-to-32-inch widths, and in lengths from 4 to 6 feet.

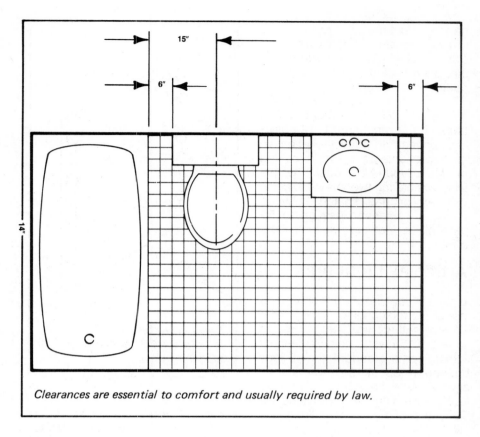

Clearances are essential to comfort and usually required by law.

Styles of toilets and lavatories also can be chosen for their space-saving advantages. A round-seated toilet takes up less space than an elongated one, although you'll have to trade a bit of comfort for that space. And, a triangular wall-mounted lavatory can help increase useful floor space in a very small bathroom. To make the best choice of fixtures in relation to floor space, you'll have to investigate the varieties of fixtures available. The Buyers Guide section of this book can be of great help to you in that respect.

You'll see a corner shower in some of the bathroom plans shown in this chapter. The dimensions given for this shower are those of a molded shower floor, not a modular shower stall. Some modular units of the same size are too big to get into an existing home. It's proof that size isn't a deterent if you're willing to install pieces and not insist on a one-piece unit. The end result is the same. However, if you can use one, the molded units do offer the advantage of having integral soap dishes, seats and grab bars.

Heating

No one likes to leave a warm bed on a cold morning for the discomfort of a cold bathroom. So, planning for adequate heating is an essential part of bathroom planning. If you are planning a new and extra bathroom, the first thing to learn is whether your furnace has the heating capacity to handle an extra room. If it will, new ducts are all you'll need. If the furnace won't supply the needed extra heat, supplemental heaters might offer the solution.

Supplemental heaters can be either electric or gas. In both cases, products and installation are strictly regulated by building codes. The code in your area might require all electrical hookups to be made by a licensed electrician. Check to learn code requirements before choosing a heater, especially if you intend to do the job yourself.

A wall heater of either type requires thoughtful planning. It must be located where it won't present a burn hazard, and can't ignite towels

or curtains. Portable electric heaters can be hazardous in the humid environment of a bathroom. Don't use one. Electrical heaters and the electrical controls of gas heaters must be grounded to prevent creation of a shock hazard. Safety demands a thermostatic control with automatic shut-off when the temperature reaches a pre-set level. Good venting and a pilot light shut-off are essential with a gas heater.

Radiant ceilings should definitely be considered for supplemental heating. A number of systems have been tried during recent years. The most successful consists of a network of wires attached by staples to a special type of gypsum board then covered with a plaster-like material. When wired into the house circuit, the system provides clean, comfortable and low-cost heat. However, installation is not for the do-it-yourselfer. Consult a reputable drywall or plastering contractor for more information—most now do radiant-heat installations.

Natural Lighting

For most bathrooms, good lighting means a blend of natural and artificial light. When one thinks about natural lighting, windows come to mind. But, windows aren't the only means for admitting natural light. Skylights also should be considered.

Should you consider a skylight for your bathroom? That depends. If yours is a single-story home, or if the bathroom is to be on the second floor of a two-story home, the answer is an emphatic "yes." For a first-floor bathroom in a two-story home, the answer is "maybe"—and the cost can be very high. Although skylights have been installed in house walls, it's not a good solution. Mounting a skylight vertically and in a way that allows it also to be opened for ventilation is tricky. And screening such an opening to keep bugs out destroys the visual appeal of the skylight. About the only way to bring skylight benefits to a first floor bathroom is to build an addition—a small extension of the bathroom with a sloping roof. In that way you not only can have the skylight but also create a potted garden on the added floor or ledge space.

Commercial skylights are available in both glass and plastic, with translucent plastic being the most popular. Clear and colored plastic domes also are popular. However, clear plastic or glass are not good choices for a skylight on the south or west side of a sloped roof. These sides of the house receive direct sunlight for much of the day; even during winter, so much direct light can have a "greenhouse effect" in the bathroom, making the room very hot. So, if you must place a skylight on the south or west side, it should be glazed with translucent, rather than clear, glass or plastic, which will filter part of the sun's rays.

Most skylights available to the home market are complete units with integral mounting flanges for ease of installation. A double-glazed dome is a must in cold climates to minimize condensation. Still, even a double-glazed skylight needs the help of a good ventilating system to keep the inside of the dome clear of condensation.

Correct placement of a window is important for both light and ventilation. The window must open and close easily, and it must be screened. Choosing and placing a window for an all-new bathroom is relatively easy. For a remodeling project there are limitations. Moving or relocating a window in an existing bathroom requires removal of outside surfacing, cutting load-bearing studs, and later patching the outside surface. It's far easier to replace an existing window with a new window of a different size or style than to install a new window in a new location. Besides, windows in existing baths usually are where they are because it's the best available location.

Often, replacing an old window with a new one can bring improvement. If the old window is a double-hung type (vertical sliding), a new casement window (side hinged) can make life more pleasant. Reaching across a tub to crank a window open is far easier than having to push a window up. And, in cold climates, wood or plastic-clad wood windows are warmer to the touch than metal windows and retain heat better.

A variety of glass and plastic panes are possible. Clear panes transmit the most light but translucent panes add privacy. Reflective glass prevents people from looking in while you look out. Thermal windows having two sheets of glass with air or gas sealed between them can cut heat loss up to 50 percent, a definite plus in cold climates.

Artificial Lighting

Lighting engineers recommend about 30 foot candles of illumination for bathrooms. That translates to about 150 watts of incandescent lighting for a standard 5-by-8-foot bathroom—about 3¾ watts per square foot of floor area. The same level of illumination is provided by 70 watts of fluorescent lighting— about 1¾ watts of fluorescent lighting per square foot of floor area. For comparative purposes you might consider the fact that a well-lighted office provides about 100 foot candles of illumination at desktop level.

The first aspect of lighting to consider is safety. And, the safest location for your bathroom light switch is outside your bathroom door. Your overall wiring plan must be drawn and submitted to your local code official for approval. In fact, it's wise to learn code requirements in advance of planning.

Luminous ceiling lighting provides the most even illumination and is not difficult to install. But, since the suspension grid that holds the luminous panels must be 6 to 12 inches below the bulbs or tubes that provide light, a modern 8-foot-high ceiling makes installation impractical. If yours is an old home with high ceilings, it can be the ideal solution to the problem of lighting the bathroom.

Localized lighting is most often chosen for bathrooms. A prime requirement is that no single fixture be overly bright. Strive for balance.

Mirrors, of course, require good

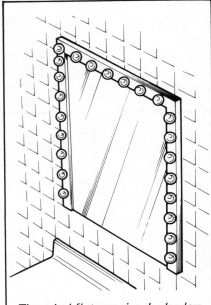

Theatrical fixtures give shadowless color-balanced light that is ideal for applying makeup.

lighting. Fluorescent tubes or incandescent bulbs behind a diffusing panel can be placed across the top and/or along each side of a mirror. Fluorescent tubes, however, because of the color of light emit-

Incandescent light looks more natural than fluorescent; at least two fixtures are needed to avoid shadows.

ted, are not well-suited to make up areas. Theatrical lighting—rows of incandescent bulbs around three sides of a mirror—give shadowless, color-balanced light that's ideal for applying makeup or for shaving. Single light fixtures installed at each side of a mirror can provide good light if they are properly placed. A good height for side lights is 62 inches above the floor. Do not, however, install a single-bulb fixture above the center of a mirror. Once popular in hotel construction, the result is harsh unpleasant light.

Lights needn't be just lights. There are combination units that also incorporate ventilating fans and heating elements. There's nothing quite so toasty warm as a heat lamp when you step from the tub or shower. And, a sunlamp can keep that fresh-from-vacation skin tone year 'round.

For compartmented bathrooms, light in toilet compartments need not be as bright as in washing and bathing areas. Usually a single 60- or 75-watt incandescent fixture suffices. And, the switch for this fixture should be located outside the compartment door.

Ventilation

Nothing contributes more to an efficiently functioning bathroom than effective ventilation. And nothing is more offensive than the dank, musty smell of a bathroom in which nothing ever gets completely dry. Windows and doors traditionally have provided bathroom ventilation. During warm weather they still can. But in cold climates and in windowless baths, mechanical ventilation is essential—not only to prevent condensation from forming on walls, ceilings, and mirrors, but also to preserve and extend life of the bathroom contents.

Exhaust fans can be wired into the lighting circuit switch, or be switched independently. Some codes require that in windowless bathrooms, exhaust fans must be controlled by the light switch.

The Home Ventilating Institute recommends that bathroom ventilators be capable of handling eight complete changes of air every

hour. How do you translate that requirement into the proper exhaust fan for your bathroom? Quite simply. Exhaust fans are rated according to the number of cubic feet of air they can move each minute—their CFM capacity. Here's how you use those two facts to calculate exhaust fan requirements for a 5-by-8-foot bath.

There are 40 square feet of floor area in a 5-by-8-foot bath. If the ceiling is 8 foot high the bath has a volume of 320 cubic feet. To change that volume of air eight times each hour means moving 2,560 cubic feet of air every 60 minutes. So, divide that volume of air by 60 and you can see that

you'd need an exhaust fan capable of moving 42.67 CFM. For an extra margin of protection figure on 10 changes per hour. That increases fan capacity to only 53.33 CFM. Apply similar calculations to your own bath and you'll know how much exhaust fan capacity you'll need.

Accessory Fixtures

You've got a lot of questions that need answers. Where should the toilet tissue holder go? How many towel bars do you need? How high should the shower head be? And many others. For some questions the answer is, "It's a matter of

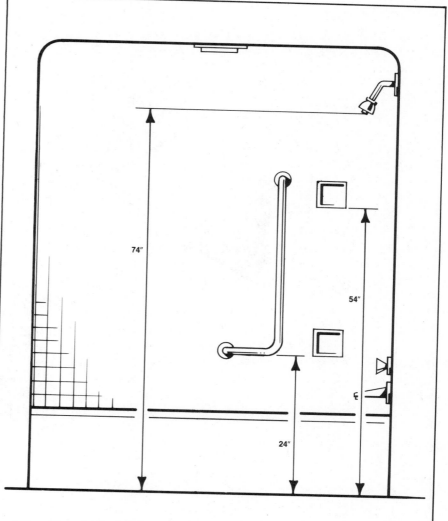

Although positioning accessory fixtures can be a matter of preference, customary clearances are based on comfort and convenience.

personal preference." For others there are established standards. However, there's an important factor to remember where some mounting heights are concerned. For example, there's a standard height for shower heads. Members of your family might want a lower or higher shower head. That's fine for now, but should you ever want to sell your home, non-standard features could hamper its sale. So, consider that fact in deciding whether to depart from the standards.

A towel bar installed above a tub should be 48 inches above the floor. Install soap dishes and grab bar 24 inches above the floor. If there's to be a shower head above the tub, allow 74 inches under the head for clearance, install a second soap dish at a 54-inch height and a second grab bar slightly higher. If you intend to use a shower curtain, install the rod 78 inches above the floor.

Since many men still shave with a blade it's best to locate the mirror above the lavatory. The mirror top should be 72 to 78 inches above the floor. Allow about 8 inches between the top of the lavatory or

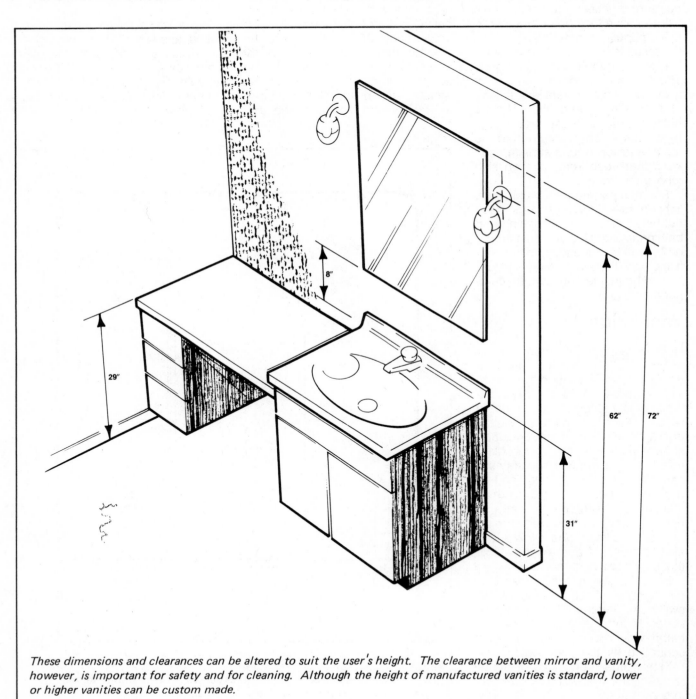

These dimensions and clearances can be altered to suit the user's height. The clearance between mirror and vanity, however, is important for safety and for cleaning. Although the height of manufactured vanities is standard, lower or higher vanities can be custom made.

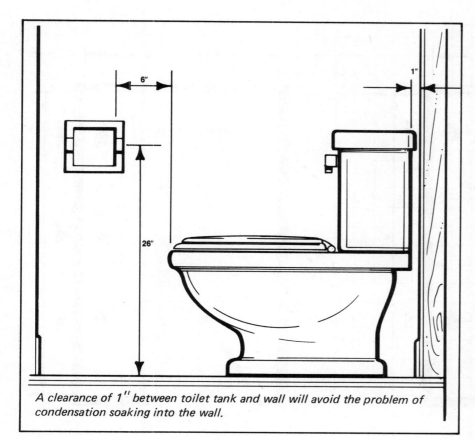

A clearance of 1″ between toilet tank and wall will avoid the problem of condensation soaking into the wall.

counter and the bottom of cabinet or mirror.

A medicine cabinet isn't mandatory, but if you want one, it should be within easy reach of the lavatory. If there are children in the household, the medicine cabinet should be placed high enough to be out of their reach. A separate lockable cabinet is also a good idea if there are children present.

Shower valves should be 48 to 54 inches above the floor and always near the shower door. Never install valves in the back wall of the shower enclosure, because you'll have to reach through running water in order to adjust them. A shower head can be as low as 60 inches or as high as 73 inches. Since there's no need to step over the side of a tub to enter a shower enclosure, minimum clearance under the shower head isn't a factor. If you install a soap dish in a shower enclosure, place it about 54 inches above the floor. The same height applies for a grab bar.

The best place for a tissue holder is on a wall next to the toilet. The edge of the roll should be 6 inches from the front of the toilet, and the center of the roll should be 26 inches above the floor.

Allow a minimum of 24 inches of towel bar for each family member. A 24-inch towel bar will accommodate a bath towel and face towel, each folded in thirds, and a wash cloth folded in half. If you prefer to fold towels only once, it will take a 30-inch bar to accommodate the three items. Install the bars about 40 inches above the floor. If wall space is limited, consider installing one 24-inch bar on the back of the bathroom door.

Standard height for a lavatory, whether wall-hung or as part of a vanity, is 31 inches. A vanity counter, without basin, is usually 29 inches high.

Designing For The Handicapped

The aged and the handicapped often need special consideration when a bathroom is being planned. The need for special features depends on the nature of the infirmity.

Although a standard 30-inch door-opening will permit access to a standard wheelchair, an extra-wide opening, say 34 inches, can make access much easier. A person in a wheelchair also will have a difficult time using a vanity, because the base cabinet does not allow the chair to be moved close enough. A wall-hung lavatory placed high enough for the chair arms to pass under the front edge is best. Also, the lavatory should be extra wide, because a person in a wheelchair needs extra elbow room. Plumbing under the lavatory should be placed so as not to obstruct the approach of the wheelchair.

Push-button or lever water controls are easier to use by people with muscle difficulties than are twist-type faucets. A temperature regulator also will help avoid scalding for people with impaired sensation in their hands.

Extra high toilets and showers with seats, rather than tubs, can be a boon to the elderly. Grab bars located both at the toilet and in the shower or tub are essential.

Begin On Paper

You'll quickly discover that planning a new bathroom, or rearranging an

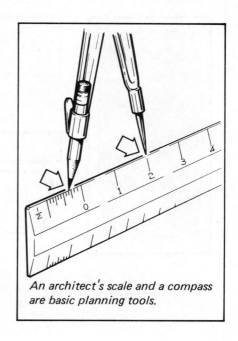

An architect's scale and a compass are basic planning tools.

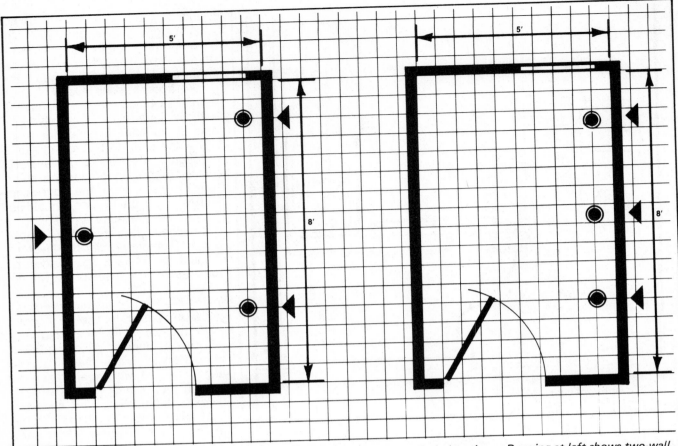

Measure your bathroom and make a scale drawing on graph paper. Mark drain locations. Drawing at left shows two-wall plumbing; at right is one-wall plumbing.

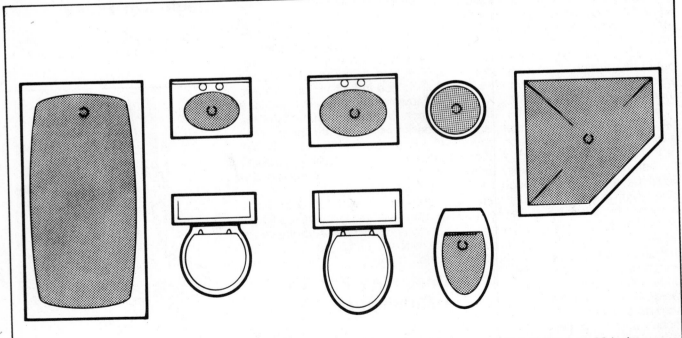

These silhouettes are 1/2" scale. Use them to trace and make cutouts for floor planning. Tub is 5 feet by 30 inches; shower base is 36 by 36 inches. Bidet is to the right of larger toilet.

old one, involves a lot of trial and error experimentation. Obviously, the best place for trials and errors is on paper. The best choice for this job is graph paper ruled in ½-inch squares. A good alternative is graph paper ruled in ¼-inch squares. In either case let ½ inch equal 1 foot when you draw your plans.

Especially useful tools are an inexpensive architect's scale (ruler) and a pencil compass. An architect's scale is a special ruler that has markings for a number of different scales. The scale you'll use is the one on which ½ inch equals 1 foot. One of the ½-inch spaces on this scale is divided to represent 12 inches. By combining feet and inch marks you can draw any dimension to scale.

You'll have only one use for the compass, but it's a very important use. The final test of a plan is to draw the arc through which the bathroom door will swing. You don't want a bathroom in which the door strikes the toilet or lavatory and can't be opened fully. Surprisingly, many of the plans published in bathroom planning books won't pass this test.

Begin by carefully measuring the inside dimensions of your bathroom, or the space in which you'd like to add a bath, down to the smallest fraction of an inch that you can accurately measure. Use these measurements to make your scale drawing. If you intend to remodel an existing bathroom, measure and locate positions for drains as well as locations of windows and doors. Be precise in locating drain positions; measure from two walls to find the exact center line of each drain.

Bathroom Layout

In order to experiment with different bathroom floor plans, you'll save time by making some cutouts for tracing fixture outlines on graph paper. You'll find it useful to make cutouts for fixtures of various sizes. Then test each layout you come up with to see how it works with large fixtures, then again with smaller fixtures. Remember, having ade-

quate clearance between fixtures is far more important than having large fixtures. If you've already purchased new fixtures, make cutouts that exactly match their dimensions. Draw their outlines to the ½-inch-to-1-foot scale. If it turns out that the fixtures you bought are too large for your bathroom, you'll want to know before you try to install them.

Mistakes To Avoid

Look at floor plans 1 through 4. At first glance all four plans may appear to be workable layouts.

Although all four use relatively large fixtures that seem to fit, each example shows something you'll want to avoid in your own plans.

In Plan 1, the open door completely blocks the lavatory. To wash your hands, you'd have to enter and close the door behind you. Hardly practical when you consider that the lavatory is the most often used fixture in the bathroom.

In Plan 2, a corner shower has been substituted for the tub, and the result gives a look of greater spaciousness. There's even room for a built-in linen cabinet or shelving. But, note the clearance be-

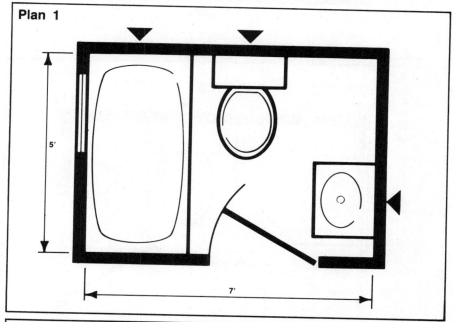

Plan 1

5'

7'

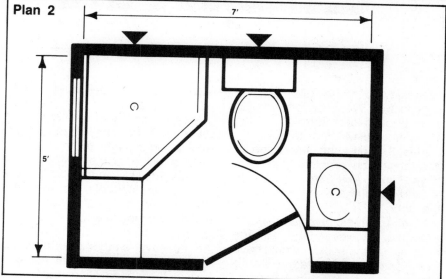

Plan 2

7'

5'

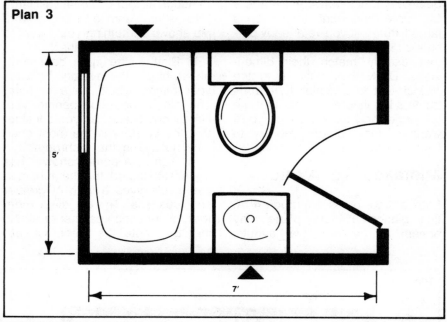

Plan 3

5'

7'

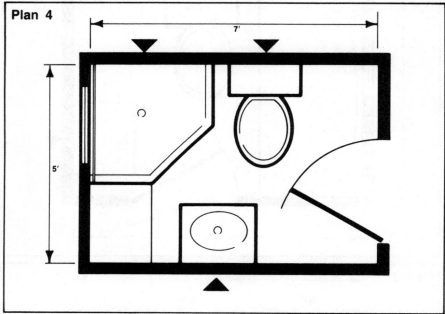

Plan 4

7'

5'

bath when the home was built. But, it's an arrangement to be avoided whenever possible. If there is no other option for placing a shower stall, a shower curtain can be hung across the window wall in the stall.

None of the above is intended to discourage you from planning a 5-by-7-foot bathroom. On the contrary, Plans 5 through 8 show that it can be done by making only minor changes in the first four plans. One of the most significant changes is the inclusion of narrower, 28-inch doors. (And this change illustrates how that compass can pay dividends in your own planning.) The other major change is the substitution of smaller toilets and lavatories than were used before. Plans 5 and 6 now have room for a wall-to-wall counter. Plan 7 now includes corner shelves, and Plan 8 has room for corner shelves plus a storage cabinet. Nothing has been taken out except space-consuming design features. So, apply that same approach to your own plans. If you arrive at a layout you like, but discover it doesn't quite work, try smaller fixtures before abandoning the plan.

Now, let's consider what can be done in an even smaller space—5 by 6 feet. Plans 9 through 12 show some possibilities that might work for you if space is extremely limited. Note that each of these utilize two-wall plumbing. One-wall plumbing simply won't work in such a small space.

Take particular note of the door arrangements in these plans. Plans 9 and 10 show 24-inch doors. That's not an ideal size, but there's not room for a wider door if it has to swing into the bathroom. Moreover, some building codes might prohibit the use of such a narrow door.

Plans 11 and 12 show how to solve the door problem by hinging 30-inch doors to swing outward. However, if you do elect to install an outward-opening door be sure to install it in a way that's compatible with traffic in your home. Most bathroom traffic will come from the direction of your living room, family room, and kitchen. So, hinge your door to swing open to receive, not block, this traffic.

tween lavatory and toilet—a bare eight inches. Would anyone want to work through that narrow opening in order to clean the corner?

Plan 3 shows the same sort of door-clearance problem that destroys Plan 1. And here, you'd have to step out of the way just to close the door.

Plan 4 comes closest to being workable. However, the storage area beside the shower would have to be open shelving rather than a cabinet, because cabinet doors—

even double ones—would be difficult to operate in the confined space beside the lavatory. And, even the lower shelves of an open unit could be difficult to use.

In addition to the flaws already described, all four plans have another undesirable feature: each has a window located within a tub or shower enclosure. It's true that many existing bathrooms have a window over a tub/shower because no other arrangement was possible within the space allocated for the

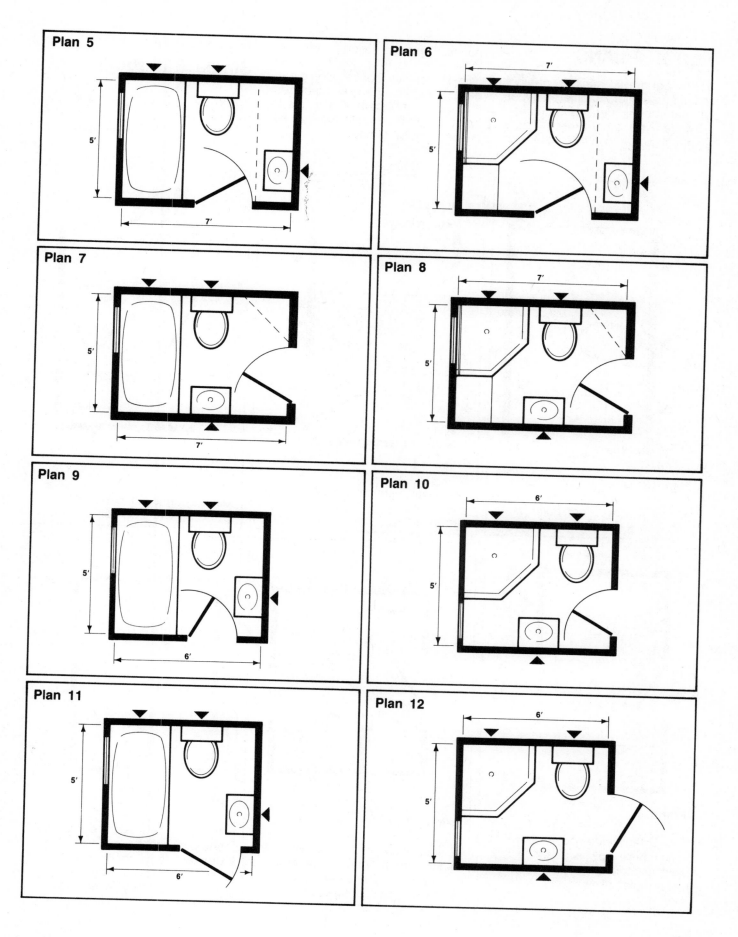

FLOOR PLANS

Following are a number of floor plans for each of the different types of bathrooms described earlier. However, you're not likely to find a single plan that exactly meets your needs. The sole reason for offering these plans is to suggest ways to utilize available space. So, glean each of them for ideas and features that will blend together to create a bathroom that best fits the special needs of your family.

Planning A Single Bathroom

You've already seen some of the ways to make 5-by-6-foot and 5-by-7-foot spaces function efficiently as

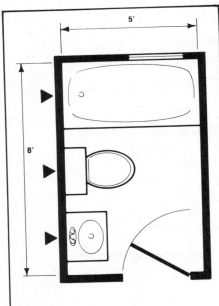

Plan 13

A typical 5-by-8-foot bathroom with one-wall plumbing.

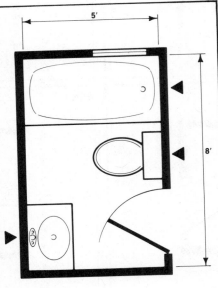

Plan 14

Two-wall plumbing allows more options for fixture arrangement.

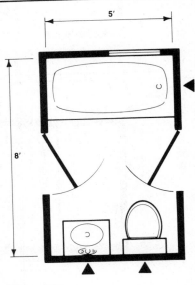

Plan 15

A 5-by-8-foot room can serve as a connecting bathroom between two bedrooms.

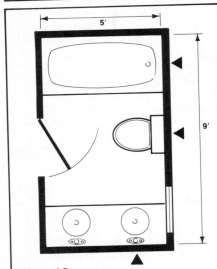

Plan 16

Still 5 feet wide, but 9 feet long, there now is room for twin lavatories. A relatively small toilet allows good clearance.

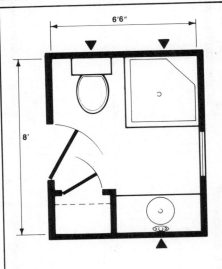

Plan 17

Using a corner tub allows space for a linen closet and a corner tub. The result is a highly efficient single bath.

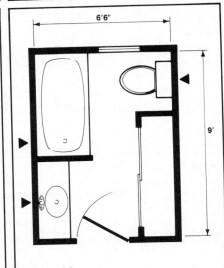

Plan 18

The wall between the lavatory and tub can be a half wall for greater elbow room at the lavatory or a full-height wall for more privacy in the tub.

single bathrooms. The more space you have to work with, of course, the more options you have. In general, it is very difficult to remodel a bathroom of 5 by 8 feet or less without capturing space from an adjacent room or without adding onto the house. Laying out a new bathroom of such small proportions is much easier, and usually much more successful, than attempting to rearrange the fixtures in a bathroom of the same size.

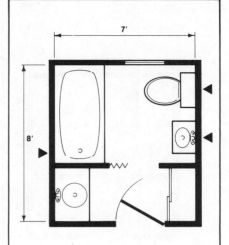

Plan 22

A 7-by-8-foot space allows excellent compartmentation with wash-up facilities in both compartments, and a linen closet. Use of a large toilet and a relatively small lavatory gives good clearances.

Planning A Family Bathroom

Compartmentation for privacy characterizes a family bathroom. The following plans suggest ways in which you can provide compartmentation in your new bath. For practical reasons, a 6½-by-8-foot space is about the smallest that can be compartmented. That doesn't mean, however, that a small family bathroom can't have many desirable features.

When laying out a compartmented bathroom, attempt to locate the lavatory in the compartment nearest the door; washing usually is not the function that requires privacy. Also, folding doors are less likely to warp and become stuck than are pocket doors (doors that slide into the wall).

Plan 19

In the same space as the preceding bathroom is a double vanity as well as either closed or open storage.

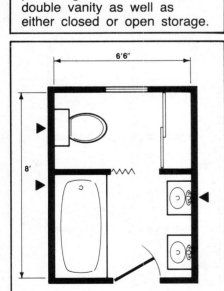

Plan 20

A 28-inch door allows for a double lavatory. If such a narrow door isn't possible, you'll have to settle for one lavatory.

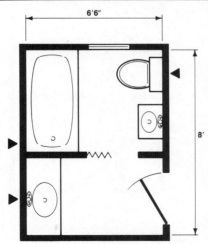

Plan 21

The space is the same as that of the preceding plan. Although the door placement won't allow for a closet, a second lavatory is possible.

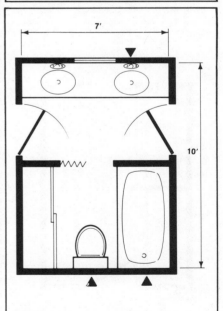

Plan 23

This plan allows complete privacy in the toilet and bathing areas even when there's traffic between bedrooms, and there's easy access to the toilet when entry doors are standing open.

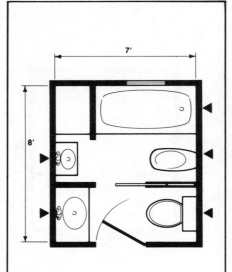

Plan 24

Although it is best to place toilet and bidet in the same compartment, space considerations sometimes make it desirable to disregard this common practice.

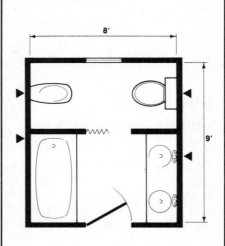

Plan 25

A more conventional layout than the preceding one places toilet and bidet in the same private compartment. Note, however, that you'd have to pass through the tub area to use the toilet—a drawback if you like long soaking.

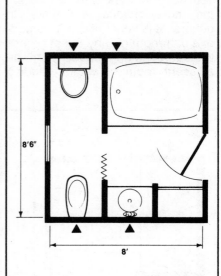

Plan 26

The size of this room makes an oversized tub possible—in this case a 3½-by-5-foot tub.

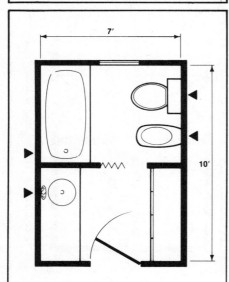

Plan 27

The long counter creates an ideal place to bathe and change a baby. And, when there's no longer a need for a baby-care center a second lavatory can be installed.

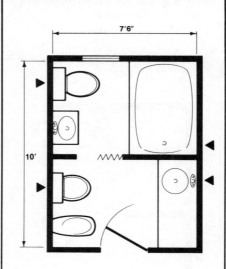

Plan 28

A more convenient compartmentation than in the preceding layout. Any function can be carried out in full privacy. A standard tub easily could be used instead of the oversized one shown.

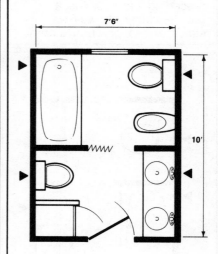

Plan 29

This plan requires the same space as the preceding one but could have more appeal to families with older children. The twin lavatories offer good wash-up convenience, and the closet is an always welcome feature.

Planning A Master Bathroom

If your initial reaction to the first of the following bathroom plans is, "Why that's just another single bath," you're entirely correct. A master bathroom can be of any type—single, compartmented, or even a half-bathroom. The factor that sets it apart from other bath-

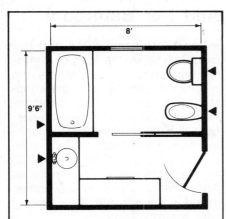

Plan 30

The prime value of this plan is its spaciousness. Also, many women prefer a dressing table that's located away from the high humidity of a bathing area, as is shown here.

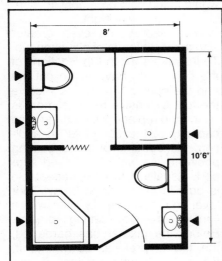

Plan 31

Want a bath with separate tub and shower? If you have the amount of space shown here you can have both without crowding.

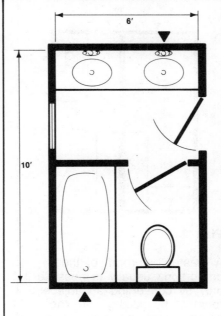

Plan 32

A double lavatory, good compartmentation, and plenty of clearance between the fixtures makes a very efficient master bathroom.

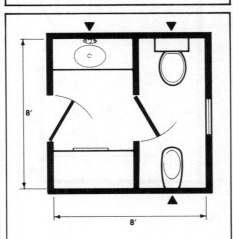

Plan 33

If you already have an adequate family bathroom, a half-bathroom can serve well as a master bathroom.

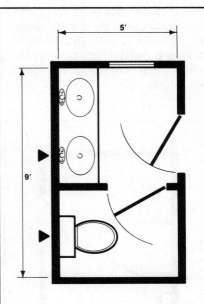

Plan 34

Still another half-bathroom, this one is a bit bigger than the traditional 5-by-8-foot single bathroom.

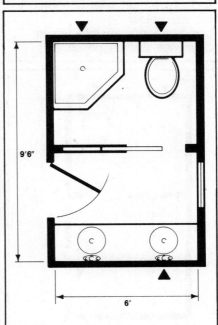

Plan 35

Shifting the partition in this plan a few inches would make room for a tub instead of the shower. And, since this is a master bathroom, a sliding entry door would be acceptable.

rooms is that access is from the master bedroom. A master bedroom with an adjoining bathroom comprise a master bedroom suite. For that reason many of the bathroom plans you've already examined should be considered eligible candidates for your master bathroom.

The benefit of a master bathroom, even if only in the form of a half-bathroom needn't be confined to the master suite. If your family includes an elderly or handicapped person, bathroom facilities connected to that person's bedroom can be a blessing.

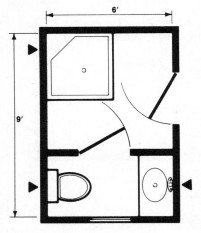

Plan 36

Replacing a fullsize rectangular tub with a corner tub can allow compartmentation that would otherwise not be possible.

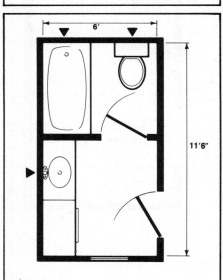

Plan 37

A long, narrow bathroom could easily be constructed across one end of a large bedroom. This kind of plan can be shortened through use of a corner tub or shower, and with an accordian-type door.

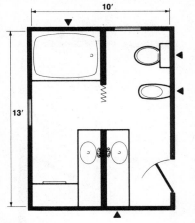

Plan 38

A master bathroom of these proportions usually is possible only by converting an adjacent room or by adding onto the house. Such ample space is, of course, the ideal of efficiency.

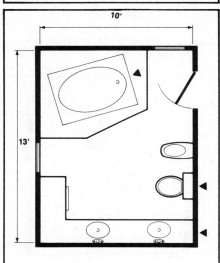

Plan 39

An oversized tub installed in a platform gives the illusion of a sunken tub, but without the plumbing problems and many of the structural problems of a sunken tub.

Planning A His And Her Bathroom

In most instances, a His and Her bathroom takes the form of a master bathroom. And, it meets the criteria set forth earlier in this chapter: it will have privacy compartmentation for toilets and lavatories, but will have a single, shared bathing area. Frequently, such a bathroom includes a large double tub for squeaky-clean togetherness. And, while one plan in this section includes such a tub, it is offered with a strong warning.

Installation of a large double tub is not recommended for a do-it-yourselfer, unless he is also an architect or architectural engineer. That same warning also applies to installation of a sunken tub. The weight of water needed to fill a double tub or bathing pool to soaking depth can exceed 1,000 lbs., and it's likely that your floor framing would need reinforcement to support that much weight.

The hazards are even greater with the installation of a sunken tub. To install a sunken tub, sections of the floor joists have to be cut out and the opening framed to receive the tub. Extensive reinforcement is needed to replace the load-carrying capacity of the cut joists. In addition, the bottoms of these bathing pools are so wide they need support. Usually a box-like receptacle is built in the opening below floor level and then partially filled with a lightweight, slow-setting plaster. Before the plaster has hardened, the tub is pressed down into it. When the plaster hardens it provides support for the tub bottom. So, you can see that installation of a large sunken tub requires special expertise. If you still want to install one yourself, there's only one safe way to go about the job: find an architect who's willing to accept small jobs and have plans drawn for the floor framing in your home.

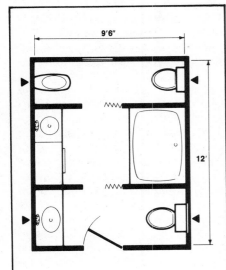

Plan 40

In this layout, the oversized tub is located on a load-bearing wall, thus avoiding the need for extra floor reinforcement.

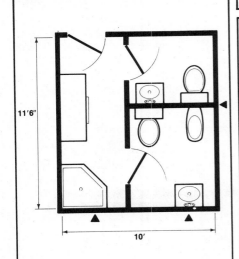

Plan 41

Many people never use a tub except as a place to stand while showering. While this plan needs only about the same amount of space as the last, due to the use of a shower rather than a tub, compartmentation is superior without sacrificing any walkaround space.

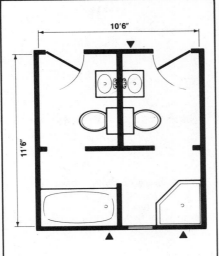

Plan 42

Not only can He and She have personal toilets and lavatories, but each can have a personal bathing facility. A folding door between the tub and shower compartments would increase privacy.

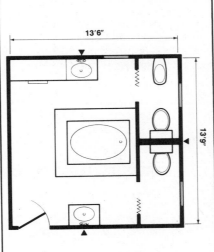

Plan 43

Since the tub is oversize and is located over the middle of floor joists, this is the kind of plan that demands an expert's evaluation of your existing floor framing.

Planning A Combination Bathroom

A combination bathroom is just what the name implies. It combines a bathroom with another and different function within the same space. Such extra facilities depend on your personal needs and desires as well as available space. Typical special functions include laundry, exercise, and/or sauna facilities. In the case of laundry and exercise facilities, all that is basically needed is space, space that can be designed into a new bathroom, or added onto or stolen from an adjacent room for an existing bathroom. A sauna, however, can require special planning.

Sauna planners have a number of options. These options range from a do-it-yourself project to having the complete installation done by a contractor. Between these extremes are sauna kits designed for homeowner erection. Kits are available in two forms—pre-cut and modular kits.

Pre-cut kits include all framing materials as well as some internal fixtures. All lumber is cut to size and detailed instructions describe every erection step. Some of these kits include a pre-hung door.

Modular saunas come in the form of factory-built panels that fit together for erection. These kits are as complete as pre-cut kits, go up faster and cost more.

Some kit manufacturers include benches and ductboards (floor boards) in kit prices, some offer them as optional extras. Heaters usually are priced separately.

Building your own sauna from sticks and boards bought from a local lumber dealer might not be the bargain it appears to be. Cutting waste and the time needed for this method can quickly outweigh the potential cost savings.

Cost can't be cut by using two walls and the ceiling of an existing room to partially enclose a sauna. A sauna is a self-contained unit. Ceiling as well as walls must be insulated and contain a good vapor barrier. And, to conserve energy

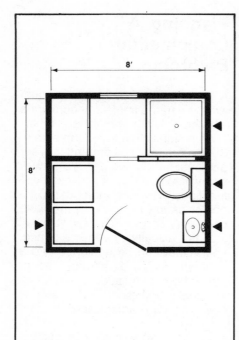

Plan 44

A small spare room can be made to function both as a laundry room and a utility bathroom.

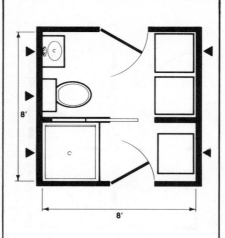

Plan 45

A "mud room" can be a necessary luxury in a house without a basement. The mud room door should be located as close to the back door of the house as possible. A second door from another room allows the mud room to double as a utility bathroom.

both need insulated doors.

The sauna floor also needs consideration. Some kit manufacturers say that a sauna can be erected over any type floor except carpeting. The reason for that exception is that sweat generated by sauna heat drips onto the floor, and carpeting would soon take on a foul smell. Sauna literature also tells you that a floor drain isn't needed, that water can be carefully poured over the heated rocks to make steam whether there's a floor drain or not. That's true, but a floor drain makes clean-out much easier.

So, if you want the utmost in sauna bathing pleasure and still must watch costs, a compromise could let you attain your goal. Have a contractor install a properly sloped floor with a drain. Then erect a sauna kit over that floor.

Planning Adjoining Bathrooms

Adding adjoining bathrooms can create the need for a special partition construction, sometimes called a plumbing wall or "wet" wall. This type of partition is thicker than conventional partitions and has an unobstructed cavity to accommodate drain and supply pipes.

with the high heat required, sauna ceilings are never more than 7 feet high. Sauna construction might be likened to that of a walk-in refriger-

ator. A sauna is an insulated box designed to keep heat in. The refrigerator is an insulated box designed to keep heat out. Obviously,

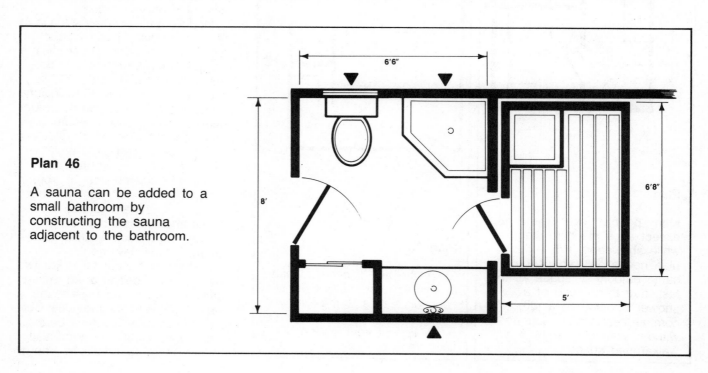

Plan 46

A sauna can be added to a small bathroom by constructing the sauna adjacent to the bathroom.

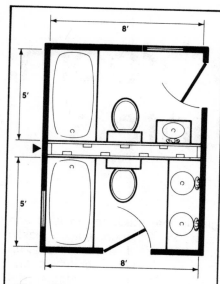

Plan 47

Bathtubs, toilets and lavatories should be positioned opposite one another along the wet wall so that one drain system can serve all six fixtures.

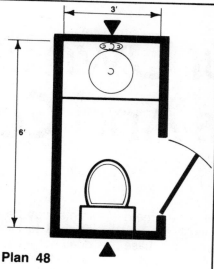

Plan 48

A half-bathroom can fit into the narrow space under a stairway.

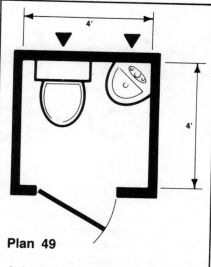

Plan 49

A half-bathroom can be added by walling off the corner of a family room.

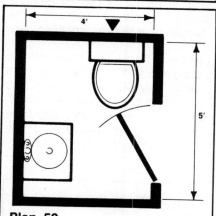

Plan 50

Usually, 4 by 5 feet is the smallest space in which the door can be hinged inward. Even here, hinging outward would be more convenient.

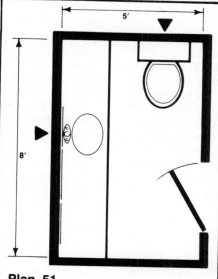

Plan 51

A powder room usually should be larger than a basic half-bathroom to include "freshening up" facilities.

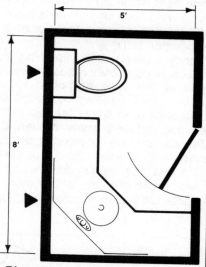

Plan 52

A corner vanity can give the illusion of more space than there actually is. Hinged mirrors are a welcomed feature.

Planning A Half-Bathroom

Where does one find space for a half bathroom? The possibilities include a large closet, space under a stairway, or in the case of an old home, a pantry. Even the corner of a room should be considered.

If yours is a two-story home with its only bathroom on the second floor, a new half bathroom should be located on the first floor. If yours is a ranch home, you'll reduce cost somewhat if you can locate the half bathroom adjacent to the existing bathroom. Alternatively, there are benefits from having a half-bathroom just off the kitchen or

near the kitchen or backdoor.

Where space is available near the front entry, you might prefer to plan for a half-bathroom that functions as a powder room and to add visual excitement with an unusual decorating scheme. Visits to a powder room are brief and the impact of the most imaginative decoration won't be traumatic.

Doing Your Own Bathroom: Vanities And Counters

How can you restyle your bathroom and make it more convenient in one easy step? Add a vanity.

There are two basic parts to a vanity: the base cabinet and the lavatory top. Usually, the cabinet is purchased separately and the top added to it.

No matter what the size or decorative style of your bathroom, there probably is a vanity that will suit it or that can be adapted to it. Most stock vanity cabinets range from 16 to 20 inches deep and from 24 to 60 inches wide. The smaller units have a single door. As width increases, more doors or banks of drawers can be incorporated.

Vanity bases usually have hardwood frames and plywood or composition board sides and bottoms. The backs of the units are open to accommodate the lavatory plumbing. Plywood sides may be stained in wood tones or in colors that allow the natural grain of the wood veneer to show through. Composition board sides usually are covered with plastic laminate or painted with a tough epoxy or urethane finish.

Oak and other hardwoods are used for the doors and drawer fronts of many of the more expensive vanity cabinets. On less expensive units, the door and drawer fronts may be of plastic that has been molded and finished to look like wood. Although molded plastic does not really equal richness of wood, it stands up better to cleaning, is more resistant to scratching, and does not warp. Plastic laminates in woodgrain and marble patterns, as well as in solid colors, also are widely used.

Ready-made vanity bases are available in many decorative styles. The most common styles are contemporary, traditional, French or Italian Provincial, and colonial. The various looks are created by the doors and the drawer fronts.

Contemporary styling is characterized by straight, clean lines, flat surfaces and simple hardware. The doors and drawer fronts usually are covered with plastic laminate.

Traditional styling features doors and drawer fronts with recessed or raised panels. The more expensive units are made of richly stained hardwoods. Less expensive units have plastic doors and drawer fronts.

Provincial-style cabinets generally have flat front surfaces to which raised molding has been added. The molding patterns can range from very simple to very

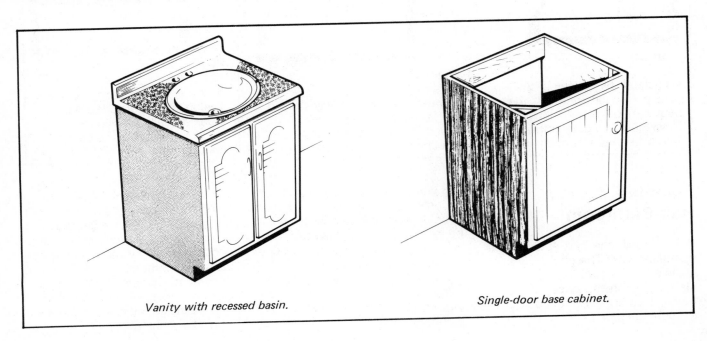

Vanity with recessed basin.

Single-door base cabinet.

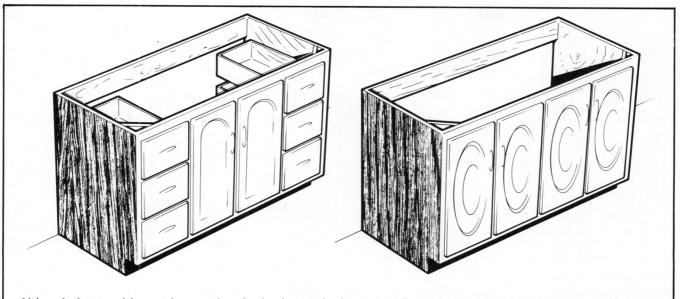

Although these vanities are the same length, the drawers in the one at left require that the basin be installed in the center.

ornate. The components may be of wood, plastic laminate, or of molded plastic, and often are finished in wood tones, although antique white with touches of simulated gold leaf also is a popular finish.

Colonial styling is characterized by a rustic look. The doors and drawer fronts often are made to resemble rough-sawn or pegged planks. Wood, plastic laminate, or molded plastic may be used in their construction, and wood tones are usual for finishing.

Customizing Vanity Bases

Most manufacturers offer companion units to match stock vanity bases. Companion units can consist only of drawers or can contain a special purpose feature, such as a laundry hamper. Companion units have the same depth as the base unit and range in width from 12 to 18 inches. Wood filler strips also are available to join a vanity base and accessory unit or to fill in between the base and the wall.

By combining base and companion units, you can assemble a vanity to fit your precise needs. A long countertop can be placed across two base units and braced with a drawer skirt panel to form a dressing table. A bank of drawers inserted between a base unit and a wall can put otherwise wasted space to use for storage. Additional counter area can be created by extending the vanity top over the toilet tank.

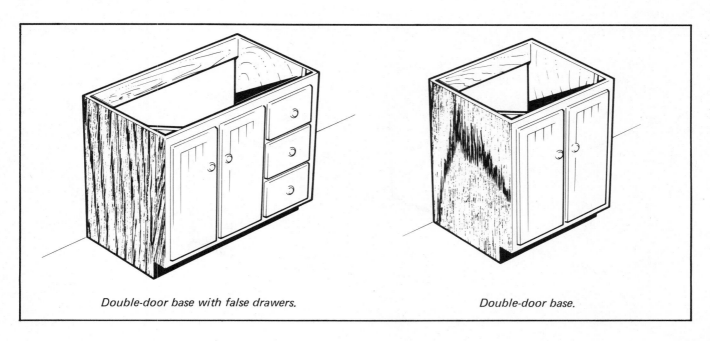

Double-door base with false drawers.   *Double-door base.*

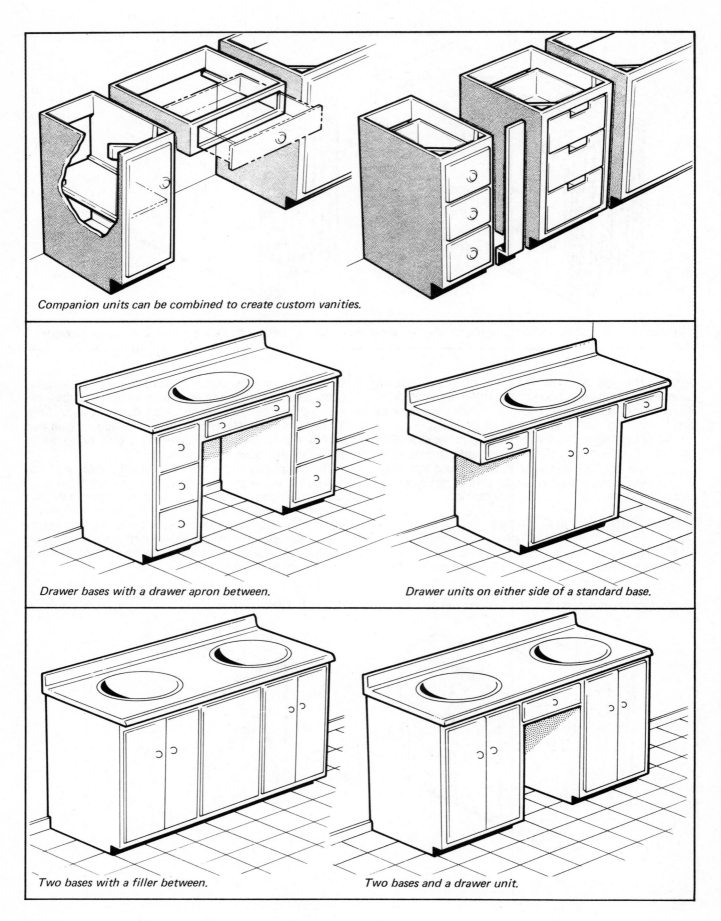

Companion units can be combined to create custom vanities.

Drawer bases with a drawer apron between.

Drawer units on either side of a standard base.

Two bases with a filler between.

Two bases and a drawer unit.

Countertops

There are four basic materials suitable for bathroom countertops: plastic laminate, ceramic tile, cultured marble, and Dupont's Corian synthetic marble.

Plastic laminate is the least expensive and most widely used of the basic countertop materials. It usually is applied to a particle-board core and comes in a great range of colors, patterns, and textures. Laminate tops are available in ready-made designs or can be custom fabricated to fit special situations. You also can buy sheets of laminate for do-it-yourself application to a core of plywood or particle board.

Ceramic tile is the most expensive countertop material. It provides a very durable surface, although the grouting can pose a cleaning problem. Almost any ceramic tile can be adapted to countertop use. Ceramic tile tops must be custom fabricated. Although most tile dealers can arrange for fabrication, making such a top yourself is not difficult and is much less expensive.

Cultured marble vanity tops are cast from a mixture of ground up marble and epoxy. Cultured marble is cast both in flat sheets and with lavatory basins cast as part of the unit. One-piece counter/lavatory tops have a smooth, elegant appearance. Fabricating a cultured marble top, however, is not a do-it-yourself project.

DuPont's Corian is a synthetic marble that is ideally suited for bathroom counters. It is nonporous and very hard, and the color runs completely through the material. Corian synthetic marble comes in a variety of marble patterns and solid colors. Ready-made DuPont Corian countertops are available with molded-in lavatory basins. Corian also is available in sheet form for custom fabrication. Unlike cultured marble, Corian can be worked much like wood.

Installing A Vanity Base Cabinet

A vanity base cabinet must be firmly attached to the wall, and the top must be level. The floor must be reasonably level, or else shims must be placed under the cabinet so that it rests against the wall as plumb as possible. Any high spots in the wall must be scraped or sanded smooth for the cabinet top to fit flush. For proper drainage and to ensure that the drawers and doors will operate smoothly, great care must be given to the installation of the base unit.

If your bathroom is small, consider putting off the vanity installation until after the painting, wallpapering, and installation of floor covering has been completed. In that way, you'll eliminate the problem of having to work around the vanity.

To install a vanity cabinet, you'll need the following tools and materials: a saw, a carpenter's level, a drill with 1/8-inch and 1/4-inch bits, a screwdriver, a supply of 2½-inch No. 10 wood screws, a supply of toggle or Molly bolts, two clamps, and a few wood shingles for shims. Make certain you have everything you need before you start. Then follow these directions:

1. Check locations of the plumbing pipes and, on paper, draw a plan of where the vanity is to be placed.
2. Cut away the base molding from the wall or walls against which the vanity is to be placed so that the unit will fit snugly against the wall.
3. Prepare the wall and floor by sanding off any very high spots.
4. Locate the wall studs where the vanity will stand, and mark them.
5. Remove the vanity base or bases from the boxes and examine them for shipping damage.

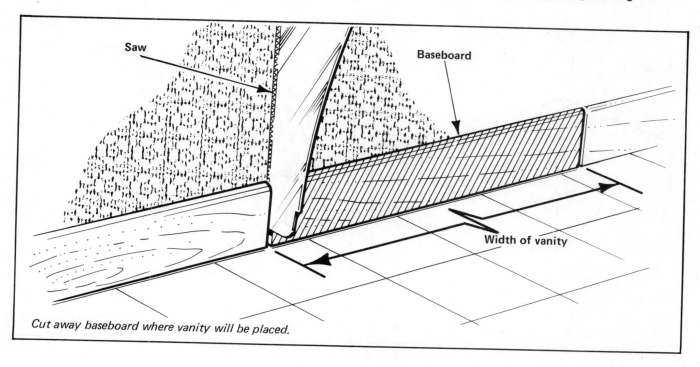

Cut away baseboard where vanity will be placed.

6. If your plan calls for a custom assembly, you should join the parts together before attaching any part of the assembly to the wall. Long double lavatory units, or those that encompass a dressing table might have to be assembled inside the bathroom. On multiple-cabinet installations, align the cabinets according to the plan and clamp them together. Drill two pilot holes through the adjoining stile of one of the cabinets and partially into the stile of the other for two screws, one in the upper quarter and one in the lower quarter of the unit.

7. Move the vanity into the bathroom and put it into position according to your plan. Place wooden shims under or behind the cabinet to level it. This will be easier if you have someone hold the cabinet level and plumb as you place the shims where there is daylight between the cabinet and walls or floor.

8. Drill a ⅛-inch hole through the top rail in the back of the cabinet and into the wall at each stud location. Place the No. 10 wood screws in the pilot holes and tighten them until they start to pull the cabinet against the wall. Before tightening them all the way, recheck the vanity; if it's level and plumb, secure everything in place. Two screws per unit are necessary, so you may need a Molly or toggle bolt if there aren't enough studs; use a ¼-inch bit for these holes.

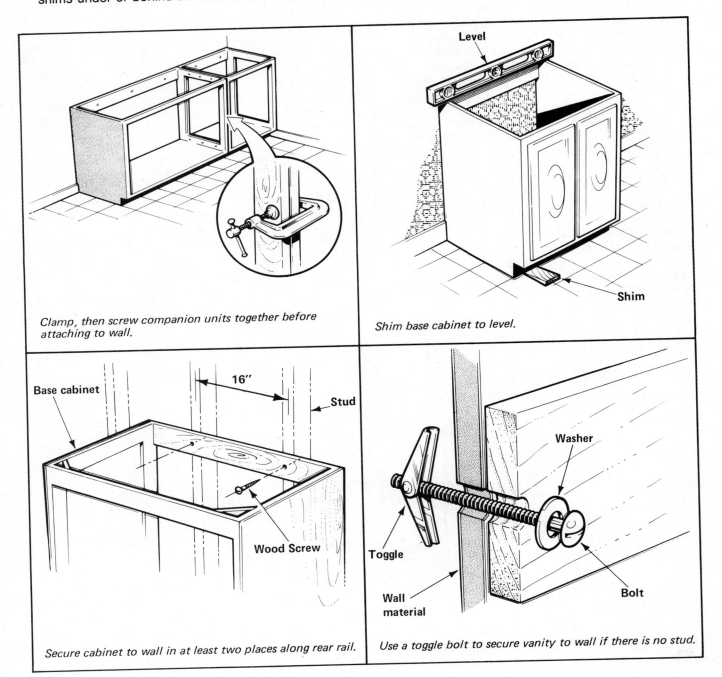

Clamp, then screw companion units together before attaching to wall.

Shim base cabinet to level.

Secure cabinet to wall in at least two places along rear rail.

Use a toggle bolt to secure vanity to wall if there is no stud.

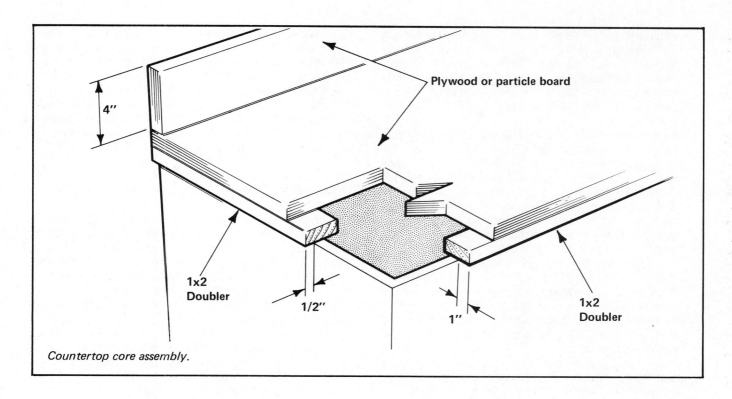

4"

Plywood or particle board

1x2 Doubler

1/2"

1"

1x2 Doubler

Countertop core assembly.

How To Make A Countertop Core

A custom countertop is easy to construct from ¾-inch plywood or particle board and plastic laminate or ceramic tile. The plywood or particle board is used for the core upon which the laminate is glued.

The first step is to plan your vanity top carefully and prepare an accurate drawing. The overall dimensions for the top should be 1 inch larger in both length and width than the base. This will give your top a ½-inch overhang on each side of the base cabinet and, when the cabinet is fitted flush to the wall, a 1-inch overhang in front. A 4-inch-high backsplash should be planned to run against the wall if you are using plastic laminate. If you are using ceramic tile, the height of the backsplash should be the height of one tile.

If the vanity is in a corner add only an extra ½ inch to the width and plan a backsplash for the side so that the top will fit flush against both walls. A recessed installation with walls at both ends calls for a wrap around backsplash and no overlap on the sides.

A ¾-by-2-inch doubling strip should be installed around the entire underside of the top to increase the edge thickness to 1½ inches. Strips of the core material or an inexpensive 1x2 can be used for this doubler.

After you have completed your plan, you'll know how much core material to purchase. For a slight extra cost, most lumber yards will cut the wood to size, thus saving you time and assuring accurate cuts. Don't forget to have the backsplash pieces cut at the same time.

To construct the countertop core you'll need the following tools and materials: measuring tape, screw-driver, hammer, drill and bits, keyhole or saber saw, sanding block and sandpaper, hard-setting wood filler, white glue, 2¼-inch No. 8 flat-head screws, 2d box nails, and a piece of brown wrapping paper large enough to cover the top surface of the core with a couple inches of overhang all around.

To assembly your vanity top follow these steps:

1. Cut the core material to size, including the back-splash and doubler strips.
2. Using white glue and 2d box nails, attach the doubling strips under the edges of the top. Space the nails about a foot apart, but don't use less than two per edge.

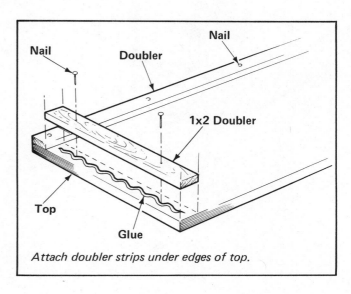

Nail

Nail

Doubler

1x2 Doubler

Top

Glue

Attach doubler strips under edges of top.

3. After the glue has set, use wood filler to fill any voids in the edges of the counter and backsplash. When the filler has dried, sand the edges smooth. This is especially important if you plan to use a router to trim the plastic laminate. Unless the edges are smooth, the cutter will bounce, giving a rough cut.

4. Drill ⅛-inch pilot holes for attaching the backsplash to the countertop piece. To do this, position the backsplash flush with the backside of the top piece and drill the holes from the underside of the top piece. Drill pilot holes 2 inches from either end and space the remaining holes about 12 inches apart. Use at least three screws per backsplash.

5. If you are going to cover the top with ceramic tile, attach the backsplash to the top piece at this time. Do so by running a bead of white glue along the bottom edge of the backsplash and then tightening it in place with screws through the pilot holes. If you're going to cover the counter with plastic laminate, set the backsplash aside for now; the backsplash will be attached after the laminate has been applied to it.

6. If you are going to apply ceramic tile, carefully lay out the opening for the lavatory basin at this time. (If you are going to use plastic laminate, the lavatory cutout will be made after the laminate has been glued down.) Most lavatory manufacturers give you a template for doing this, but you can use the basin itself. Bore a starting hole in each corner of the outline if the pattern is for a rectangular lavatory basin. You'll need only one starting hole if

the basin is round or oval. Be careful to bore inside the outline. Use a keyhole saw or a saber saw and cut along the basin outline. Remove the center and sand any split edges.

7. Check for imperfections. Test fit the top to the base and check the fit of the backsplash against the wall. It's easy to adjust the fit now before the tile or the plastic laminate is applied. When you're satisfied, its time to start laminating.

Applying Plastic Laminate

For this project you'll need all the tools you used in constructing the core, as well as the following tools and materials: block of wood, hacksaw, (or metal-cutting blade for saber saw) small block plane, fine file, inexpensive paintbrush, contact cement, caulking compound, and (helpful but not necessary) a rolling pin. The following additional power tools and special-purpose tools will make the job go faster and produce professional results: saber saw, sander, router with a carbide bit designed to trim laminate, safety glasses, and a J roller. After you've completed the countertop, you'll need a caulking gun and a tube of mastic to attach the top to the vanity base.

To apply the plastic laminate to the core, follow these steps:

1. Using a hacksaw or a saber saw equipped with a metal-cutting blade, cut strips of laminate slightly oversize for the counter edges and the top edge of

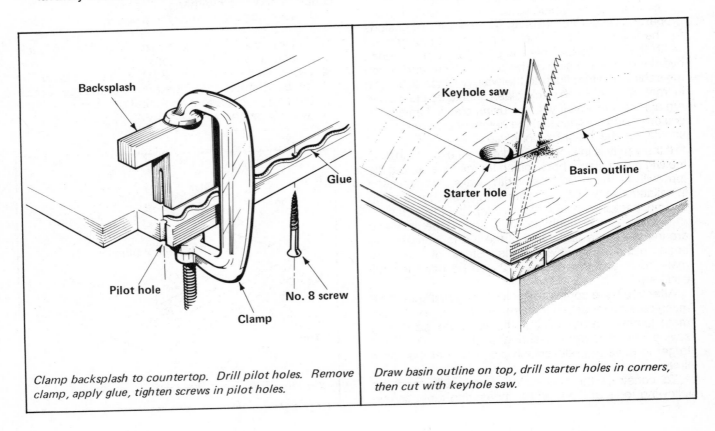

Clamp backsplash to countertop. Drill pilot holes. Remove clamp, apply glue, tighten screws in pilot holes.

Draw basin outline on top, drill starter holes in corners, then cut with keyhole saw.

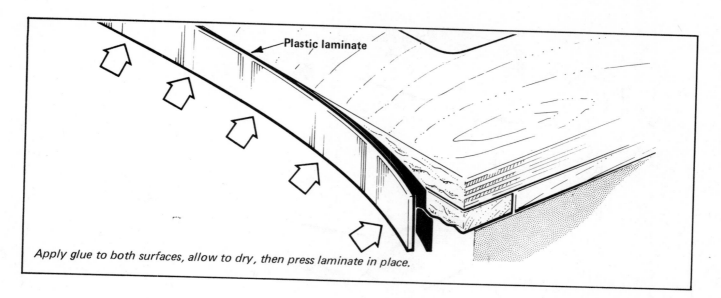

Apply glue to both surfaces, allow to dry, then press laminate in place.

the backsplash. Allow at least a ⅛" overlap on all sides. If you use a saber saw, keep the laminate face down and well supported as you cut it. A hacksaw cuts best with the material face up.

2. Use a brush to apply an even coat of contact cement to the back of the strips of laminate and to the edge of the countertop. Allow the glue to set according to the manufacturer's directions.

3. Start on one side of the countertop and carefully apply the laminate to the edge. Make the first contact at the center of the strip for better control. Work carefully, because contact cement grabs instantly; you will not be able to slide the laminate once the two glue surfaces have made contact. Work your way around the top, applying the laminate first to a side, then to the front, and finally to the remaining side if there is one. Do the same with the backsplash.

4. As you finish each side, apply pressure using a hammer and wood block. Heavy blows are not necessary; use a tapping motion and slide the block along the edge for even and complete distribution of pressure.

5. Using a block plane, or a router with carbide cutter,

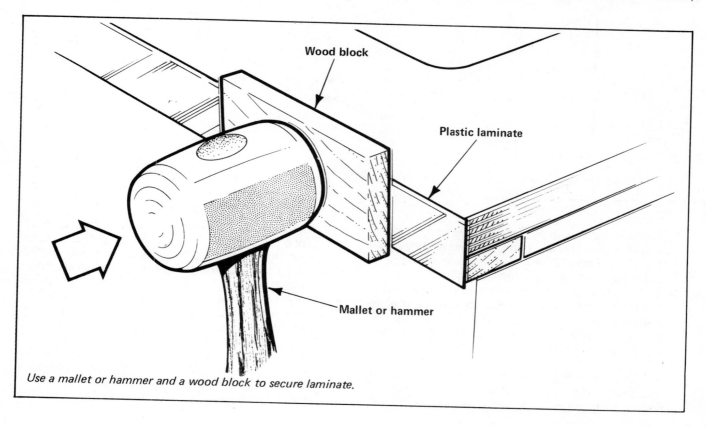

Use a mallet or hammer and a wood block to secure laminate.

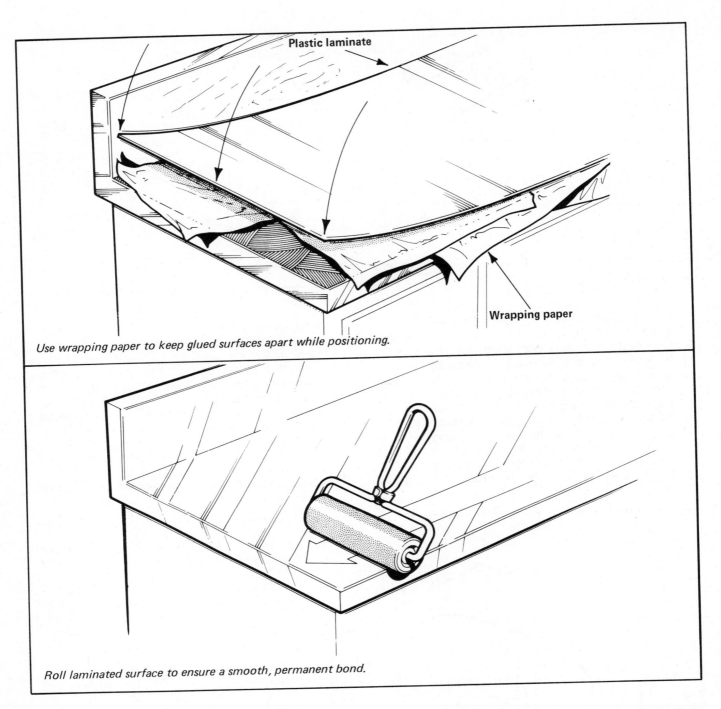

Use wrapping paper to keep glued surfaces apart while positioning.

Roll laminated surface to ensure a smooth, permanent bond.

carefully and evenly trim off the overhang. On the corners use a fine file to smooth and slightly bevel the joints. Remove any excess glue by using a scrap piece of laminate as a scraper.

6. Carefully measure the countertop and backsplash. The top laminate must overlap the side pieces, so make sure you allow for an overhang of at least 1/8'' on all sides. Mark the laminate and cut it as before. When you've finished cutting, test the laminate for fit.

7. Apply an even coat of contact cement both to the countertop and to the laminate and let it set as before. After the glue has set, cover the countertop with a piece of wrapping paper. Then, carefully place the laminate in position on top of the paper. Slide the paper from between the two pieces, pressing the laminate in place as you do so. When the surfaces are in full contact, use a hammer and wood block or a roller to apply pressure over the entire surface. Give special attention to the edges; they must be perfectly tight. Apply laminate to the face of the backsplash in the same manner.

8. Use a block plane or router to trim the laminate. Hold the plane at a slight angle to avoid scuffing the laminate on the edges of the assembly.

9. Use a fine file to smooth and bevel the joints. The

router has a special bevel cutter for this, but test it for proper adjustment before using it on a conspicuous place on the vanity top.

10. Using the template or lavatory basin as a pattern, mark the location of the cutout. Double check its position for drawer clearance inside the vanity base.

11. Mark the corners of the cutout and use a nail or punch to make a dent in the laminate so that when you drill the starter holes for sawing, the drill will not skid. Drill a hole in each corner if the basin is square, one hole on the perimeter if the basin is round. Carefully cut along the layout lines with a keyhole saw or a saber saw and dress the rough edges with a file.

12. Turn the vanity top over and drill through the laminate for the backsplash screws. The holes are already there; all you have to drill through is the laminate, so use very little pressure.

13. Apply a generous bead of caulk along the bottom of the backsplash and fasten it in place using 2¼-inch No. 8 flat-head screws. Immediately clean up the excess caulk with water and a rag.

14. Set the top onto the base and use a carpenter's level to make sure it does not slant from side to side and from front to back. Remove the top and apply a bead of mastic along the top edge of the base. Position the top on the base and press it in

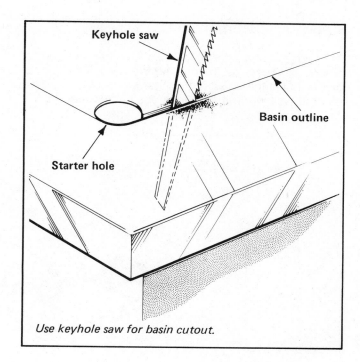

Use keyhole saw for basin cutout.

place. If leveling is necessary, use thin wooden shims between the top and the edge of the base, setting them in place with mastic.

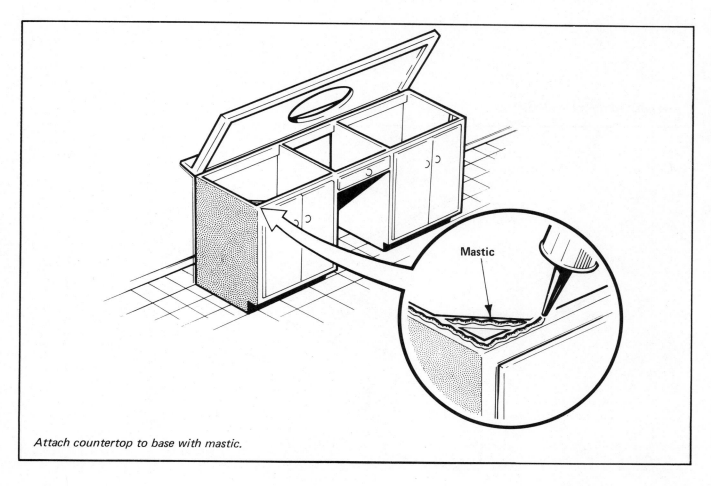

Attach countertop to base with mastic.

Applying Ceramic Tile

This project is a little more involved than laminating plastic because you're dealing with many individual pieces of tile that must fit together to form the top. The effort is well worth it, because you'll have a beautiful, lasting vanity top when you're finished.

Planning the job is half the battle. You'll need face tiles for the front edge of the counter; if they're not available they can be cut from full tiles. Bullnose tiles, or tiles with a rounded leading edge, are then placed along the top edge as a starter row to give the edge a

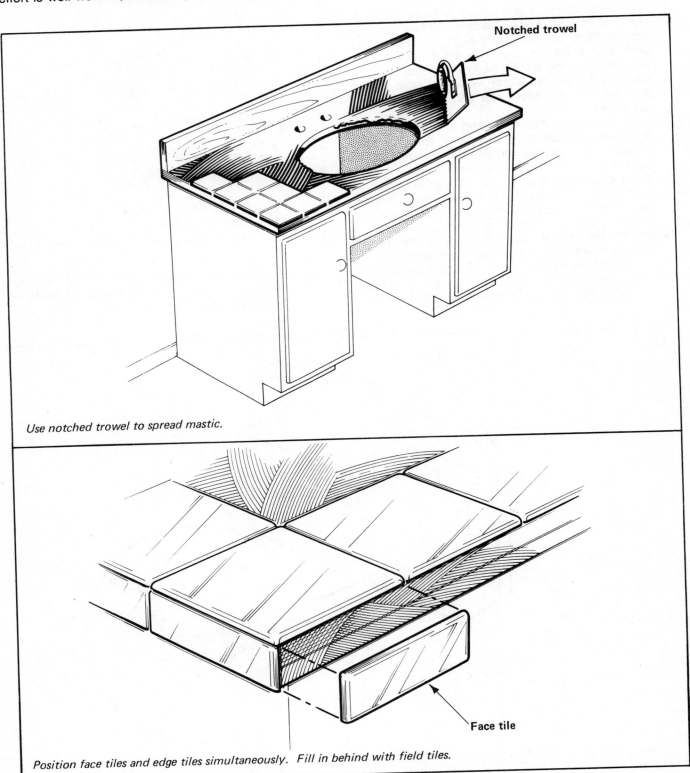

Notched trowel

Use notched trowel to spread mastic.

Face tile

Position face tiles and edge tiles simultaneously. Fill in behind with field tiles.

finished appearance. Then the regular field of tiles is laid with the rearmost row cut to fit against the backsplash. Tiles are then set on the backsplash to hide the rough-cut edges of the last row. Bullnose tiles finally are cut to cap off the top of the backsplash.

Keeping that general scheme in mind, prepare a plan that you can follow for laying the tile. Here is a list of tools and supplies you'll need in addition to those you used for making the core top: a saber saw with carbide blade, a carpenter's level, epoxy or organic tile adhesive, grout, silicone sealer, caulking compound, wood shims, and an old toothbrush or paint stick. You'll also need the following, which you can rent from your tile supplier: a tile cutter, tile nippers, a rubber grout trowel, and a notched trowel.

With your plan in hand follow these steps:

1. Install the countertop core on the vanity and make sure it's level. Apply a small amount of tile adhesive to the edge of the vanity base to secure the top

2. Lay out a test area of tiles. Most tiles have small tabs attached to their sides for proper grout spacing, but if they don't you'll have to decide on the width of the groutline. A narrow groutline—about 1/16-inch wide—usually looks best and is easy to keep clean.

3. When you're satisfied that your plan will work, use a notched trowel to spread an even coat of adhesive over as much of the counter as you can cover with tile in the suggested "wet edge" time given by the manufacturer of the adhesive.

4. Lay in the tile starting at the front edge. Set a bullnose and face tile together and fill in behind the field tiles. Press them in place; don't slide them. Sliding the tiles will force the glue from under the tile and up through the grout lines. If necessary, insert a finishing nail between the tiles to maintain even spacing as you lay them. Cut the tiles to fit in the last row against the backsplash and continue up the backsplash and finish by cutting bullnose tiles to cap off the backsplash. Don't worry about the lavatory basin cutout. Place the tile so as to overhang the edge of the opening. After the glue has set they can be trimmed off with a saber saw equipped with a carbide blade, thus avoiding the tiresome task of nipping and cutting each tile. When you're finished, clean off the excess glue and let the installation dry overnight.

5. Use a carbide blade in a saber saw to cut the overhanging tiles of the basin cutout. Move slowly with light pressure; don't force the blade.

6. Apply the grout according to the manufacturer's directions, using a rubber trowel to force it between tiles. Use the end of a toothbrush or a thin piece of wood, such as a paint stick, to force the grout deep into the grooves. Wipe off excess grout with a wet rag.

7. When the grout is completely dry, a light polishing with a rag will remove the light film of grout left on the tiles. Seal the grout with a silicone sealer to prevent dirt from discoloring it.

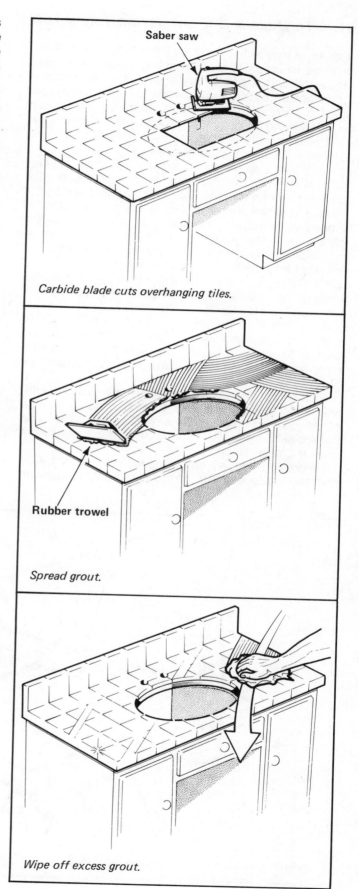

Carbide blade cuts overhanging tiles.

Spread grout.

Wipe off excess grout.

How To Make A DuPont Corian Vanity Top

Corian, a synthetic marble manufactured by DuPont, may be worked like ordinary wood using power tools equipped with carbide-tipped blades. Planning and construction methods are the same as for a wooden-core countertop. Corian synthetic marble is available in sheets 25 and 30 inches wide, up to 145 inches long. A 25-by-98-inch sheet is the smallest available and will probably be larger than needed.

The first step is to measure the base cabinet accurately. Plan for the countertop to overhang the base by ½ inch on each side and by 1 inch along the front. Therefore, if neither side of the cabinet is to be placed against a wall, the overall length of the counter should be 1 inch greater than the width of the base. If one side of the cabinet is to be against a wall, the length of the counter should be ½ inch greater than the width of the cabinet. If the cabinet is to be enclosed by walls on all three sides, the length of the top must be the same as the width of the base.

Also plan for a backsplash along the wall or walls against which the vanity is placed. The backsplash should be about 4 inches high, although the actual height can be varied to make the most economical use of material.

Plan to cut the Corian sheet crosswise, to length, first. Then trim it lengthwise, to width. The lengthwise cutoff can be used for the backsplash. The side backsplash, if needed, can be cut to the same height from left over stock.

Before you start, assemble the following tools: power drill and sharp drill bits, circular and saber saw with carbide blades, 400-grit sandpaper and sanding block, router and carbide-tipped bits, caulk, and neoprene glue. With your tools and plans ready, follow these steps:

1. Accurately lay out the dimensions on the Corian sheet. Using the circular saw and a sharp carbide blade, cut the top to length first. Corian is heavy and must be supported at all times. Then trim for width by cutting off the long section that will be the backsplash.
2. Smooth the edges with sandpaper. A fancy edge can be cut using a router equipped with a carbide blade.
3. Apply a bead of sealing caulk along the top edge of the base cabinet and set the Corian top in place.
4. Mark the lavatory basin cutout using the template provided by the manufacturer or use the basin as a pattern. Double check to be sure that the basin will be properly located in relation to the plumbing hookup.
5. Drill a pilot hole in each corner of the basin outline if the lavatory is rectangular; if the lavatory is round, drill one pilot hole just inside the perimeter of the outline. Using a saber saw with carbide-edged blade, cut out the lavatory opening along the outline.
6. Install the backsplash by running a bead of neoprene glue along the bottom of the backsplash and press the backsplash in place. Seal the backsplash by caulking the small gaps between the wall and the backsplash and wipe off any excess glue and caulk.

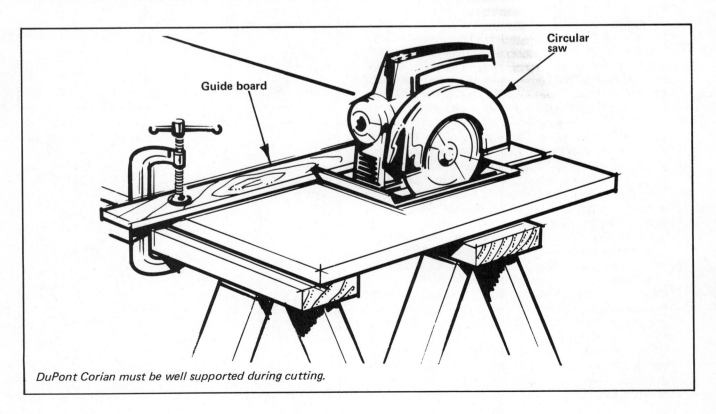

Guide board

Circular saw

DuPont Corian must be well supported during cutting.

Doing Your Own Bathroom: Storage

Storage space is at a premium in the bathroom. Although most of the floor and wall space must be allotted to the tub, lavatory, and toilet, creative use of shelving and medicine cabinets can make useful storage out of hard-to-reach corners and put space over toilets and lavatories to good use.

Installing a new medicine cabinet is an easy way to increase the storage capacity of your bathroom. The wall-mounted units come in many attractive styles and shapes. Different looks are achieved by varying the mirror frames. Any style ranging from the deeply carved and ornate to the streamlined contemporary look are available to suit your taste and match your decor.

Single medicine cabinet units are available to fit above a small vanity or wall-hung lavatory. Double and triple units provide maximum storage space and can cover up unsightly walls that might be left when an old cabinet is removed. Corner cabinets also are available and can be used in those dead spaces or over the toilet combined with a mirror to create a customized unit.

Multiple cabinets come with built-in mirrors that are hung on hinged doors or used as sliding panels. The triple units have the added advantage of the two outside mirror panels providing three-dimensional viewing for easy grooming. The swing of most cabinet doors can be adjusted to open to the right or left by turning the cabinet upside down.

Many medicine cabinets come equipped with built-in lighting. Fluorescent is the most popular but some units are available with a combination of incandescent and fluorescent for a more natural light.

Most older custom-built medicine cabinets are recessed into the wall. Today they come ready to install on the surface of any smooth wall. A few screws hold them securely in place making it one of the items easiest to install in the bathroom, a natural for an easy bathroom makeover.

There are cabinets designed for recess mounting where space is at a premium or where the look of a flush mounting is desired. Most surface-mounted units can also be recessed; the opening left by the old cabinet can be used or enlarged to fit the new unit.

Installing A Surface-Mounted Cabinet

Ready-made surface-mounted cabinets are quick and easy to install. Removal of the old cabinet, if there is one, is the hardest part of the job. When shopping for a cabinet, choose one that will completely cover the opening left by the old cabinet. If there is a light over or in the old cabinet you can choose a style with a built-in light or select a new matching fixture.

Before you begin, gather the following tools and supplies: hammer, screwdriver, level, drill and bits, tape measure, and wall anchors (not necessary if you use existing wall studs). If the old cabinet must go, or you plan to install a light in the cabinet, the following tools will be needed: small pry bar, wire cutter, pliers, and wire nuts (if not supplied with cabinet).

After you've read the installation instructions supplied by the manufacturer and have everything on hand, follow these directions:

1. Turn off the electricity by pulling out or tripping the main circuit breaker or fuse. This is necessary only if a light is close to, or part of, the old cabinet.
2. Remove the old cabinet. If it's a metal unit it will come out in one piece. Remove the hold-down screws in the back or sides of the unit and force the pry bar under the front flange of the wall. If the cabinet is of wood, remove the door and dismantle it, starting with the trim moldings
3. Disconnect any wires running to the old cabinet, and remove the cabinet.
4. Lay out the location of the hanging fasteners for the new cabinet according to manufacturer's specifications, and drill small pilot holes where these screws will go. If you feel resistance as you drill into the wall, you're on a stud and a screw will hold; but if there is resistance for only an inch or so, you'll need a Molly bolt, toggle bolt, or plastic wall anchor.
5. Secure the two top fasteners and hang the cabinet on them. Check for level and that the cabinet is correctly centered; then mark the location of the

two bottom fasteners using the cabinet as a guide.

6. Remove the cabinet and drill pilot holes for the bottom fasteners and install wall anchors if needed.

7. If your cabinet is equipped with a light, carefully read the wiring instructions. In most cases two or three wires are all that have to be connected. The cabinet back is equipped with knockout holes close to where the wires should enter the fixture. Remove the most convenient knockout by prying it out and twisting it off with pliers. Attach the end of the BX armored cable to this hole and tighten it securely in place.

8. Always attach the same color wires together. Take the two black wires and skin off about ½ inch of insulation; grip the bare ends with the pliers and twist the two wires tightly together. When they are completely twisted, turn on a wire nut and tighten. Do the same for the white wires. If you're using a nonmetallic cable, attach the green ground wires in the same way.

9. Push the wires carefully into the enclosure and put on the cover and install the cabinet on the wall. Tighten the top mounting screws; then install and tighten the bottom screws.

10. Install the light bulbs and trim, put in the shelves and turn the electricity back on.

Installing A Recessed Cabinet

Space can be saved by recessing the medicine cabinet into the wall. It's easiest if you remove the old cabinet and install a new one the same dimension in the ready-made recess. But if you want a larger cabinet or there was no cabinet, you'll have to cut a recess for the new one. Whatever your situation, take these instructions and use what applies to your particular situation.

Before you begin, the following tools and supplies are necessary: hammer, screwdriver, measuring tape, keyhole saw, saber saw, level, extension cord, drill and bits, putty knife, patching plaster, wallboard tape, wallboard taping compound, No. 8 nails, 2x4 lumber, ½-inch wallboard, wire cutter, pliers, and wire nuts. After you have everything ready, follow these instructions:

1. Turn off the electricity to the bathroom.
2. Remove the old cabinet according to steps 2 and 3 in the preceeding section, "Installing A Surface-Mounted Cabinet."
3. Lay out the dimensions of the new cabinet on the wall. You have to cut away the plaster and studs in this area and install a 2x4 sill and header to frame the cabinet.

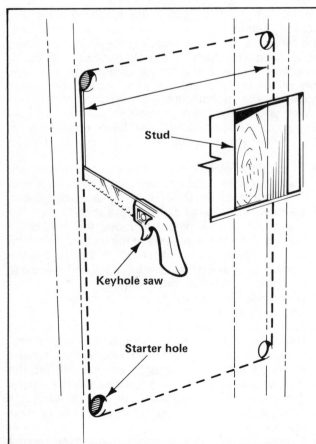

Mark the position of the cabinet on the wall, then use a keyhole saw to remove wall material between studs.

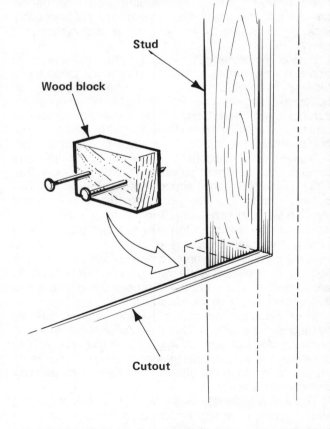

Position wood blocks, or use nails by themselves, to support the sill and header for toenailing.

4. Using a keyhole saw or saber saw, cut the wall opening along the layout lines. Go slowly and watch for electrical or plumbing lines. Then remove the plaster. The header and sill 2x4s have to be nailed into a stud, so you'll probably have to widen the opening to the next full stud on each side. Cut two 2x4s to fit the top and bottom opening and toe nail them into place by driving No. 8 common nails at 45 degree angles through the base of the 2x4 into the stud. To hold the 2x4s in place while nailing, drive two nails into the vertical wall studs on both sides about 1½ inches below where you want the sill and 1½ inches above the header. Be sure the nails are level across.

5. Cut two 2x4s to fit vertically between the header and sill and toe nail them in place to frame the opening for the cabinet. Then cut pieces of wallboard to enclose the opening. Shim out and nail these flush with the existing wall and patch the cracks between the wallboard and the plaster with patching plaster. When the plaster is dry, sand the joint smooth. If the wall is wallboard, apply a coat of joint compound and then drywall tape. Then apply a thin second coat after the tape is in place, and let dry. Apply a top coat, feathering the edges three or four inches on each side of the tape, and let it dry;

then sand the surface smooth.

6. Paint the wall and patch area, and when it's dry install the cabinet in the recess. Place the cabinet in position and check that it's level. Mark the location of the placement screws and remove the cabinet and drill pilot holes for these screws.

7. If the cabinet has a light, wire it as described in steps 7, 8 and 9 of "Installing A Surface-Mounted Cabinet."

8. When the wiring is in place, screw the cabinet permanently into position, replace light bulb and install the shelves. Then turn on the electricity.

Other Storage

Creative use of shelving can solve some of the storage problems found in the small bath. Ready-made shelving that is easy to install can be purchased wherever hardware products are sold. By painting or wallpapering construction grade lumber to compliment your bathroom decor, you can construct custom-made shelves inexpensively.

Locate the shelves in the dead wall space next to vanities, over toilets, and behind doors. They are out of the way and will not obstruct movement.

Added storage may be created by making a shelving

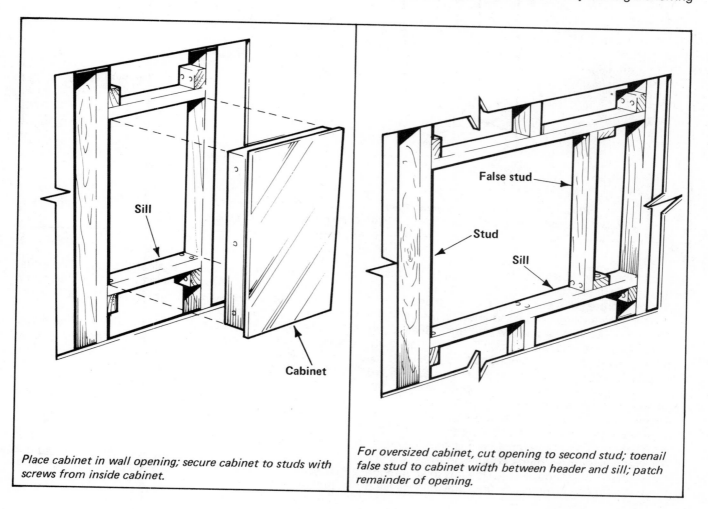

Place cabinet in wall opening; secure cabinet to studs with screws from inside cabinet.

For oversized cabinet, cut opening to second stud; toenail false stud to cabinet width between header and sill; patch remainder of opening.

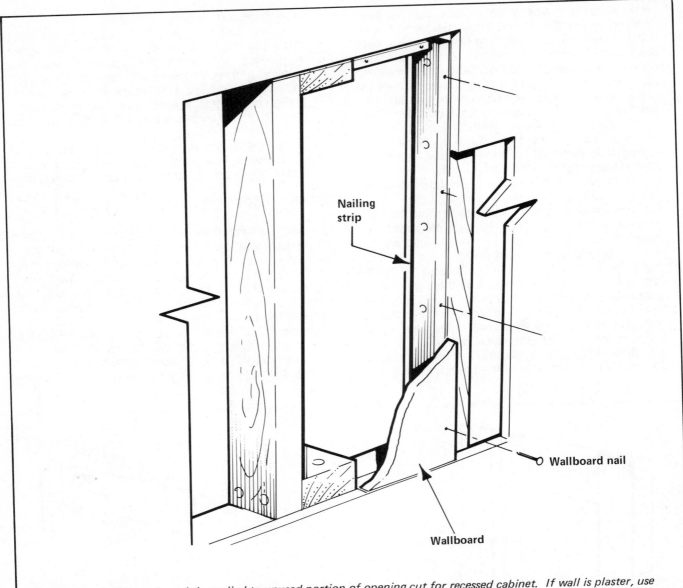

Nailing strip

Wallboard nail

Wallboard

Detail of how wallboard patch is applied to unused portion of opening cut for recessed cabinet. If wall is plaster, use patching plaster to patch joint; if wall is wallboard, use joint compound and joint tape.

unit to fit the space between the vanity and the toilet. By extending this unit to the ceiling you receive the bonus of increased privacy for the toilet area.

Narrow shelves also can be mounted on the backs of doors. This shelving will allow storage of cleaning equipment, soaps and shampoos. The backs of vanity cabinet doors and linen cabinet doors are naturals for this type of shelving. Don't forget to provide a lip for the shelves; otherwise, everytime you open the door, the contents of the shelves will spill out.

Recess-shelving offers the same storage space as surface-mounted shelves but doesn't project into the room. This type of storage must be built into the walls.

The wet wall of most baths containing the soil stack is thicker than the standard wall. Use this to advantage and plan a recessed shelving unit that can fit flush behind a door that opens against the wall. The soffit over a bath and shower enclosure is another good location for recessed shelving. Sliding doors can be added to hide the contents.

The wall has to be cut away between the studs for this type of shelving to be installed, so check that wiring or plumbing pipes do not pass behind where you plan to cut. The installation of these units is straightforward. Cut the wall as you would for a medicine cabinet and line the enclosure with wallboard or wood, and trim the front edge with molding to hide the joints.

Whatever type of shelving you choose, it should be planned from the beginning of your remodeling project to receive the most benefit. Ready-made or custom-cut shelves are an inexpensive solution to the storage problem of every small bath.

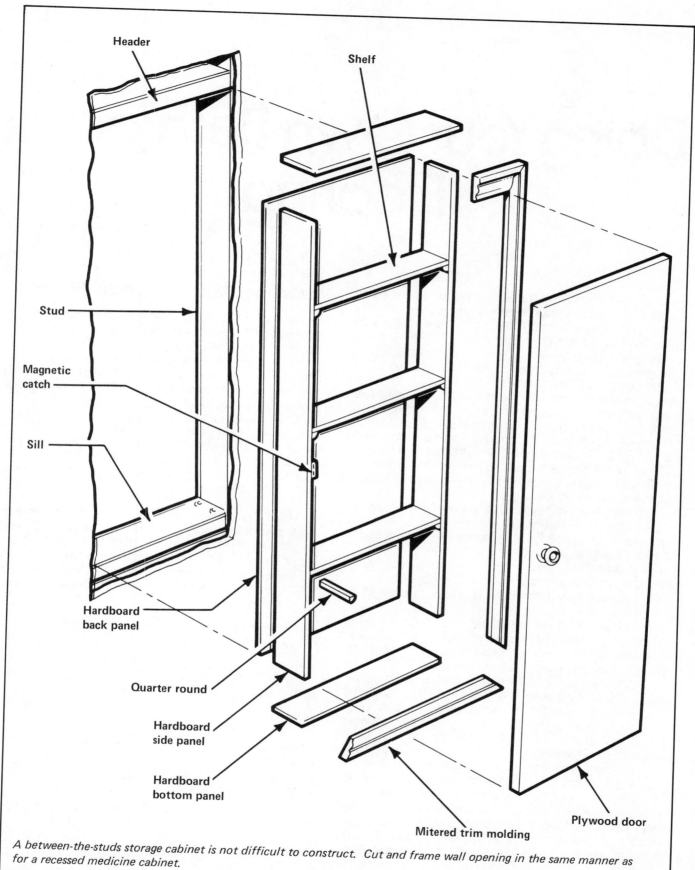

Header

Shelf

Stud

Magnetic
catch

Sill

Hardboard
back panel

Quarter round

Hardboard
side panel

Hardboard
bottom panel

Mitered trim molding

Plywood door

A between-the-studs storage cabinet is not difficult to construct. Cut and frame wall opening in the same manner as for a recessed medicine cabinet.

Doing Your Own Bathroom: Flooring

Bathroom flooring can be either hard or soft, easy to care for or difficult, inexpensive or expensive. Yet the various materials have one thing in common: nearly all can be laid by the do-it-yourselfer.

Resilient flooring—which is the modern successor to linoleum (not manufactured in the United States since Armstrong abandoned it in 1974)—ranges from inexpensive asphalt tiles to somewhat more expensive vinyl asbestos sheets and tiles, to vinyl sheets and tiles that can range in price from moderate to expensive. Generally, resilients in tile form are less expensive than sheet goods. As you might expect, the resilient tile that comes with a self-stick backing is more costly than its plain counterpart, but that backing makes the tiles extremely easy to lay.

Asphalt tile is an inexpensive material that offers no advantages over the other resilients except price. Its colors are not as good; it is not as wear-resistant; and it breaks easily.

Vinyl asbestos tiles have less gloss than vinyl flooring, and the colors are duller. Their appeal lies in the fact that they offer no-wax ease of care at a moderate price.

The vinyls range from the least expensive rotovinyls to the most expensive no-wax vinyls. All vinyls are available with or without cushioning. The best, of course, are the well-cushioned no-wax vinyls.

Ceramic tile is a traditional bathroom flooring material. There is good reason for its continuing popularity; it is elegant, relatively easy to care for, and very durable. If you opt for ceramic tile, you can choose from many colors and shapes and create your own patterns when laying it.

Carpeting is soft and warm to walk on but poses a cleaning problem if it is used near any of the fixtures. If carpeting is a must for you, it is best to get a carpeting specifically manufactured for bathroom use. It is inadvisable to make a permanent installation as you would in any other room. The carpeting should be laid loose to allow it to be taken up and laundered as necessary. Fitting carpeting into your bathroom is nearly the same as fitting sheet vinyl.

Installing Resilient Sheet Flooring

Sheet floor covering is nearly always installed with adhesive. Adhesive is especially needed on subfloors subject to seasonal changes in humidity.

Before buying the material, always check the installation instructions. You may find that the resilient flooring you want does not lend itself to easy do-it-yourself installation.

The following instructions apply specifically to Sundial, an Armstrong cushioned no-wax vinyl sheet, but the steps are quite similar for installing other types of resilient flooring. You'll need a chalk line, knife, straight edge, trowel, rolling pin or roller, the correct adhesive, and some cardboard.

1. Read the instructions that come with the flooring.
2. Measure the room as accurately as possible, and diagram the floor plan on graph paper, noting the position of fixtures, closets, doorways, offsets in the walls, etc. Measure twice to verify your figures.
3. Take the roll of sheet flooring into another room

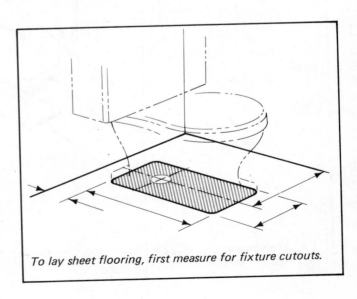

To lay sheet flooring, first measure for fixture cutouts.

where it can be spread out. Use the chalk line to transfer the measurements from the graph paper to the flooring, allowing some extra for trimming. Put cardboard underneath the flooring to protect the floor. Then cut along the chalk lines with a sharp knife and straight-edge.

4. Carry the flooring back to the bathroom and put it in place; it should fit almost exactly. Trim all overlap with the knife.

5. Roll back half of the flooring and spread the adhesive on the exposed floor with a trowel.
6. Press the flooring material back onto the adhesive before it dries.
7. Then roll up the other half of the flooring and repeat the procedure.
8. Finally, roll out the bumps in the material either with a rolling pin or with a special roller available from your flooring dealer. Trim edges tight.

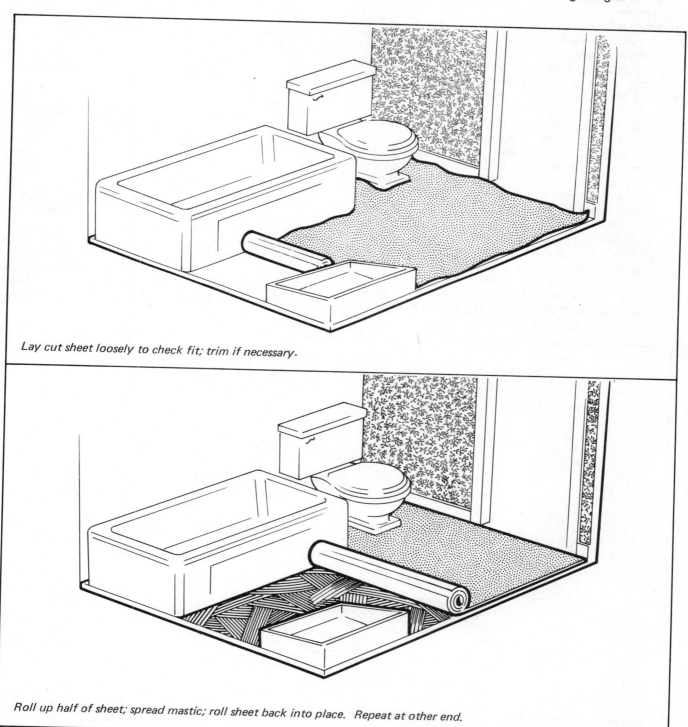

Lay cut sheet loosely to check fit; trim if necessary.

Roll up half of sheet; spread mastic; roll sheet back into place. Repeat at other end.

Laying A Tile Floor

Floor tiles now come in a wide range of prices and materials. The two most popular types are asphalt tiles and vinyl tiles. The use to which you put the room, the type of subflooring that is already down, and the availability of patterns will have much to do with your selection of tile. Spend some time in choosing; you might as well get it right the first time. Purchasing the right adhesive is important too. Different materials and different subfloors require different mastics. No matter what type of tiles you choose, however, the procedures for installation are about the same. Besides the tile and the appropriate adhesive, you'll need heavy-duty scissors, rolling pin, paintbrush or roller or thin-notched flooring trowel, sandpaper, and chalk line.

1. The first step—preparation—is the most important one of all. Pry up the moldings; remove all wax and dirt from the floor surface; search for and sand down any high spots; and make sure there are no nails sticking up. Since resilient tiles are flexible and will conform to whatever is under them, any irregularities in the subfloor will eventually show through.
2. Next, find the exact center of each wall and snap a chalk line from these points across the floor. Where the two lines intersect is the center of the room.
3. Lay a full run of loose (uncemented) tiles from the center of each wall within one quarter of the room. If the last tile in either direction is less than half the width of a full tile, draw a new chalk line beside the actual center line, moving the original line half a tile in either direction. This technique will give you even-sized end tiles at both ends of the room.
4. Now you are ready to start cementing the tiles down. Work on a quarter of the room at a time. Be sure that you check the back of each tile to see that all of the arrows are aimed in the same direction. This keeps the pattern, if any, aligned. If you are using a mixed tile pattern, you should lay it out without mastic before putting the tiles in place. If you have tiles with the adhesive already on the backing, peel off the release paper. Start at the center point, and place the tile down precisely on both lines. It will not slide into place; once down, it is down for good. If you have tiles without mastic, spread the cement over the first quarter only, bringing it right up to the lines. Be sure to use the proper mastic, and follow the directions regarding how long to wait before setting the tiles in place. Usually, you are instructed to wait until the adhesive is tacky.
5. After you get the first center tile in place, lay tiles alternately toward each wall, building a sort of pyramid until the entire quarter is covered except for the tiles along the edges.
6. To cut and fit the border tiles, first place a loose tile (#1) on the last tile in the row. Then butt another loose tile (#2) against the wall, with its sides aligned with those of the #1 tile. Now, make a mark on the #1 tile, along the edge of #2 where the two

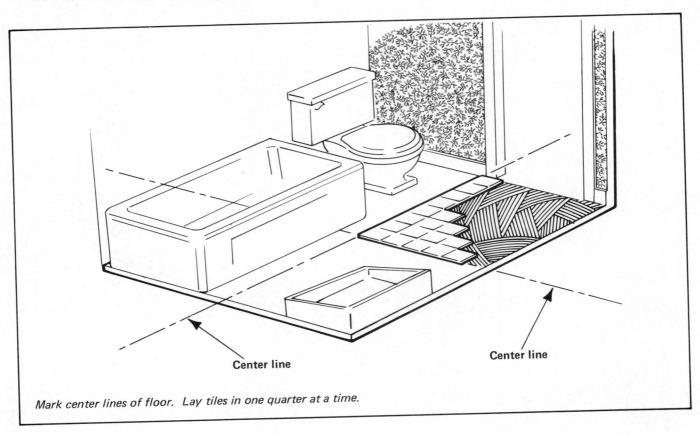

Center line

Center line

Mark center lines of floor. Lay tiles in one quarter at a time.

tiles overlap. If you then cut the #1 tile along the line, you will have an exact fit for the border tile. If you have any irregularities (such as pipes) to fit tiles around, make a paper pattern of the obstacle, trace it onto the tile, and then cut along the line. You should be able to cut most tiles with ordinary heavy-duty scissors.

7. Go over the tiles with a rolling pin.
8. Follow the same procedures for the other three quarters, and then be prepared to receive pats on the back for doing such professional-looking work.

Installing A Ceramic Tile Floor

Installing a ceramic tile floor can be transformed from a very messy and difficult job to one that is relatively simple and clean. You can buy tile with a self-stick backing that requires just peeling off the protective paper and pressing the tile in place. Other tile comes in pregrouted sheets, containing hundreds of those little mosaic tiles that can all be laid simultaneously.

You can lay ceramic tile over wallboard, exterior grade plywood, tempered hardboard, or almost any firm base. But never lay tile on a surface that is not perfectly firm or one that has dirt, wax, or flaking paint. Always use the proper mortar, adhesive, and primer (i.e., those recommended by the tile manufacturer); the adhesive must be compatible with the surface being covered and with any primer and grout.

If your present bathroom floor is wood, make sure it is sound and firm. Then cover it with ¼-inch exterior grade plywood or underlayment board. Nail down the covering material every 4 inches with ring shank or ring-grooved nails. The nails must be long enough so that more than half the length of the nail penetrates the floor. Long (1¼ inch) staples will work as well and are less tedious to install.

If your present floor is linoleum, rubber, vinyl, vinyl asbestos, or asphalt tile, you can apply the ceramic tile directly to it. But again, make sure the floor is structurally sound, firm, and free of any grease, wax, or dirt. The entire surface should be lightly sanded to ensure good adhesion, and badly worn spots should be leveled with underlayment cement.

To lay tile with pregrouted ceramic mosaic tile sheets you will need a tape measure, a chalk line, a V-notched trowel, a tile cutter, tile nippers, a razor knife, adhesive, and a carpet-covered roller. For caulking around the walls or any plumbing fittings, you'll need a tube of sealant and a caulking gun. For cleanup when finished, you'll need cheese cloth and high-flash-point mineral spirits.

Follow these steps for a neat and attractive ceramic tile floor:

1. Find the center of each of the four walls, disregarding fixtures, alcoves, etc. Snap chalk lines between opposing walls. The lines must be perfectly perpendicular to each other.
2. Starting at the center point, lay several sheets of tile along one chalk line. Then lay several sheets

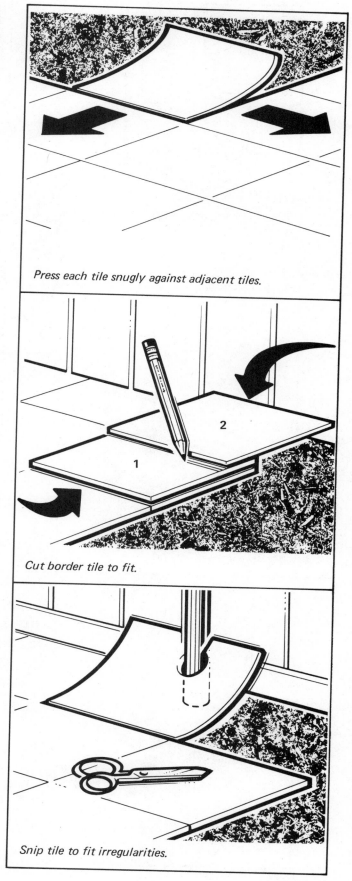

Press each tile snugly against adjacent tiles.

Cut border tile to fit.

Snip tile to fit irregularities.

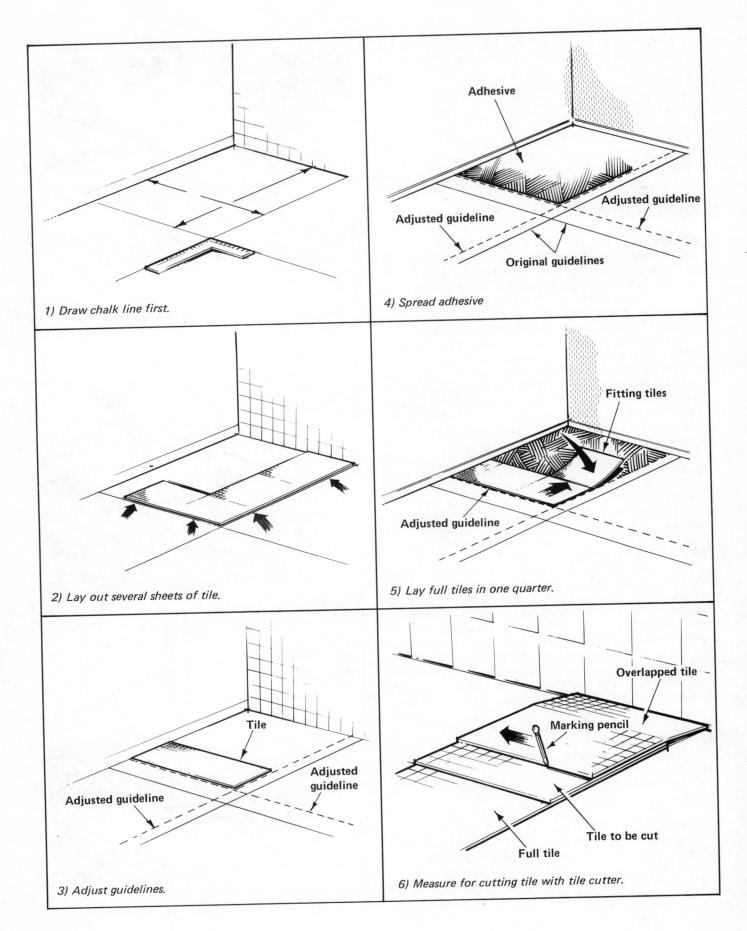

1) Draw chalk line first.

2) Lay out several sheets of tile.

3) Adjust guidelines.

Tile

Adjusted guideline

Adjusted guideline

4) Spread adhesive

Adhesive

Adjusted guideline

Adjusted guideline

Original guidelines

5) Lay full tiles in one quarter.

Fitting tiles

Adjusted guideline

6) Measure for cutting tile with tile cutter.

Overlapped tile

Marking pencil

Tile to be cut

Full tile

along the other line, all within the same quarter of the room.

3. When you approach the wall, overlap the last sheet to see where you must cut. If the cut line is in the middle of a tile, push all the sheets back so this cut will fall on a grout line. Do this with the two adjacent walls to minimize tile cutting.

4. Now go back and adjust the original chalk lines accordingly. If you are laying the tile sheets on a subfloor, adjust the sheets of subflooring so that the seams are at least 3 inches from any joints between tile sheets.

5. Starting at the intersection of the adjusted center lines, spread adhesive with the trowel over one quarter of the room—or over that part of it you can finish in one hour or less. If there is an area for which you will have to cut the tile (like a far corner), don't spread adhesive there yet.

6. Lay the first sheet of tile on the adhesive with its two edges precisely meeting the chalk guidelines. Butt each sheet tight against other sheets, holding the far edge upward so it doesn't get into the adhesive before the near edges are butted. Put the sheets straight down; never slide the tile into place.

7. Finish laying all the full sheets of tile before cutting any sheets. Next, fit all sheets that require cutting only at the grout lines. Butt the tile sheet against the wall to determine the grout line to be cut, then cut it with a razor knife.

8. Spread adhesive and lay the cut sheets, pressing them into place between the wall and the other sheets. If your measurement was slightly off and the space is too small, causing the sheet to buckle slightly, take it up and trim along the wall edge with tile nippers or a hacksaw.

9. To determine the cut line for tile sheets that must be cut with a tile cutter, place a sheet of tile precisely on top of the last full sheet of laid tile, and then lay another sheet of tile on top but butted against the wall. Use the edge of the top sheet as a straightedge to draw a line on the sheet below.

10. Cut the sheet along the line with a tile cutter (a tool which you can rent). Spread adhesive and lay in the cut sheet, putting the cut edge along the wall.

11. If you must make contour cuts, such as those around pipes or fixtures, use a soft pencil and draw the shape as precisely as you can. Cut out all the whole tiles within the line with a razor knife, and then use tile nippers to finish the contour.

12. Wait at least an hour after the installation is completed, and then go over the entire floor with the carpet-covered roller to make sure that the tile makes a good bond with the adhesive. In corners where the roller won't fit, pound the tile gently with a carpet-covered board.

13. Make a ⅛-inch bead of sealant along the joint at the wall. The sealant, available in colors to match the grout, prevents moisture seepage.

14. Seal around any plumbing fittings in the floor.

15. Clean any sealant or adhesive from the tile floor with mineral spirits or paint thinner.

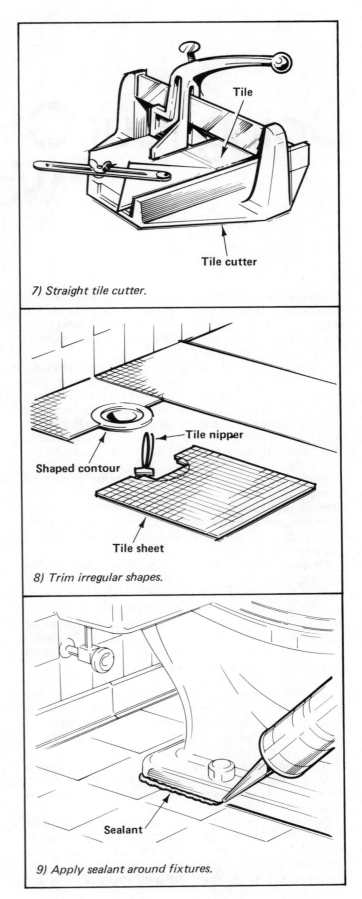

7) Straight tile cutter.

8) Trim irregular shapes.

9) Apply sealant around fixtures.

Doing Your Own Bathroom: Walls

Two objectives should be kept in mind when planning your bathroom walls. First, the walls must be able to withstand the moisture and water vapor so prevalent in the bathroom and, second, they should be easy to maintain and keep clean.

Plaster, wallboard, wood studs, and insulation will quickly deteriorate if not effectively shielded from water. The area around the tub and behind the vanity and toilet are particularly vulnerable to moisture damage. Small but constant leaks that keep the wall or floor framing damp will lead to rot and decay, and pipes and electrical fixtures will rust away if not protected by the walls.

Waterproof or water resistant material should be chosen for the splash area of the tub, the walls of the shower, and the backsplash area of the lavatory. Many products are available to the do-it-yourselfer to completely seal off moisture and provide an attractive easy-to-care-for surface.

Ceramic and marble tile. Ceramic and marble tile are old standbys in the bathroom—and for good reason. The tile is held in place by a mastic that acts as an effective vapor barrier. It can be applied over any structurally sound surface, including old ceramic or plastic tile. The hard surface of the tile is completely waterproof, scuff proof, and if the grout is properly sealed, it's easy to keep clean.

The 4¼-inch square ceramic tiles are the most popular, but many mosaic designs or larger quarry tiles are equally at home on the bathroom wall. Marble is available in 6-inch-square tiles. If these tiles are properly installed on sound walls, they'll provide a lifetime of service in your bathroom.

Synthetic marble. Cultured, or synthetic, marble is easy to clean with a damp sponge and mild detergent and is completely waterproof. Easy-to-install kits are available for do-it-yourself installation.

DuPont's Corian synthetic marble is available in ¼-inch thick sheets. These come in precut bathroom wall kits designed to cover three walls of any 5-foot recessed tub. The panels are easy to install with adhesive and caulk. There are a minimum of joints and

they have an easy-to-care for surface. Corian synthetic marble also is available in larger sheets for wall application anywhere a waterproof wall covering is needed. This material is also a natural for the backsplash behind the vanity and will match or compliment a Corian vanity top perfectly.

Plastic laminate panels. High pressure plastic laminate has been a favorite for easy-care countertops for a little over two decades. This versatile material also makes sense for the bathroom walls. It is waterproof, stain resistant, and when cleaned with compatible products, its finish is long lasting.

The laminate is available in 4-by-8-foot panels that may be cut to size and glued in place. Special trim moldings join the panels to assure a watertight joint.

Fiberglass. Molded fiberglass is a natural for the bath and shower enclosure. Both waterproof and rotproof, fiberglass panels have a tough, easy-to-clean surface with the added convenience of molded-in soap trays and handholds. These attractive units are especially easy to keep clean since the rounded corners offer no hiding places for dirt and soap scum.

Tub Surrounds: Preparing The Walls

Installing your own surround is easy if you use tile or one of the tub/shower surround kits. In most cases the hardest part of the job is preparing the wall to receive the new covering. All types rely on a mastic bond. Therefore, the wall must be structurally sound. Loose plaster, tile, wallpaper, etc. must be removed for the adhesive to have a firm, smooth surface to stick to.

Depending on the condition of your walls, some of the following tools will be needed: hammer, pipe wrench, keyhole saw, putty knife, razor knife, patching plaster, ½-inch wallboard, wallboard nails, wood shingles for shims, and measuring tape.

Follow these instructions to repair and prepare the tub walls for receiving a new surface:

1. Use a wrench to carefully remove the handles and trim of the water supply to the tub. Put masking

tape around the chrome to protect it from the teeth of the wrench and put these in a safe place for reinstalling later.

2. Push hard on the wall, any movement of the plaster, especially around the perimeter of the tub is a sign of infirm plaster that should be removed. Using a putty knife, pry off any loose tiles and probe the plaster for crumbly spots. Continue around the tub, probing for weak spots; mark any such places.

3. Use a hammer to give the bad spots a few sharp blows. Bad plaster crumbles and comes off easily. The same is true for wallboard; the paper will separate easily from the gypsum back. Don't get carried away; just remove what's bad.

4. If the bad areas are small and the lath is firm, mix up some patching plaster. Wet the lath and trowel the plaster into the void to about half the thickness of the original plaster. Let the plaster dry, then apply more plaster to fill the void level with the surrounding wall surfaces. Be sure that the patched area is level with the existing wall; a high spot will create a bulge in the wall surround.

5. If you have to patch large areas, use a patch made of wallboard. First, square off the edges of the holes and remove the lath. Remove the plaster and lath until you reach a stud at both sides of the bad area.

6. Cut some scrap pieces of wood for backers and nail them along the studs to support the ends of the wallboard.

7. Measure the opening and lay it out on the wallboard. Using a razor knife, score the face of the wallboard along your layout lines and give the sheet a sharp blow from behind to crack it; then cut through the backing paper with the razor. Use a keyhole saw to cut the wallboard if the patch is L-shaped.

8. Shim the drywall flush with the existing wall and nail it in place. If you're installing ceramic tile, fill in the small gaps between the wallboard and wall with patching plaster, and sand the joints smooth.

9. After all patching is complete re-examine the walls and sand down any high spots.

When all the walls are smooth and structurally sound you're ready to install the tub or shower surround of your choice.

Installing A Fiberglass Surround

Installation of a fiberglass tub surround is quick and easy. Assemble the following tools before you begin: drill, keyhole saw or saber saw, wall mastic, tub caulk (if not supplied in the kit), and a measuring tape and marker.

Carefully read the directions supplied by the manufacturer, then follow these steps:

1. The surround consists of two end panels and a center panel, or else a single semi-flexible wrap-around panel. These sections are not interchange-

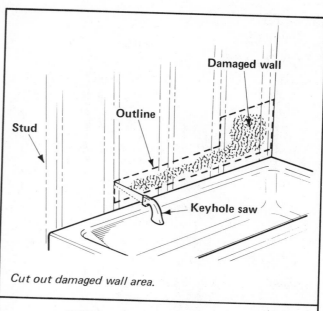

Cut out damaged wall area.

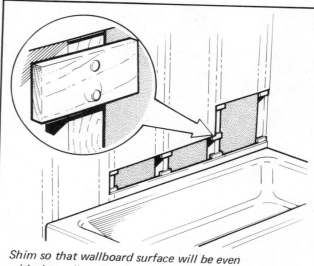

Shim so that wallboard surface will be even with the wall surface.

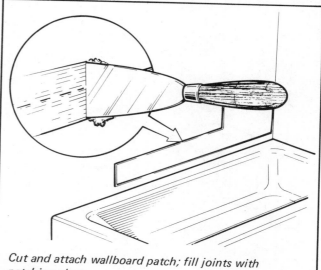

Cut and attach wallboard patch; fill joints with patching plaster.

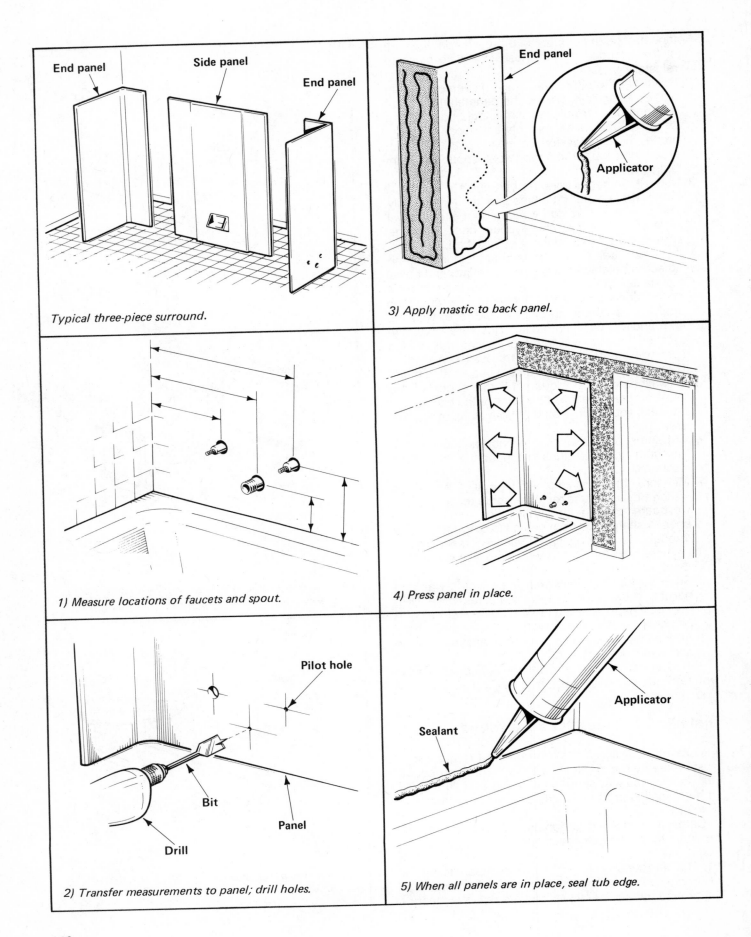

Typical three-piece surround.

3) Apply mastic to back panel.

1) Measure locations of faucets and spout.

4) Press panel in place.

2) Transfer measurements to panel; drill holes.

5) When all panels are in place, seal tub edge.

able and have a top and bottom. Before you begin, check to make sure that all parts and supplies are included and not damaged.

2. Measure the location of water outlets and controls on the plumbing wall, then transfer your measurements to the correct end panel. A paper template can be helpful if you're not sure of your measuring. Protect the surface of the surround with masking tape, then drill a pilot hole and use a saber saw to cut the openings.

3. Dry fit all the panels, checking for a tight fit in the corners and at the overlaps.

4. Apply the end panels first unless the manufacturer states differently. Run a generous bead of adhesive around the perimeter of the panel about 1 inch from the edge. Some adhesives are highly flammable, so take proper precaution against open flames and provide proper ventilation. Make a large figure 8 with the mastic in the center of the panel and apply extra adhesive around the back of hand holds or soap dishes.

5. Apply the panel to the wall, and press it all over to make complete contact with the wall. (Some glues require that you pull the panel away to vent the adhesive and, then, press the panel again to the wall.)

6. Apply adhesives to the other end and side panels and press them in place. After about 20 minutes, go back and press all the panels again to make certain they're in full contact with all the walls.

7. Run a bead of caulk along the panel joints (or as directed by the manufacturer) and apply caulk around the holes where the water supply pipe and faucets penetrate the panel. Clean up any finger prints or sealant mess immediately. If it's latex caulk, use water; if it's Butyl, use the proper solvent, making sure it won't harm the panel surface. Solvents are flammable so provide for proper ventilation and don't allow any open flames in the room.

8. Allow the sealant to dry for at least 8 hours before you use the tub.

Installing A Ceramic Or Marble Tile Surround

Installing ceramic or marble tile is easy using modern fast-setting mastics, sealants, and grout. Many styles of ceramic tile are available pregrouted with flexible latex grout. Whatever style or size you choose to install, the principles are the same.

Measure carefully the area you want to tile and take these dimensions to your tile dealer. He'll help you lay out the job and suggest soap trays and towel bars and other compatible accessories. You can also rent from him the special tools needed to help the job go faster.

Before you begin, assemble the following tools and supplies: hammer, chalk line, level, two pieces of 2x4, saber saw with carbide blade (very helpful but not necessary for ceramic tile), rubber gloves, a gallon of tile mastic, 5 pounds of tile grout sealer, tiles, (edging cap and two outside corner edge caps for ceramic tile), and a paint stirring stick or old toothbrush to use for forcing grout deeply into the tile joints. Rent the following: grooved trowel, tile nippers, tile cutter, and rubber squeegee. When you have everything ready, follow these instructions:

1. Inspect the walls; they must be smooth and free of loose plaster, dust, or peeling paint. Read the mastic instructions; on new plaster or unfinished wallboard, a primer might be suggested.

2. Starting at the back wall (the wall opposite the faucet end of the tub), use a level and draw a vertical line from the outside edge of the tub upwards as high as you want the tile. Check the tub for level, and if one side is higher or lower by more than ⅛ inch you'll have to adjust the starter row of tiles.

3. Temporarily place a row of tiles (including an edge

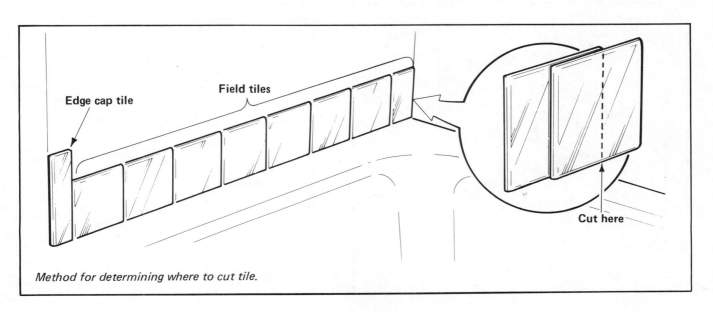

Edge cap tile

Field tiles

Cut here

Method for determining where to cut tile.

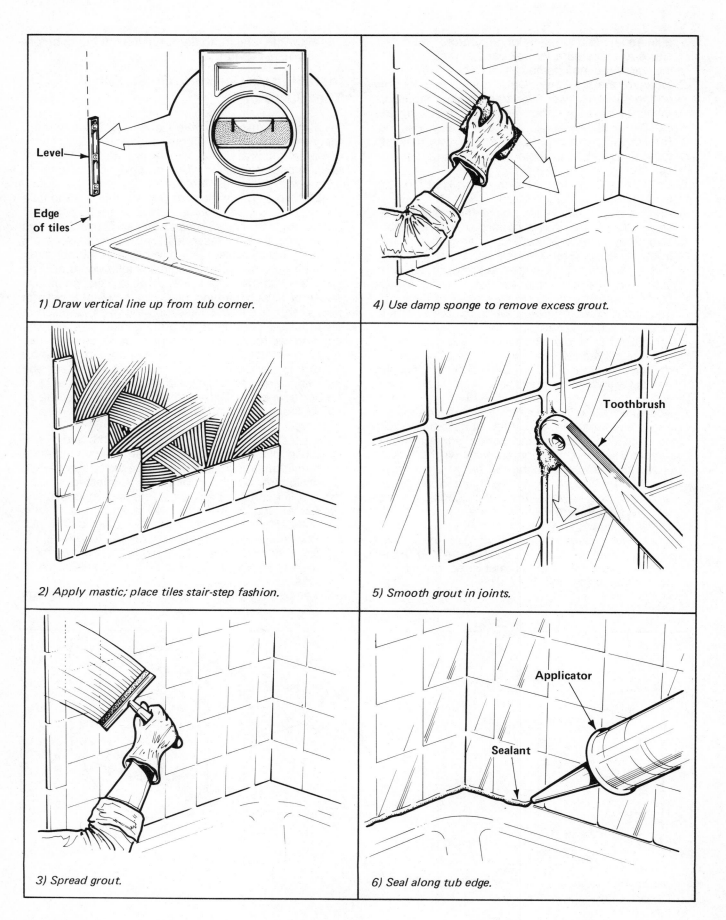

1) Draw vertical line up from tub corner.

2) Apply mastic; place tiles stair-step fashion.

3) Spread grout.

4) Use damp sponge to remove excess grout.

5) Smooth grout in joints.

6) Seal along tub edge.

Level

Edge
of tiles

Toothbrush

Applicator

Sealant

cap tile) along the top edge of the tub. The tile next to the wall will have to be cut to fit. Adjust the run slightly so that not less than half a tile will have to be cut off.

4. Spread the mastic along the wall of the tub as high as you'll be able to cover with tiles in half an hour. Spread more mastic as needed as you progress upward with the tiles.

5. Place the first row of tiles in place. Push each tile in place with a slight twisting motion to spread the mastic, but don't slide the tile around or the mastic will rise in the grout line. If the tub is not level, you'll need to nip the bottoms of the tiles to keep their edges level. Leave 1/8-inch gap between the tub and the first row of tiles.

6. Put the edge cap and first two tiles of the next row in place. Then put the edge cap and first tile of the third row in place. You now have the beginning of a stair-step pattern. Continue placing tiles in a stair-step pattern until all except the top row of cap tiles are in place. Finish by placing the row of cap tiles along the top of the tiled area, starting with an outside corner cap.

7. The tiles are placed on the long wall in the same stair-step fashion. Start by placing a row temporarily along the top of the tub to determine how much of the last tile to cut off.

8. Spread the mastic as you did for the first wall, and install a row of tiles along the edge of the tub. Then place the tiles of the next two rows to start a stair-step pattern. Fill in the rest of the wall, and finish the top with a row of cap tiles.

9. The faucet wall is next. The layout procedure is the same as it was for the other two walls. Use a saber saw equipped with a carbide blade or use tile nippers to cut the openings for the spout, faucets, and shower arm. The openings don't have to be exact, because the chrome trim rings (escutcheons) will cover minor imperfections.

10. When you've finished placing the tiles, clean up any excess mastic and clean the tools. Allow the mastic at least a day to dry thoroughly.

11. Mix the grout to a creamy consistency and set it aside. Use a sponge and wet the tiles so that they won't draw the moisture out of the grout. Wear gloves and spread grout evenly over half of the back wall. Then use a rubber squeegee to work the grout well into the tile. Wipe the excess away with a wet sponge.

12. Use a blunt stick (the end of a toothbrush or paint stirrer are ideal) to force the grout deep into the tile joints. Remove the excess grout with a sponge and continue in the same manner for the remaining area.

13. Allow the grout to dry overnight and polish off the thin film of grout that has dried on the tile. Run a bead of tub caulk around the joint between the tub and the first row of tiles. If you have tiled around a window be sure also to caulk it carefully.

14. Apply a grout sealer according to the manufacturer's directions.

Paint In the Bathroom

The ceiling and woodwork are best covered with semi-gloss enamel. This surface resists moisture well and is easy to care for. Both oil and latex enamels are available, and both do an admirable job of protecting woodwork from moisture. Epoxy and urethane paints are more difficult to work with but are tougher and more waterproof. They make an excellent coating for the ceiling of a shower where water and mildew often is a problem.

When painting walls, you can use either a brush or roller. The quickest method is to use a roller, but only after you use a brush to "cut in." That is, you put a few inches of paint around areas you don't want to touch or mark up with the roller. You should cut in a brush width close to all areas to be left unpainted, after shielding the area with masking tape or a hand-held sheet of cardboard. The ceiling is painted first, then work downward.

When using either brush or roller, make sure the walls are clean, smooth and even. Any old, flaking paint must be scraped and the edges sanded, or the new paint will not adhere. If you are right-handed, start at the left edge or corner and go to the right, working from the top down. A roller requires that you even the coverage by going crosswise after the up and down strokes. Go from one side to the other, from top to bottom, always painting against the wet edge. Try to time it so you can finish in one day. If you start wet paint against a dried edge it will show a mark.

Don't go too fast with either brush or roller. Speed causes splatters and makes for unnecessary cleanup problems.

Wallpaper: Taking It Down Or Putting It Up

The wallpaper you put up in your bathroom shouldn't really be a paper at all, but rather a vinyl-covered fabric or metallic foil. You can buy these materials prepasted. It's a good idea, if possible, to buy one that's strippable, because these can be peeled off easily if you want to change later.

A standard roll of wall covering will cover 30 square feet, with 6 square feet in the roll that allows for overlapping, wastage, and so forth. Rolls come 24 inches wide by 18 feet long or 27 inches wide by 16 feet long. Both cover the same wall area. A few of the new metallic foils are 29 1/2 inches wide. You can also buy double and even triple rolls in the same widths but longer.

Before choosing the wall covering, measure the area you want to cover and add 20 percent to that figure for wastage. You will then be prepared for any length or width your chosen material comes in. If you have one door and one window in the area to be covered, deduct one roll.

To prepare a wall that has a prior coating of flat paint, wash it thoroughly, fill all cracks, and remove any loose paint and sand the edges. Then apply a coat of wall sizing, a form of glue that makes wall coverings stick.

If the wall is covered with gloss or semi-gloss paint, sand it down lightly with medium-grit sandpaper, just enough to remove the shine. Wash it with an ammonia solution made of one part ammonia mixed with six parts water. Rinse, apply sizing as above and proceed.

A textured wall surface must also be sanded reasonably smooth. Then fill any cracks or holes, rinse, and apply sizing. Bare wallboard or unpainted plaster, if smooth and sound, needs only a coat of sizing.

Should there be old wallpaper on the wall, it is best to remove it first. Vinyl paper will pull off easily; but often there are one or more layers of old paper. Many wallpaper stores rent steamers, and you will need a wallpaper scraper. Hold the steamer head to the wall and when the paste underneath has softened, use the scraper to peel it off. Wash the wall with steel wool and a washing compound to remove any old paste and sizing, rinse thoroughly, and patch any holes. Apply sizing and the wall is ready.

To hang the new wall covering you will need the following: A chalk line with a plumb bob at the end, paste brush, smoothing brush, seam roller, natural sponge, and a razor trimming knife. You also will need a pasting table. This can be rented, or use a sheet of plywood—ideally about 6 feet long and 3 feet wide—resting on two sawhorses. If you can not do that, you can make do with two card tables placed together and covered with brown wrapping paper. If you are using a prepasted wall covering, the store will sell you an immersion tray, which is usually made of waxed cardboard or plastic; you can also use the bathtub for immersing the wallpaper rolls.

Though it seldom happens in a bathroom, if you are going to paper entirely around the room start in the most inconspicuous corner. This is because you will not be able to index (match the pattern) at the last seam.

Now follow the steps below.

1. When hanging wallpaper, you should work from left to right if you are right-handed. Measure out from the corner along your first wall a distance of one inch less than the width of the roll. Mark the wall. Then tack your chalk line to the wall near the ceiling so that it drops through the mark; hold the weight steady, and snap the line against the wall. This gives you a true vertical on which to line up the paper so that it will be straight.
2. Lay the first sheet of paper on the pasting table, and cut it lengthwise to 4 inches more than your floor-to-ceiling height. Hold it up to the wall to check. There should be about a 2-inch overlap at the ceiling and floor.
3. If it is right, lay it back on the table face up and unroll paper for the second strip. Make sure that the pattern matches at the left edge of the new strip and the right edge of the first strip. Don't cut until it indexes. Repeat this to get a stack of several strips ready to hang. Turn the stack over pattern side down and you are ready to start.
4. Mix your paste according to the manufacturer's instructions. Avoid lumps. Tying a string across the top of the paste bucket to hold the brush will keep the handle clean.
5. Apply the paste first on the top half of the roll in a figure 8 and then the remainder, making sure to cover the whole surface. Any unpasted spot will make a blister. Fold the top half over, paste to paste, and apply paste to the bottom half. Fold this in the same way. This will make it easy to carry the strip to the wall.

At the wall unfold the top half, carefully and accurately position the edge next to the chalk line,

Chalked string

Chalk line

Weight

To make chalk line, hold weight in place, stretch chalked string away from wall, let string snap back to wall.

and start smoothing toward the corner with your hand. Smooth it well into, and an inch around, the corner. When finished, unfold the bottom half and smooth it the same way.

6. Use your smoothing brush to work out excess paste and air bubbles, always working toward the edges. Use the edge of the brush to ease the material tight into the corner along the ceiling and the floor or baseboard. Turn the brush vertical to smooth the paper into the vertical corner. Make sure the material sticks.

7. Proceed as above with the next panel, butting it against the edge of the first, and so on, working along the wall.

8. Roll the seams with the seam roller about 15 minutes later. Do not roll hard, but firmly. Rinse each strip after rolling with a natural sponge and clear water, squeezed dry enough so the water will not run. Trim off any excess material at floor and ceiling with the razor knife. Have plenty of blades on hand so you can throw the blade away after five or six cuts. They dull rapidly, and when dull will easily tear the material.

9. When you reach a corner, measure from the edge of the last strip to the corner, and add a half-inch. Subtract the total from the width of the roll strip. Measure this total along the new wall, make a mark, and snap a new chalk line to be sure all strips on the new wall will be vertical.

For example, say you have 15 inches from the edge of the last strip to the corner. Add a half-inch and you get 15½ inches. Subtracting this from the width of your roll (say it's 24 inches) and you get 8½ inches. Measure along the new wall a distance of 8½ inches and make your mark for the new chalk line.

When you hang the last sheet on the first wall (the sheet that turns the corner), butt its left edge against the right edge of the previous strip. Smooth it and tap well into the corner, then trim it vertically a half-inch from the corner on the new wall. Slide the remaining section to the left, into the corner and over the half-inch you already have pasted. Line up the right edge with the new chalk line on the new wall.

10. Do not try to piece small strips in over windows and doors. Hang a full strip just as though the window or door was not there. Use scissors and cut diagonally from the inside of the door or window and across the corner like a miter joint. This will let you paste the paper flat against the wall around the corner, and you can trim off excess paper with your razor knife.

To hang prepasted wall covering, follow the same procedure as above, cutting strips to length and indexing them. To apply a strip, reroll it from bottom to top with the glued side out, loosely, and immerse it in the tray. Follow directions on immersion time. Then carry the whole tray to the wall, lift the end of the roll to the ceiling, index to the line, and stick it down. Again rub and brush out air bubbles; then trim as before.

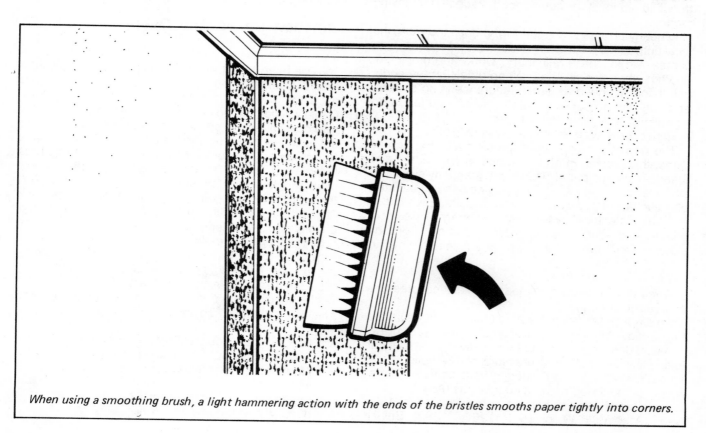

When using a smoothing brush, a light hammering action with the ends of the bristles smooths paper tightly into corners.

Doing Your Own Bathroom: Light, Ventilation, Heat

If you plan to install lighting yourself—or make other sorts of electrical connections—the first thing you must know is whether you are permitted to do any wiring at all. Most communities have wiring and electrical codes, and many of these specify that all wiring and electrical work must be done by a licensed electrician. The first step, therefore, is to go to the town hall or county seat and get a copy of the electrical code to check whether you are permitted to do the work.

Also, unless you know something about electrical work, it would be wise to have the work done for you by a licensed electrician. Wiring is dangerous, and electrocuting yourself is not a good tradeoff for saving money.

In nearly all cases, no matter who does the work, the local authorities will make at least two inspections. One comes when the preliminary work is completed, another when it is finished. When obtaining the code, ask if you will need a permit. Ignorance is no excuse, and you can be subject to fines later if you fail to do something that local law requires.

Here's how your electrical system works:

The power company supplies electricity through its wires, this passes through a meter in your home and then to a service panel. The power company's responsibility ends at the meter. The service panel is the start of a number of separate, discrete circuits. Each circuit is a small electrical system with a variety of electrical outlets, and each circuit is guarded and controlled by either a circuit-breaker that trips or a fuse that blows in case of overload.

Terms you should know:

A *volt* is the unit used to measure electrical pressure or current strength.

An *ampere* (or "amp") is a unit used to measure the rate of flow of electricity or intensity of current draw.

A *watt* describes current drain relative to voltage. For example, 120 watts at a pressure of 120 volts is one amp (W/V = A). Watts divided by volts equal amperes. Amperes multiplied by volts equal watts (A × V = W).

A typical 15-amp circuit in a home can deliver 1800 watts (A × V = W, or 15 × 120 = 1800). Before adding outlets on a circuit, you have to know what the load already is on that line. You can do this only by checking circuit by circuit and adding up the wattages of all the lights and appliances on each. Take out the fuse or trip the circuit breaker to see what doesn't work. You can not assume everything in one room is on the same circuit. The ceiling light in the bathroom might be on the same circuit as the wall outlets of the upstairs bedroom; the bathroom wall outlet might share a circuit with a room on the first floor.

The service panel will be found in a metal box near the meter. Called the panel box, it usually has blank spaces for additional circuits.

Junction Boxes And Cable

If you wish to install a new switch or receptacle outlet, you will have to cut into the existing wall or ceiling to mount a junction box. This box provides an anchor point for the electrical cable and the actual fixture. Cable will have to be run from an existing circuit to this new box. Often, it is possible to drop a wire through into the basement or go up into the attic; if not, you will have to do some "fishing." This process is what happens when you put a wire through a blind wall or other location where you cannot conveniently reach to pull the cable. Fishing tape is springy, flat steel wire 1/16 x 1/8 inch that comes in coils of 50 or more feet. With a couple of 12-foot lengths, you can do about all the fishing you need to do.

To fish for a wire, you will require the following equipment: A keyhole saw, brace and bit, some fish tape (sold in rolls in the hardware store), the proper cable, junction box, patching plaster and the wall finishing materials. To install a new box:

1. Locate where you want the new junction box, mark and then saw out that section of the wall or ceiling. Mount the box securely to the stud. Determine where the cable will run from the existing circuit. Try to have it come up through the basement or directly through a party wall.

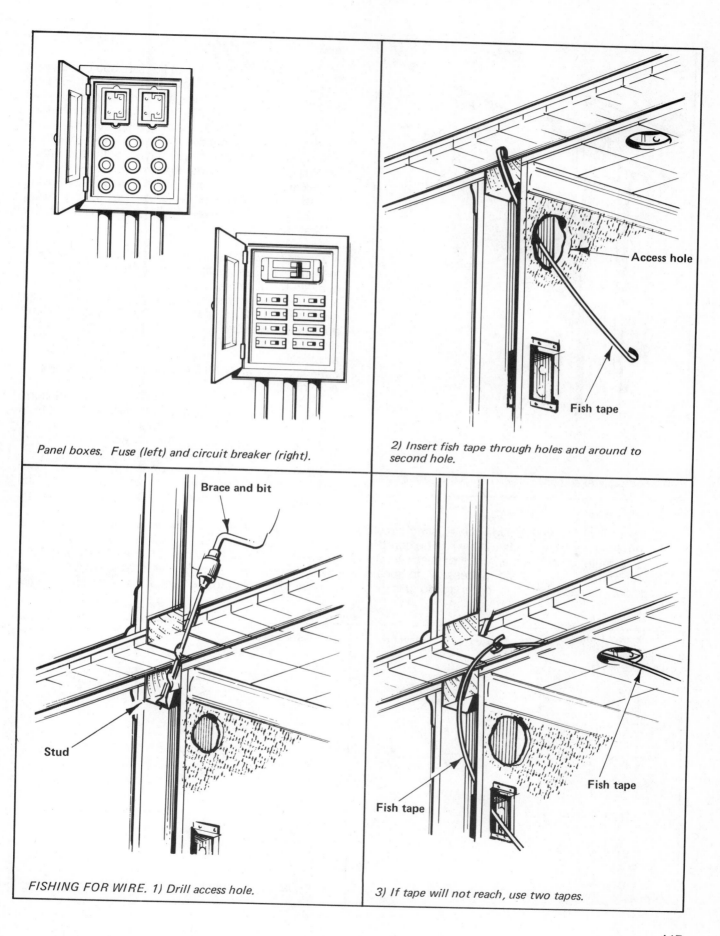

Panel boxes. Fuse (left) and circuit breaker (right).

2) Insert fish tape through holes and around to second hole.

Access hole

Fish tape

Brace and bit

Stud

FISHING FOR WIRE. 1) Drill access hole.

3) If tape will not reach, use two tapes.

Fish tape

Fish tape

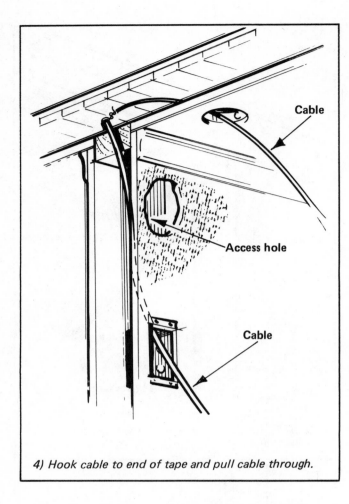

4) Hook cable to end of tape and pull cable through.

careful to avoid plumbing and electrical lines that are already in place.

3. Bend hooks at the ends of the fish tape by applying heat from a gas stove or a propane torch. This will prevent it from catching on obstructions and will give you a place to attach your cable. Run the tape through the holes and along where the cable will run. It may be necessary to use two tapes from opposite sides before you have a sufficient length.

4. Pull cable through with the fish tape and make the necessary connections into the junction box using the appropriate connectors. The fishing holes should then be covered with plaster. Refinish the wall and/or ceiling.

Junction boxes come in standard sizes, and there are special ones to fit into the ceiling. All general-purpose circuits require at least No. 12 two-conductor wiring; a three-way switch will require three-conductor wiring with an attached ground. If you are installing an appliance receptacle, heavier gauge wire will be required if the appliance takes 220 volt current. Your electrical code will tell you what type of wire and/or conduit to use and should always be consulted prior to any installation.

Single-pole switches control a single outlet or fixture, while three-way switches control a fixture or light from two locations (as on opposite doors in the same room). Standard plugs are called duplex receptacles. Any of them will fit into a standard junction box.

Wire nuts are solderless connectors for joining two or more wires. These are available in many sizes and are simply screwed over the exposed ends of the wires.

Electrical cable comes in many types and sizes. According to your local code, standard in your area may be Romex or BX cable. The latter is armored in a metal sheath, while the former is typically run through conduit or stapled to the stud. If you strip off the outer

2. Cut a hole in the wall beside the existing circuit. Determine how many studs will have to be bored in order to route the cable; then drill the holes with the brace and bit. It may be necessary to locate additional access holes in order to do this. Be

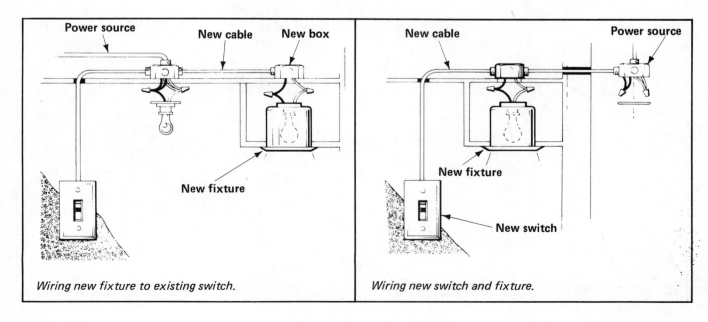

Wiring new fixture to existing switch.

Wiring new switch and fixture.

covering on the cable, you will find one bare wire, one with black insulation, and a third with white insulation. The black wire is always the hot wire. It attaches to another black wire or to the brass-colored attachment screw in the device you are hooking up. The white wire is neutral and always attaches to another white wire or to the silver-colored screw in the device. The bare wire is the ground and is attached to the green colored screw.

If your electrical code calls for conduit to route the cable to the outlets, you must install such conduit first. Take care to make accurate bends in the tubing. Fish tape is the method by which the Romex cable is led through the conduit.

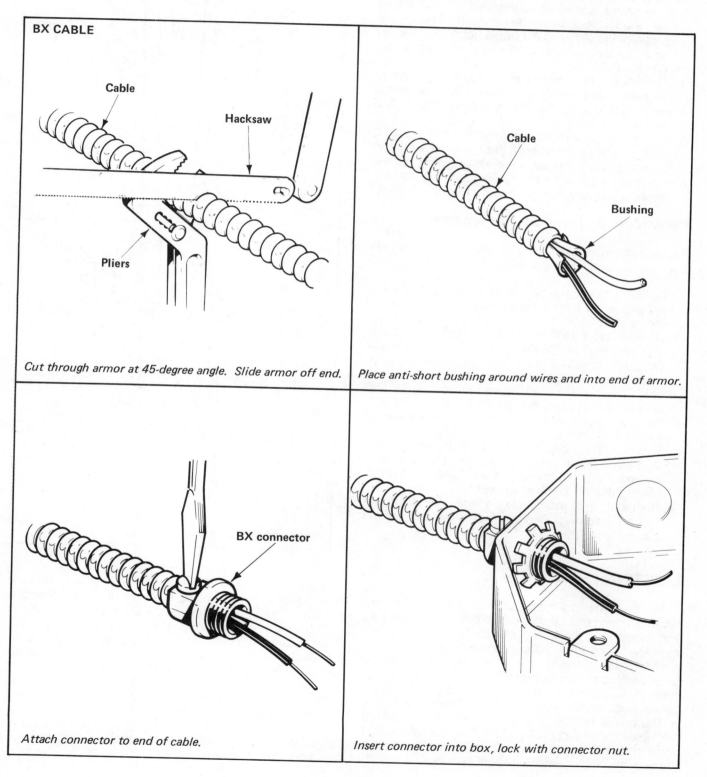

BX CABLE

Cable

Hacksaw

Pliers

Cut through armor at 45-degree angle. Slide armor off end.

Cable

Bushing

Place anti-short bushing around wires and into end of armor.

BX connector

Attach connector to end of cable.

Insert connector into box, lock with connector nut.

Replacing A Single-Pole Switch

If you need to replace a switch because it no longer operates or because a newer type would fit your remodeling plans, here is how to go about it:

1. Shut off the current to the switch. Remove the cover plate, and use a voltage tester to make sure the switch has been deactivated. Touch one probe of the tester to the brass hot screw and the other to the metal box. If the light is dark, the current is off.
2. Remove the two screws at the top and bottom of the switch that hold it to the box. Pull the switch completely out, loosen the screw terminals, and remove the wires.
3. Align the new switch so the lever is down in the off position. Attach the wires in the same sequence as in the old switch. Replace the entire switch into the box and secure with the same mounting screws. Replace the cover plate and restore the current.

Replacing A 120-Volt Receptacle

If a receptacle cracks and you wish to install a new one, the procedure is as follows:

1. Be sure the electricity is shut off. Test with a voltage tester to make sure no current is going to the receptacle.
2. Remove the mounting screws and pull the receptacles from the box. Check carefully to see how many wires are attached to the receptacle. With four or more wires, there will be two cables entering the box. This is the "middle-of-the-run" type and means other receptacles are on the same circuit. If there is only one cable, then the receptacle is the end of a circuit.
3. Remove the wires by removing the attachment screws on either side. Wire up the replacement in the exact same manner as the original receptacle. Make sure all screws are tight.
4. Remount the receptacle in the box with the mounting screws. Replace the cover, and turn on the current.

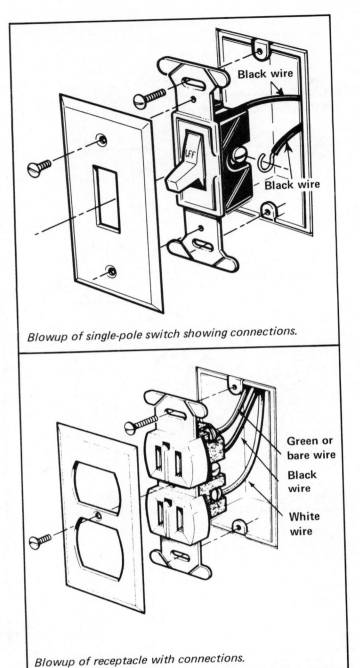

Blowup of single-pole switch showing connections.

Blowup of receptacle with connections.

LIGHTING

A few basic design concepts should be kept in mind when planning the lighting for the bathroom. There are two areas that must receive special consideration: overhead lighting and facial lighting for mirrors.

Overhead lighting is only absolutely necessary in a large bathroom. This type of lighting is usually mounted on or recessed into the ceiling. It can be combined with an exhaust fan or heater in one multipurpose fixture.

The use of natural lighting shouldn't be overlooked. Windows and skylights are sources of free natural light. Most older bathrooms have windows, but those small second-floor bathrooms that might be tucked under the eaves can be dramatically brightened by the addition of a skylight. A skylight can be installed by framing a simple shaft from lumber and facing it with wallboard.

Special purpose lighting must be planned for the mirror area to provide proper illumination of the face for makeup application and for shaving. Many medicine chests have built-in lighting, and there are fluorescent fixtures designed to be mounted over the mirror. Special surface-mounted incandescent fixtures that look like theatrical lighting are also available and can be mounted above or along the sides of a mirror. Track lighting is easy to install and can provide illumination in hard-to-reach areas.

Recessed lighting is also popular for the mirror vanity area. A very attractive and functional lighting soffit can be constructed to enclose these fixtures if they can't be mounted directly in the ceiling.

Depending on the size of the ceiling joists there is usually enough room for a recessed light. But, if there is inadequate clearance, a drop ceiling can often contain the new lighting. Fluorescent tubes mounted on the old ceiling can create a totally illuminated ceiling when opaque diffuser panels are suspended below these fixtures.

All the lights should be controlled by wall switches located away from the shower or tub area. A wall outlet should be planned for the vanity and mirror area where electric razors and curling irons are used. Most electrical codes call for ground fault circuit breaker protection in the bathroom.

Installing A Recessed Lighting Fixture

The installation of a recessed lighting fixture is straightforward and requires a single hole to be cut in the ceiling. These fixtures get very hot and must have proper clearance all around to provide ventilation. If the ceiling is open to an attic above there is no problem. But, if there is a second floor over the bathroom, a clearance of at least 10 inches between the ceiling of the bathroom and the floor of the room above is necessary to accommodate a recessed fixture.

Before you start, read the directions supplied by the manufacturer of the recessed fixture you plan to install. When you're familiar with the special requirements, gather the following tools and supplies: hammer, tape measure, drill and bits, keyhole or saber saw, hacksaw, pliers, wire snips, screwdriver, wire nuts, electrical current tester, 2-wire No. 12 BX cable or Romex cable, BX or Romex box connectors, BX or Romex staples, patching plaster, putty knife and safety goggles.

Follow these steps to install your recessed lighting fixture:

1. Turn off the electricity to the bathroom and test the circuit with your current tester to make sure it's dead.
2. Lay out the location for the new fixture. Slight adjustment in position might be required for proper clearance of a joist.
3. After you've marked the location for the fixture use a keyhole saw or a saber saw to cut the opening in the ceiling to receive the fixture. Wear safety goggles to protect your eyes from falling debris.
4. If a switch is needed to control the fixture see the "Junction Boxes And Cables" section in this chapter.
5. Disassemble the fixture if necessary and remove one of the wiring knockout plugs by prying it back and forth until it breaks off. Insert a BX or Romex cable connector into the hole and tighten the lockdown nut on the connector.
6. Remove about 6 inches of the protective cover of

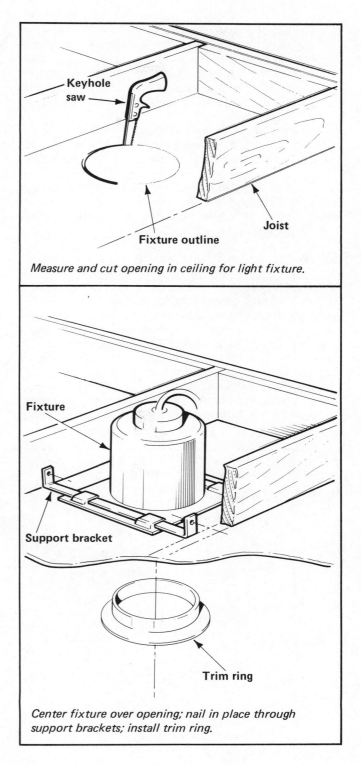

Measure and cut opening in ceiling for light fixture.

Center fixture over opening; nail in place through support brackets; install trim ring.

the BX or Romex to expose the conductors. Cut the BX cable partly through with a hacksaw and then twist open. Strip about ½ inch of the insulation off the ends of the conductors. Then insert a plastic or fiber anti-short bushing between the outer cover of the cable and the conductors.
7. Insert the mounting frame into the cutout hole according to the manufacturer's directions. Thread

the BX or Romex cable through the connector at the top of the housing and tighten the set screw. Connect the black wire of the cable to the black wire of the fixture by twisting them together with pliers; then thread on a wire nut. Do the same for the white wires, and connect the ground wire to the green screw.

8. Reassemble the light, making sure the wire connections are all inside the junction box. Then slide the fixture into place and secure it with the screws provided.

9. Paint or repair any small cracks in the ceiling. Then install the trim frame.

10. Install lightbulbs and turn on the electricity to test the fixture.

Building A Lighting Soffit

If the ceiling over your bathroom doesn't have sufficient clearance for recessed lighting you can build a lighting soffit over the vanity. The instructions given are for a continuous soffit that runs from wall to wall. Using simple framing of 2x4 and 2x2 lumber and ½-inch wallboard, you can quickly construct a professional looking soffit to enclose the recessed lighting.

Collect the following tools and supplies before you begin the soffit: hammer, tape measure, level, saw, razor knife, square, ½-inch wallboard, outside metal bead, wallboard tape, joint cement, wallboard nails, No. 8 common nails, No. 16 common nails, wall anchors or toggle bolts, safety goggles and 2x4 and 2x2 lumber.

Before you begin the soffit, make an accurate drawing to aid in construction and in purchasing the correct amount of lumber. Plan for a 2x2 nailer for the ceiling and wall the full length of the soffit. One 2x4 will be used as a front beam the full length of the soffit and two 2x4s will be used as side nailer supports the width of the soffit. Also plan on a 2x2 vertical nailer every 16 inches along the length of the soffit.

After you've made the plan and purchased the materials, follow these instructions to construct the lighting soffit:

1. Measure down from the ceiling and use your level to draw a horizontal line from wall to wall for the bottom nailer.

2. Cut two 2x4 end wall nailers to size; remember that they should be 1⅝ inches shorter than the total width of the soffit because the front 2x4 beam is nailed to these. Nail these to the end walls level with the back wall layout line. Drive the nails into studs or use wall anchors.

3. Cut a 2x2 back wall nailer to fit between the end wall nailers and nail this in place using No. 16 nails driven into the studs (or use toggle bolts).

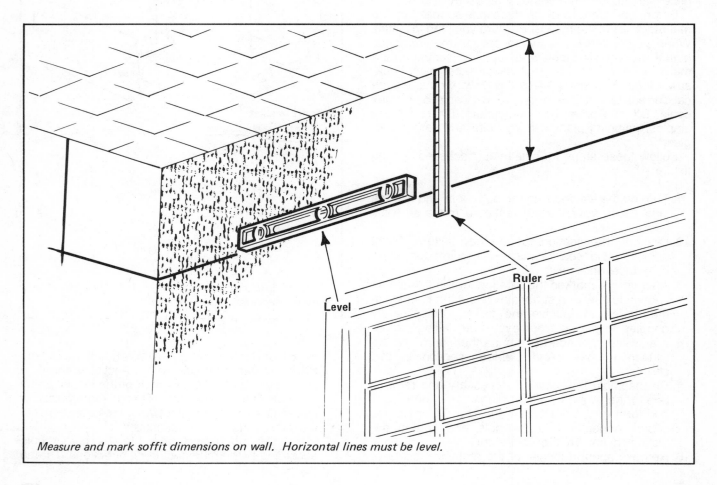

Measure and mark soffit dimensions on wall. Horizontal lines must be level.

4. Cut the front 2x4 nailer beam and nail it in place against the ends of the wall nailers. Check for levelness, then set the level against the face of the 2x4 beam and, when the level is vertical, mark the location of the top ceiling nailer in several locations along the ceiling.

5. Cut and nail the top 2x2 nailer to the ceiling joist (or use toggle bolts).

6. Place a vertical and horizontal 2x2 nailer every 16 inches and toenail these in place using No. 8 nails. Don't place a nailer where a recessed fixture will be located.

7. Cut a piece of wallboard to fit the bottom of the soffit. Use a razor knife to score the face of the board and give it a sharp blow on the back to crack it, then cut the backing paper with a knife. Nail the wallboard in place with wallboard nails driven along the front 2x4 beam and 2x2 nailer. Cut a piece of wallboard to fit the front of the soffit; set this piece aside for now.

8. Cut out holes in the wallboard to receive the light fixtures according to the manufacturer's specifications. Install the fixture mounting frame in the opening, then install and wire the fixture as described in steps 5 through 8 in the section "Installing a Recessed Lighting Fixture."

9. In multiple-light installations, connect the switched power line to one of the fixtures and then run a BX or Romex cable from this fixture to the next fixture in line and so on. Securely fasten the cable to the soffit framing between.

10. When all the wiring is complete, reassemble the fixtures and turn on the electricity to test the installation. Then install the front piece of wallboard, nailing it in place along the top and bottom. If the soffit is more than 18 inches high place a few nails in the center of the sheet along the vertical nailers to prevent the wallboard from sagging outward over time.

11. Cut the outside corner bead to fit. If there are any joints in the soffit, apply a coat of taping compound and lay on the wallboard joint tape. Smooth the tape down with a putty knife and apply a second coat of compound over it. The ceiling and wall joints can be taped or molding can be used to hide the joints. Apply a coating of joint compound to the metal outside corner using the raised corner as a guide, then slowly draw the knife along the edge. Three coats are usually necessary for a smooth job. When the joint compound is dry, sand all joints smooth.

12. Apply a coat of primer paint to seal the wallboard and the joint compound. You can then paint or paper the soffit.

13. Finish off the job by installing the trim ring around the fixture.

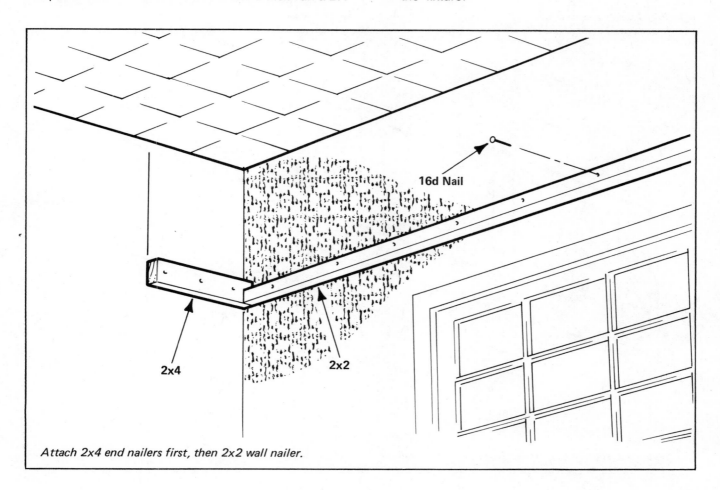

16d Nail

2x4

2x2

Attach 2x4 end nailers first, then 2x2 wall nailer.

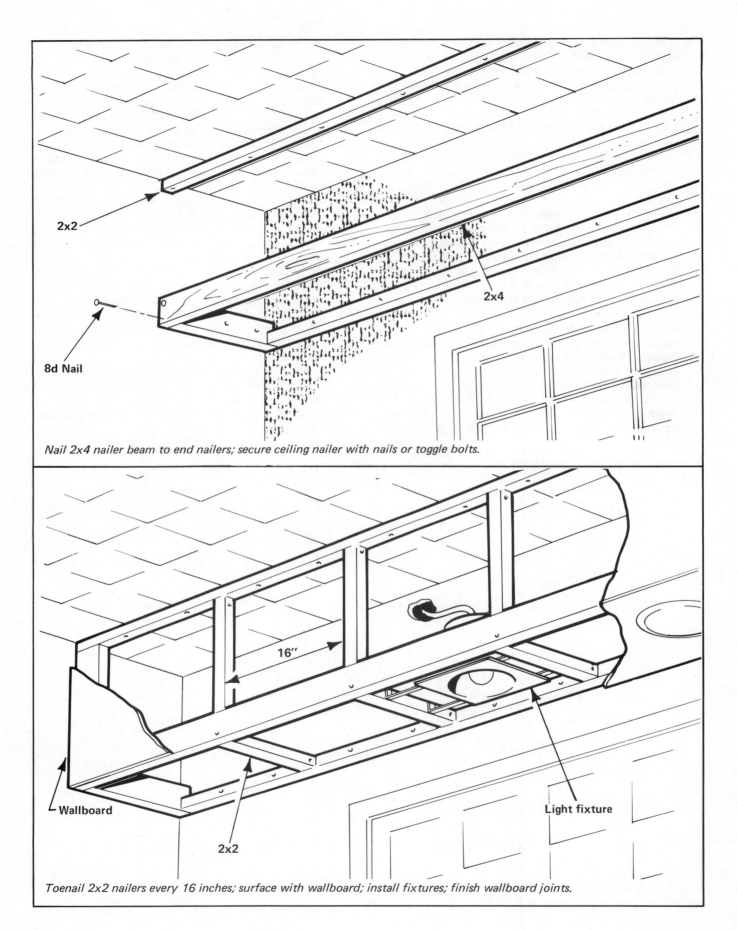

2x2

8d Nail

2x4

Nail 2x4 nailer beam to end nailers; secure ceiling nailer with nails or toggle bolts.

16"

Wallboard

2x2

Light fixture

Toenail 2x2 nailers every 16 inches; surface with wallboard; install fixtures; finish wallboard joints.

Installing A Skylight

A skylight can add both drama and natural daylight to the bathroom. Best of all, it can be installed fairly easily in a day, if the roof is flat.

If the roof is sloped, the way to do it is to construct a "light shaft" from the skylight in the roof, through the attic and to a hole in the ceiling of the bathroom. The light shaft can be made of ½-inch wallboard nailed to 2x4s placed vertically between the ceiling and the roof.

First, though, check the ceiling and the attic to make sure there is a place for a skylight. You might find cooling ducts, wiring or other mechanical elements that can't be moved out of the way. If the way is clear, buy the skylight to fit between the rafters. These can vary from 16x16 inches to 48x48 inches. The roof opening generally will be cut about 3 inches less on both dimensions. Try to find a skylight that is doubled-glazed with a dead air space between, to avoid heat loss in winter or summer cooling problems.

To install a skylight, do the following:

1. Up in the attic, drive a 3-inch nail up through the roof at each corner where you want the opening. Follow the same procedure with sloped or flat roofs.
2. Climb onto the roof and locate the nails. Remove the roofing material about 12 inches all around the skylight area. Drill pilot holes within the corners of the cutout and cut the holes for the skylight with a keyhole or saber saw. You may have to cut one rafter in doing this.
3. Frame the opening at top and bottom between the rafters with the same size stock as used for the rafters. Normally these will be 2x6-inch pine. If the rafters are too far apart to align with the skylight, add framing at the sides. If it was necessary to cut a rafter, you will have to tie it into the framing with other 2x6s.
4. Apply roofing mastic around the entire opening, about ¼-inch thick. Cover all exposed wood surfaces.
5. Position the skylight over the opening, drill small holes for nails, and nail each corner down into a rafter using 8-penny nails. Use rustproof roofing nails around the flange itself, spaced about 3 inches apart.
6. Apply more mastic over the edge of the skylight. Stop short of the cutout and any parts that will be visible from below. Cut strips of roofing felt wide enough to go from the flange to overlap the felt on the roof decking. Put the side pieces on first, then the top piece; and then a piece at the bottom overlapping the sides to prevent a moisture trap.
7. Apply another coat of mastic over the felt strips and replace the roof shingles. When all shingles have been replaced, apply a bead of mastic across the bottom edges of the skylight. The result will let light in and keep moisture out.

The above instructions are for a low-profile skylight,

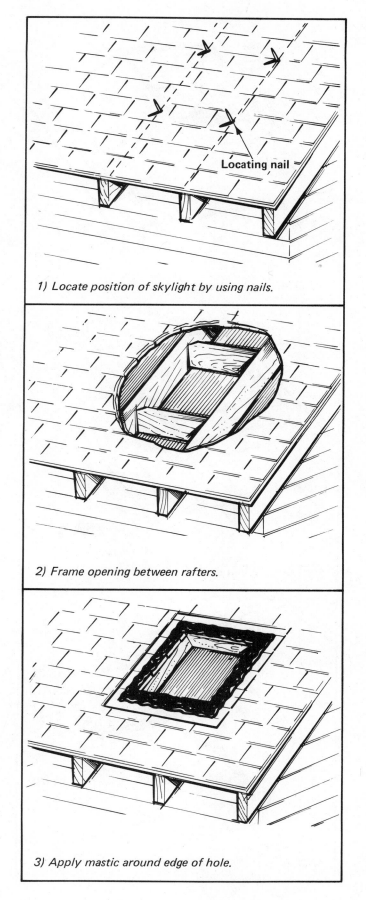

1) Locate position of skylight by using nails.

2) Frame opening between rafters.

3) Apply mastic around edge of hole.

125

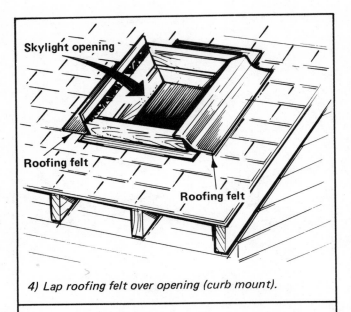

4) Lap roofing felt over opening (curb mount).

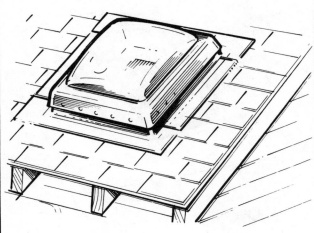

5) Skylight unit in position after installation.

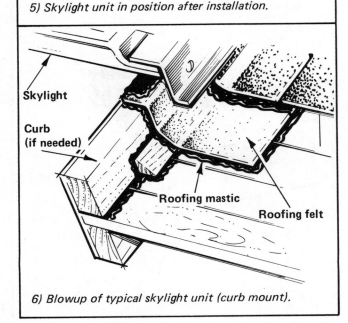

6) Blowup of typical skylight unit (curb mount).

mounted flush to the roof. Others are mounted on a curb. The process is the same except that you build a "curb," a box of 2x6 inch lumber to fit on top of the cutout. The skylight fits over the top of the curb.

VENTILATION

Proper ventilation will not only make the bathroom more comfortable, but it will extend the life of paint, wallpaper, and fixtures. Removing the humidity from the bathroom can be accomplished by an open window or an exhaust fan.

An open window is not practical for year-round ventilation in most climates. A ceiling- or wall-mounted exhaust fan provides the best way to keep air circulating in the bathroom.

Ceiling fans are recessed between the joists and vented through a duct to the roof or eaves. Wall fans are inserted between the studs and vent directly outside through the wall. Both types of units are effective and will remove the moisture from the bathroom.

A 50 cubic-feet-per-minute capacity fan is adequate for a small bathroom, but choose a 70 cubic-feet-per-minute unit for a larger room. For efficient operation, the ducting should be as short as possible and have as few bends as practical.

If the ceiling clearance is a problem, the fan can be mounted in a soffit built over the tub or shower, or it can be installed in a lighting soffit.

The fan needs a source of power, so locate the blower as close to an existing light or outlet as possible. Sometimes a cable can be fished up a wall from the basement or across the bathroom from an existing light fixture. The fan can be wired to work simultaneously with a light fixture, or it can be wired to its own switch.

Installing the ceiling-mounted exhaust fan is fairly easy. But providing a path for the exhaust ducts can be a problem. If there is an attic overhead, the job is considerably easier than if there is a second floor. If you can vent the fan through an attic, try to place the exhaust outlet in the eaves or run the duct to an existing roof vent if possible. Cut through the roof only as a last choice. If there is a second floor overhead, run the duct parallel with the ceiling joists and vent through the wall between floors.

Before starting the installation of an exhaust fan, assemble the following tools and supplies: hammer, tape measure, keyhole or saber saw, hacksaw, drill and bits, wire snips, pliers, BX or Romex cable, BX or Romex box connectors, safety goggles, circuit tester, flexible ducting to fit the exhaust unit, and a weather cap for the duct outlet.

After you've read the installation instructions for the particular fan you plan to use, follow these steps:

1. Turn off the electricity to the bathroom and test to be sure that the circuit is dead.
2. If you are installing the fan in the wall, locate the nearby studs; if you are installing it in the ceiling,

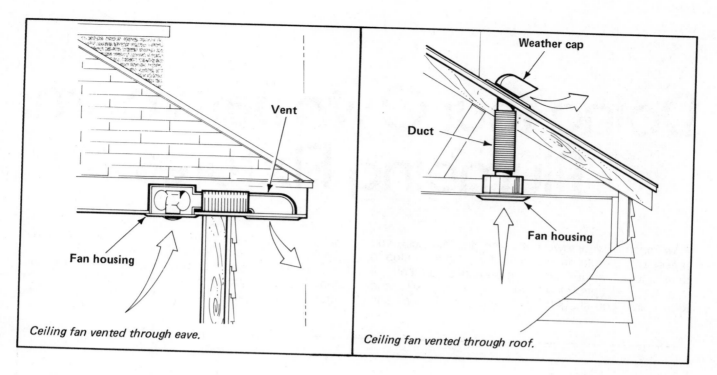

Ceiling fan vented through eave.

Ceiling fan vented through roof.

locate the joists. The fan must be positioned between studs or joists. Mark the outline for the cutout according to the manufacturer's specifications.

3. Wear goggles to protect your eyes. Drill a large starting hole in each corner of the outline. Then use the keyhole or saber saw to cut a hole the proper size.

4. Lay the ducting next. If you can get into the eaves through the attic, drill a pilot hole in the floor of the eave where you want the vent to go. Then, from outside the eave, saw a hole the diameter of the sleeve of the weather cap. If you are installing the fan in a wall, drill a pilot hole from the inside of the bathroom through the outside wall of the house; then go outside and saw the opening for the outside portion of the vent. If the ducting is to be vented through the roof, you will be able to saw the outlet hole from inside the attic.

5. Install the weather cap over the outside opening and attach the ducting to the sleeve of the cap according to the duct manufacturer's instructions.

6. Fish the necessary electrical lines to service the fan. It can be switched with the main lighting, or it can have a switch of its own next to the light switch. See the "Junction Boxes And Cables" section earlier in this chapter.

7. Dismantle the fan assembly and remove one of the knockouts in the electrical connection box by bending it out and then twisting it off. Insert a BX or Romex box connector and tighten the lock nut. Cut 6 inches off the cable armor or covering and skin ½ inch off the insulation at the ends of the conductors. Use pliers to twist the bare ends of the black wires of the cable and the fixture tightly together; then twist on a wire nut. Do the same for the white wires,

and connect the green wire to the grounding screw on the fan housing.

8. Attach the ducting to the fan, and secure the fan housing in place against the studs according to manufacturer's instructions.

9. Turn on the electricity and test the unit. Then repair and paint the ceiling before you put the cover and trim ring in place.

HEATING FIXTURES

The high cost of energy has made many homeowners lower their thermostats. To take the chill out of the bathroom, a space heater can easily be installed that may be used only when necessary. Attractive wall and ceiling heaters are available in many styles and sizes. Most are made to be installed against combustive surfaces, so no special precautions need be taken. However, since these units use a resistant element to provide heat they need heavy-duty wiring. In planning for your heater, figure in the expense of an additional 20 amp circuit needed to operate most units.

There are heaters that use infrared heating bulbs that can be installed in the ceiling and look like normal light fixtures. Sun lamps are also available that can be incorporated in these units.

There are also combination fixtures that provide light, heat, and ventilation from one single overhead source. These install like any recessed light fixture; they also require outside ducting like an exhaust fan and heavy duty wiring for the heating element. Combination units are ideal for small bathrooms that don't have the wall space for a separate heater. They are installed in the same way as single ventilation units, and wiring instructions are provided by the manufacturer.

Doing Your Own Bathroom: Plumbing Fixtures

How much of your own bathroom plumbing can you reasonably plan to do yourself? If you have to stop to think about that question, you should be cautious. If you have doubts about your plumbing skills and knowledge, you should stick to replacing fixtures and other plumbing parts visible inside the room; leave in-the-wall plumbing to a licensed plumber.

Every bathroom has two separate plumbing systems—a water supply system and a waste disposal, or drain, system. Complete separation between the two

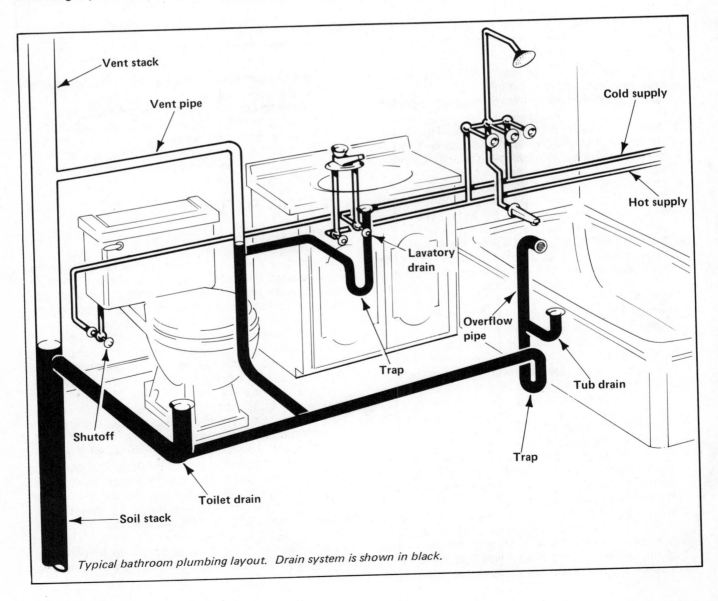

Typical bathroom plumbing layout. Drain system is shown in black.

systems is essential to prevent contamination of the water supply by bacteria from the drain system. For that reason, an improperly designed, constructed, or modified plumbing system—especially a drain system—is a health hazard. In fact, most communities have detailed codes governing all aspects of plumbing. Before doing any plumbing work, obtain from your local government a copy of the code for your community. Also, be sure that you know how your plumbing system works.

Water enters your house via a main supply pipe. At the point where the main pipe enters, there is a main shutoff valve. It's important to locate this valve; as long as the valve is open, the water in your household supply system is under pressure and ready to flow from any disconnected pipe. At some point after entering the house, the main supply pipe branches in two directions. One of the branch pipes carries water to the water heater, so that you now have two supply pipes—one carrying cold water and one carrying hot water. At some point, both pipes disappear into a wall and continue on to the bathroom, where branches direct water to the individual fixtures.

In a neatly designed supply system, the hot and cold pipes follow roughly the same route to the bathroom and run parallel through the wall, or walls, behind the fixtures. But, in an old house, or in one that has been remodeled, you can't count on this to be true; if you intend to do any more than replace an old fixture, proceed cautiously and be ready to call in expert help.

The water supply system is not difficult to rearrange if you have the time and have had some experience assembling pipes. The drain system is a different story, however.

The drain system often is referred to as the DWV—Drain, Waste, and Vent—system. Its central feature is the large pipe that runs down from the toilet into the ground under your house and from there connects with your septic tank or your community's sewage system. An extension of the soil stack, called

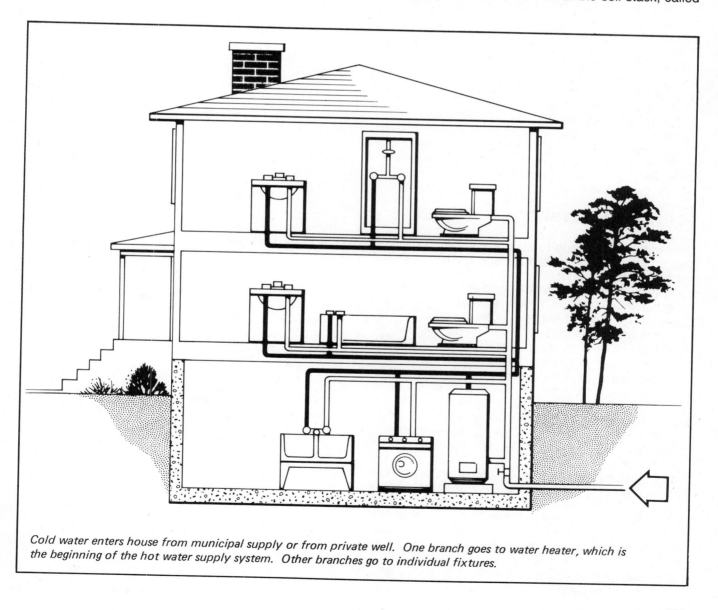

Cold water enters house from municipal supply or from private well. One branch goes to water heater, which is the beginning of the hot water supply system. Other branches go to individual fixtures.

the vent stack, runs straight up through the roof of your house. The protruding end of this pipe is open to allow decay gasses to escape and to allow fresh air to enter the drain system. Unlike the supply system, the drain system works by gravity; water will not flow through it unless it is properly vented. And, unless the system is properly vented, siphon action will empty the water traps under the fixtures. A trap is a hook-shaped section of pipe that retains enough water in its curve to form a seal that prevents sewer gasses and insects from entering your house. Traps are essential for sanitation and never should be bypassed. Toilets, however, are self-trapping and therefore require no trap in the pipe.

The location of the soil stack almost always is the factor that determines the extent to which bathroom plumbing can be remodeled. Rearranging the lines that drain into the soil stack requires removing portions of the bathroom walls and floor and often involves disruption of the structural members of the house. Although the tub, shower, and lavatory drain lines can be moved more easily than the toilet drain, remember that all the drain lines work in conjunction with the vent stack. Relocating a drain may mean redesigning the vent connections. Also, because the drain system works by gravity, horizontal runs of piping must be pitched slightly downward.

Because of the complex nature of the DWV system, and the necessity of following code specifications carefully, placing new fixtures in the locations of the old ones is always a safer course than relocation. Even professional designers and plumbers will attempt to work with existing drain lines before turning to more drastic measures.

REPLACING BATHROOM FIXTURES

Removing and installing a lavatory or a toilet is easily a one-person job, although an assistant often can be helpful for lifting and balancing a cumbersome unit. A fiberglass bathtub also can be handled by one person, if necessary. However, a steel tub can weigh more than 250 pounds and requires at least two people. A cast iron tub will weigh even more, and it will take at least three people to maneuver it.

Before disconnecting any fixture, you must turn off the water supply. If your present fixtures don't have individual shutoff valves, turn off the water at the main supply valve. Then, disconnect the supply lines to the fixtures and screw pipe caps on the open ends. You can then open the main valve, which will restore water to the rest of the house. Pipe caps are available at most hardware stores.

If any fixture doesn't presently have individual hot and cold supply valves—except the toilet, which requires only one valve—it's an easy matter to add them when you replace the fixture. Supply valves and fittings for connecting them to the fixture are available in kit form from plumbing supply stores and most hardware stores.

The method of connecting a valve to a supply pipe may depend on whether your supply system is constructed of steel, copper, or plastic pipe. Special adaptor fittings are available for joining the valve to any of these kinds of piping. Your hardware or plumbing dealer can recommend the correct adaptor for your situation.

If your supply system is of galvanized steel pipe, you may have to add a short extension to the supply pipe at the wall and screw the valve onto the extension. You can get short sections of galvanized steel pipe, pre-threaded, at a hardware store. When joining sections of steel pipe, always smear the threads with plumbing compound to prevent leaks. Plumbing compound is available in hardware stores.

When connecting a valve to a copper pipe, use an adaptor that has a compression fitting, if possible. This type of fitting doesn't require soldering. However, if you must solder the fitting, make sure that both the fitting and the end of the pipe are absolutely dry and have been "brightened" with steel wool or emery cloth. Apply a coating of soldering paste, or flux, to the surfaces to be joined, then slip the parts together. Using a small propane torch, heat the copper at the joint. As you heat the metal, touch solder to the joint. The solder will be drawn into the joint. Don't apply heat directly to the solder.

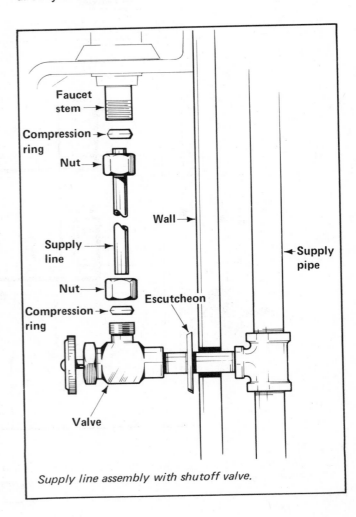

Supply line assembly with shutoff valve.

For joining an adaptor fitting to a plastic pipe, a special glue called solvent cement must be used. You can get this glue wherever you buy the fitting. The surfaces to be joined must first be thoroughly cleaned. Then, apply the glue to one of the surfaces to be joined. Press the fitting over the end of the pipe, giving it a slight twist as you do so. Allow the glued joint to dry thoroughly.

Replacing A Wall-Mounted Lavatory

A wall-mounted lavatory is supported by a metal hanger that is anchored by screws to a wood support in the wall. Although the lavatory may have thin metal legs at the front corners, these legs provide only additional support and do not carry the entire weight of the fixture.

If you are replacing an old lavatory with one of the same style, the existing hanger bracket will serve. However, if your new lavatory is of a different style, you may need a bracket specifically designed for it. When you buy the new fixture, find out from the dealer whether you'll need a new bracket.

To remove an old lavatory and install a new one, you'll need the following tools and supplies: a smooth-jawed adjustable wrench with a jaw opening of 2 inches, a smaller adjustable wrench, a basin wrench, a bucket, plumber's putty, and an old rug to cushion the new lavatory fixture. If you need to install a new hanger bracket, you'll also need, besides the bracket, a screwdriver and a drill and bit to drill pilot holes for the hanger screws.

Removal

1. Shut off the water supply. If there are not shutoff valves at the fixture, turn off the main valve where the main supply pipe enters your house.
2. Place a bucket under the trap and unscrew the clean-out plug if the trap has one. The water in the trap will pour into the bucket. If the trap doesn't have a plug, proceed carefully with the next step.
3. Loosen the two slip nuts that hold the trap in place. If you intend to reuse these fittings, use a smooth-jawed adjustable wrench to remove them; a pipe wrench will damage their surfaces. When the nuts have been loosened, pull down on the trap to free it. If the trap has no drain plug, remove the trap carefully and empty the water into a bucket or into the tub or toilet.
4. Pull the metal cover plate (escutcheon) away from the wall. Loosen the compression nut that holds the

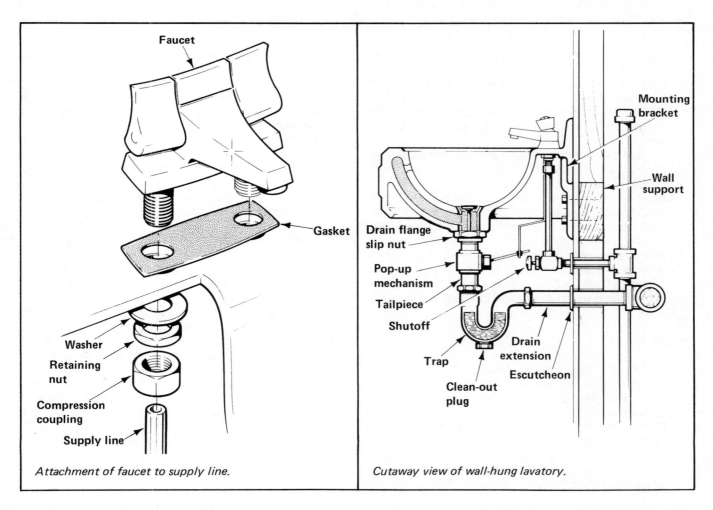

Attachment of faucet to supply line.

Cutaway view of wall-hung lavatory.

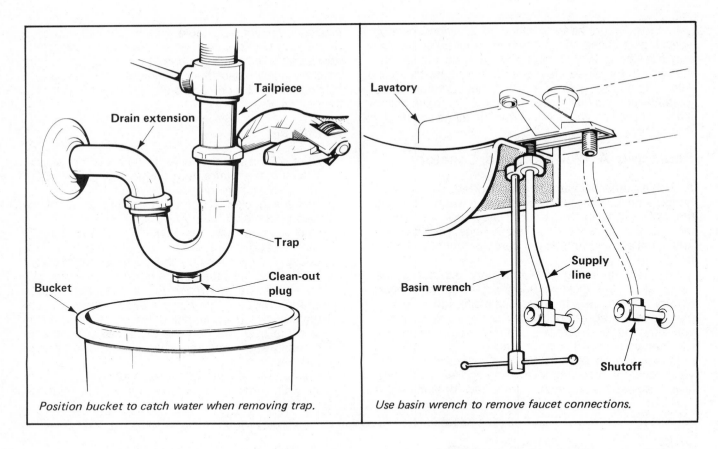

Position bucket to catch water when removing trap.

Use basin wrench to remove faucet connections.

drain extension in place. Pull out the drain extension.

5. Use a basin wrench to loosen the coupling nuts from the faucet stems if you can't reach the nuts with another type wrench. If the nuts are too rusted or corroded to turn, use a hacksaw to cut the supply pipes.

6. Loosen the nuts that couple the fixture supply pipe to the shutoff valve or to the wall supply pipes. Remove the fixture supply pipes.

7. When all supply and drain lines are disconnected, lift the lavatory straight up from the hanger bracket and place it on the floor, face down, atop an old rug or other padding material.

8. Remove the nuts that hold the faucets in place and remove the faucet assembly.

9. Loosen the slip nut that holds the drain flange and the tailpiece of the drain pipe in place and remove both.

Installation

1. Attach the new hanger bracket to the wall, if necessary. Also, if you wish to install shutoff valves at the wall inlets, do so now. Then proceed with the lavatory installation.

2. Place the lavatory on the floor on its side atop padding to avoid damage. Apply plumber's putty (or the gasket supplied with a new faucet and spout assembly) around the base of the faucet and spout fixture and put that fixture in place. Reach behind

the lavatory and screw the retaining nuts onto the faucet stems. Install the drain strainer and tailpiece. Turn the lavatory face down and tighten all nuts with a wrench. Attach the supply line sections to the faucet stems and tighten the unions with a wrench.

3. Lift the lavatory and slide it straight down over the hanger bracket.

4. Install the trap and drain extensions, and connect the supply lines.

5. Restore the water supply at the fixture valves or at the main supply valve.

Replacing A Counter-Top Lavatory

Counter-top lavatories may be surface mounted or frame mounted. The two types have identical plumbing hookups, however.

A surface-mounted lavatory supports itself by a lip around the edge. To remove such a fixture, simply remove the plumbing lines as you would for a frame-mounted lavatory. Use a thin knife to break the seal around the lip and, then lift out the lavatory. To install a surface-mounted lavatory, obtain the proper mounting sealant from your supply dealer, apply it liberally under the lip of the lavatory, then lower the lavatory gently into place. Don't press it down tightly. Using a damp cloth, immediately wipe up any sealant that squeezes out under the lip. The plumbing lines may be connected after the sealant has cured for four hours.

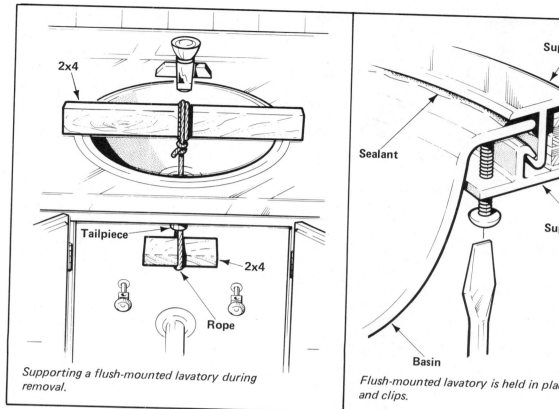

2x4

Tailpiece

2x4

Rope

Supporting a flush-mounted lavatory during removal.

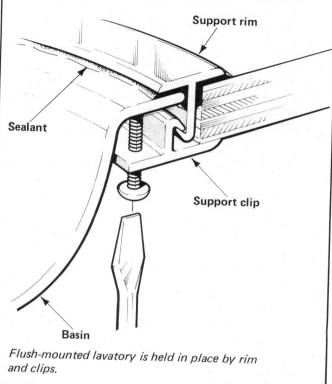

Support rim

Sealant

Support clip

Basin

Flush-mounted lavatory is held in place by rim and clips.

A frame-mounted lavatory is held in place by clips and a band-like metal frame that circles the edge of the lavatory. Care must be taken during removal and installation of a frame-mounted lavatory so that it doesn't fall through the opening in the counter top. The following procedures are for a frame-mounted lavatory. To remove or install a frame-mounted lavatory, you will need the following tools and materials: an adjustable wrench with smooth jaws that open at least 2 inches, a basin wrench, a pair of pliers, a knife, plumber's putty, a bucket, an 18-inch and a 6-inch length of 2x4, and a piece of clothesline about 3 feet long.

Removal

1. Shut off the water supply at the fixture inlet valves or at the main supply valve to your house.
2. If there is a drain plug in the bottom of the trap, place a bucket under the trap and remove the plug. If there is no drain plug, you'll have to empty the water when you remove the trap.
3. Use a smooth-jawed adjustable wrench to loosen the slip nuts at each end of the trap. Pull down on the trap to remove it.
4. Use a basin wrench to loosen the coupling nuts from the faucet stems and from the inlet valves or wall inlets. Remove the supply lines.
5. Drop a loop of lightweight rope, such as clothesline rope, through the drain hole. Insert a length of wood through the top end of the loop so that the ends of the wooden piece rest on the counter top.

Insert a small wood block through the bottom end of the loop and twist the block until it is wedged tightly against the bottom of the drain tailpiece. This arrangement will hold the lavatory in place when you remove the supporting clips.

6. Unscrew the bolts that hold the supporting clips in place under the lavatory and remove the clips.
7. As you support the lavatory from below with one hand, turn the wood block with the other hand to untwist the rope. When the rope is loose enough, remove the block and let it drop. Then lower and remove the lavatory.
8. If you plan to use the faucet and spout assembly again, use a pair of pliers or a wrench to loosen the retaining nuts on the faucet stems. Remove the nuts and lift off the assembly.
9. Insert a thin knife blade between the edge of the metal support rim and the counter top to break the putty seal, and remove the rim.

Installation

1. Install shutoff valves at the wall inlets at this time if you want to do so.
2. To install the faucet and spout assembly on the new lavatory, apply a bead of plumber's putty (or a gasket) to the base of the faucet and spout assembly and press the assembly into place. Reach behind the lavatory and tighten the retaining nuts on the faucet stems. Attach the supply tubing to the faucet stems and install the drain flange and

drain tailpiece assembly.

3. Put a continuous bead of plumber's putty around the inside and outside lips of the mounting rim. Position the rim on the edge of the hole in the counter and press the rim firmly in place.

4. Use the rope and block technique described in the removal procedure above to support the lavatory in place. Put the mounting clips in place, spacing them evenly around the perimeter of the lavatory, and turn the bolts down firmly.

5. Remove the rope and block support apparatus.

6. Attach the trap assembly and connect the supply lines to the wall inlet valves or to the wall inlet pipes.

7. Restore the water supply.

Replacing A Toilet

If you are going to replace a toilet, you must select a new one that will fit into the same space as the old. If the drain opening for your present toilet is 12 inches from the wall, a toilet that requires a 14-inch clearance won't fit. And, although a toilet requiring only 10 inches of clearance will fit over a drain located 12 inches from the wall, there will be a gap of at least 2 inches between the wall and the toilet tank.

Standard toilet clearances are 10, 12, and 14 inches, measured from the center of the drain opening to the back of the tank. Because the two floor bolts that hold your present toilet in place are centered on the drain opening, you can measure the distance from one of these bolts to the wall behind the toilet to determine the clearance. The bolts, located on the foot of the toilet, might be covered by small plates or by knob-like caps; if so, measure from the center of one of these covers to the wall.

Although the toilet will appear to be empty of water when you remove it, there actually will be quite a lot of water in the trap. The easiest way to get rid of this water without making a mess is to place the disconnected toilet bowl in the bathtub and tip it to pour out the water. So, before you begin removing the toilet bowl, place an old rug in the bathtub to protect the tub's surface.

To install a toilet, you'll need a special wax sealing ring. This seal is used for making a watertight connection between the toilet base and the drain pipe. You can get such a seal from a plumbing store or a

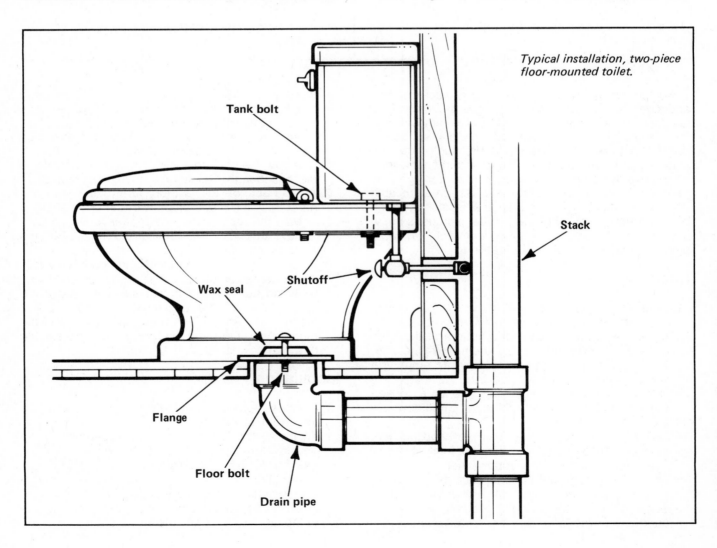

Typical installation, two-piece floor-mounted toilet.

Tank bolt

Stack

Shutoff

Wax seal

Flange

Floor bolt

Drain pipe

hardware store. Besides the wax seal, you'll need the following tools and materials: a yardstick or carpenter's rule, a pair of pliers or a small adjustable wrench, a screwdriver, a putty knife or scraper, a knife, and plumber's putty. If you discover that a portion of the floor beneath the toilet has rotted, you'll also need a circular power saw and wood, as well as wire nails, for patching.

Removal

1. Turn off the water supply at the wall inlet valve or at the main supply valve.
2. Flush the toilet to empty the tank. Sponge the remaining water out of the bottom of the tank.
3. Loosen the retaining nut that connects the supply line to the bottom of the tank, and disengage the supply line from the tank.
4. There are two bolts that hold the tank to the bowl. You can see the slotted heads of these bolts in the bottom of the tank. The nuts that secure the bolts are under the rear ledge of the bowl. Use a wrench or a pair of pliers to remove the nuts. If necessary, use a screwdriver to keep the bolt heads from turning as you remove the nuts. When you have removed the bolts, lift the tank off the bowl.
5. There are two bolts in the base of the bowl that hold the bowl to the floor. The bolts are inserted upward through a flange attached to the floor then through holes in the base of the toilet. The nuts securing the bolts are concealed by small ceramic plates or caps that are held in place by putty. To get at the nuts, pry off the plates or caps. Then use a wrench or a pair of pliers to remove the nuts.
6. There is a wax or putty seal under the toilet bowl. It was placed there when the bowl was installed in order to make a watertight seal between the toilet and the drain pipe. Break this seal by rocking the toilet gently.
7. Carefully lift the bowl off the bolts to avoid spilling the water remaining in the trap. Set the bowl in the bathtub and spill the water out.
8. You can now see the opening of the drain pipe in the floor. Attached to the floor around the opening is the metal flange, or ring, to which the toilet was bolted. The flange also serves as a joining device between the toilet and the drain pipe. Remove the bolts that held the toilet to the flange (they slip out easily). Then scrape away any sealing putty or wax remaining on and around the flange.
9. Stuff a wad of rags into the drain pipe opening to block sewer odors until you are ready to install the new toilet.

Installation

1. If the seal under your old toilet had deteriorated, water may have seeped into the flooring beneath the toilet and caused the wood to rot. Test for rot by probing the flooring around the toilet flange with a knife blade. If the wood is rotten, the blade will cut easily into it; in extreme cases, the wood will crumble.
   Rotten flooring should be replaced. If you find evidence of rot, proceed with steps 2 through 7. But, if the flooring is firm, go on to step 8.
2. Remove the screws holding the toilet flange in place and remove the flange.
3. If there is underlayment over the flooring, cut out an approximate 2-by-2-foot section of the underlayment. This job is best done with a circular saw set to the thickness of the underlayment (usually ¼ inch). If the damage does not extend to the flooring below, cut a square of new underlayment to fit the opening, cut out the drain hole, and nail the new section of underlayment into place.
4. If there is damage to the flooring itself, a section of flooring must be replaced. Before doing any more cutting, shut off all electrical circuits to the bathroom. If the flooring is plywood, or if it is tongue and groove boards laid at right angles to the joists, you can cut out a square or rectangular section of flooring. But, if the boards are diagonal to the joists, cut out a diamond-shaped section with the angled cut parallel to the floor boards.
5. When the opening is completed, inspect the joist nearest the drain for rot. If there is rot, nail a section of 2x4 to the side and flush with the top of the joist. And, if you terminated the opening at the side of a joist, nail pieces of 2x4 lumber to the side of the joist to support the floor patch.
6. Determine the total thickness of the flooring material that you've removed and match it as closely as possible with two thicknesses of plywood. If yours is an old home, the flooring might be thicker than your replacement pieces. In this event, place shims atop the joists to bring the patch level with the surrounding floor. Wood shingles make good shims. When the shims are adjusted to give the proper thickness, tack them down with short wire nails so that they don't shift position. Then nail the patch pieces down, one piece at a time.
7. Put the toilet flange in place over the drain opening and attach the flange to the floor with screws. Place the hold-down bolts in the flange slots with their heads down. Use a dab of putty to hold them in place. If the flange is not slotted, place the bowl over the drain, position it exactly and, using a pencil, mark the position of the bolt holes on the floor. Remove the toilet bowl and drill starter holes for the bolts. Screw the bolts into the floor to their full depth.
8. If you want to install a shutoff valve, do so now.
9. Invert the bowl on the floor atop padding. Place the wax sealing ring into the recess around the toilet drain hole and mold it into place.
10. Turn the bowl right side up and put it into position over the drain, with the hold-down bolts protruding through the holes in the bowl base. Apply your full weight to the bowl while gently twisting and rocking it to get a complete seal from the wax gasket.

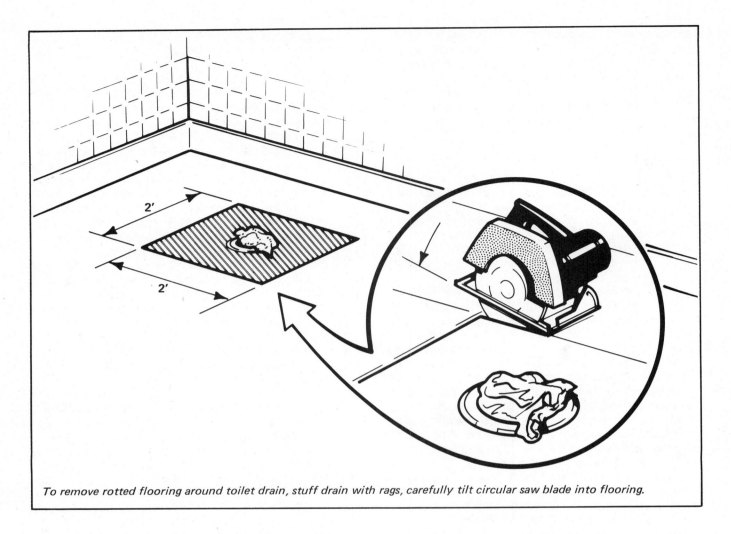

To remove rotted flooring around toilet drain, stuff drain with rags, carefully tilt circular saw blade into flooring.

When the base is solidly in contact with the floor, put washers and nuts over the bolts and tighten the nuts. Be careful not to turn the nuts down so tightly as to crack the bowl. Apply plumber's putty to the nuts and press the porcelain caps or plates into place.

11. Install the tank and flushing mechanism according to the manufacturer's directions.
12. Install the seat and lid.
13. Restore the water supply.

Replacing A Bathtub

The bathtub is the most difficult of the basic bathroom fixtures to replace. In fact, if you have a recessed tub, there are certain circumstances under which it is inadvisable to attempt to replace it yourself. A recessed tub has a flange, or lip, that usually is attached directly to the wall studs. The wall finishing materials— wallboard or plaster, tile, etc.—are applied over the flange. So, if your present recessed tub extends the full width of your bathroom, the tub may actually be longer than the bathroom is wide. Such circumstances may require that part of the wall be cut away and that the tub be removed through an adjacent room. Before decid-

ing to replace your recessed tub yourself, take a close look to determine exactly what removal and replacement may entail. You may decide to leave the work to a plumber, after all. If you do decide that you can handle the situation yourself, remember that the existing drain is plumbed for a tub of a specific width. Installing a wider or narrower tub will require slight relocation of the drain.

Removing a tub-on-legs usually is much simpler than removing a recessed tub, because the drain connections are exposed. However, replacing it with a recessed tub will require matching the drain opening to the new tub. Also, you will have to remove the wall material below the edge of the new tub in order to attach the tub flange to the studs.

The following general procedures are for removing and installing a recessed tub. However, you will have to adapt them to the design of the tub you are working with. The basic tools required are an adjustable wrench or a pair of adjustable pliers, a screwdriver, a hammer, a cold chisel, and a pry bar. Other tools and materials will be necessary, but they, also, will depend on the tub design. If you are removing a tub-on-legs, removal of the drain connections are basically the same as for a recessed tub.

136

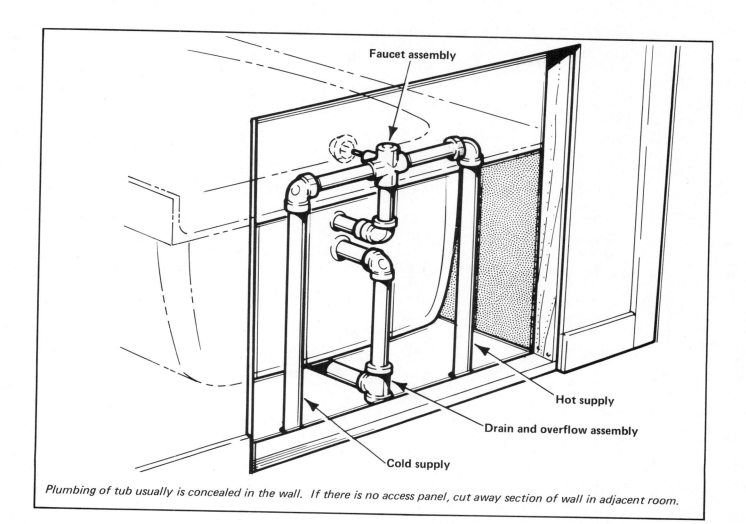

Faucet assembly

Hot supply

Drain and overflow assembly

Cold supply

Plumbing of tub usually is concealed in the wall. If there is no access panel, cut away section of wall in adjacent room.

Removal

1. Turn off the water at the main supply valve.
2. Remove the screws that hold the overflow plate/stopper control in place. Remove the overflow plate and pull out the stopper control mechanism.
3. Remove the access panel in the opposite side of the wall at the drain end of the tub. If there is no such panel, you have two options. First, you can cut into the wall where the access panel should be. (After you have replaced the tub, you can tack a panel in place over the opening.) Second, you can disconnect the tub from the drain pipe through the drain opening in the tub itself.

   If you are able to reach the drain connections through an access opening, use a wrench or adjustable plier to loosen the slip nuts that join the overflow pipe and the drain elbow to the main drain pipe. Remove the overflow pipe.

   If there is no access opening, unscrew and remove the drain strainer from inside the tub. Then, use a pair of pliers to remove the sleeve inside the tub drain opening. That will disconnect the tub from the drain elbow.
4. Remove the faucets and tub spout from the wall.

Remove the nipples (short lengths of pipe) to which the faucets and spout were attached, and remove anything else that projects beyond the face of the studs and might interfere with removal of the tub.

5. Free the tub flanges. Using a cold chisel and a hammer, cut away the wall surface along a line about 4 inches above the back of the tub and 3 feet above each end of the tub. Some tubs are anchored to the studs with nails or screws. If your tub is so anchored, remove all the fasteners.
6. Insert a pry bar under the tub skirt at one end of the tub. Raise, wedge, and raise again until a 1x2-inch wood strip can be placed under that end of the tub to hold it off the floor. Repeat the process at the other end.
7. Here's where you'll need help. If your tub is cast iron, you'll probably need two assistants in order to safely move the tub out. Two people can handle a steel tub. In either case have a dolly handy to move the tub through your house to the outdoors.

   Your helpers (or helper) should pull outward on the tub while you use a pry bar to force the tub away from the studs. Work the tub outward until there's space behind it to stand. Then get behind it and tilt the tub forward until it's standing on the front

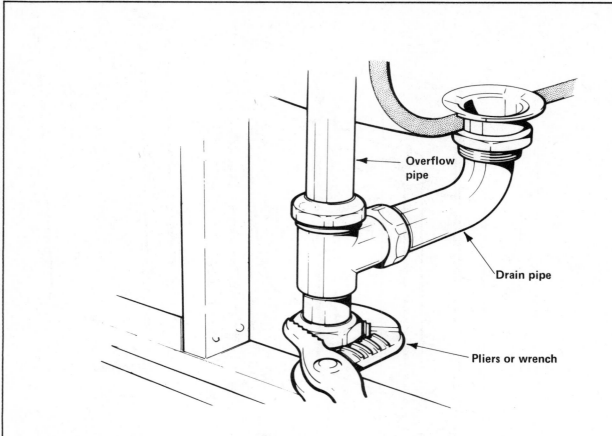

To disconnect tub from drain system, loosen slip nut connecting drain and overflow pipes to drain system.

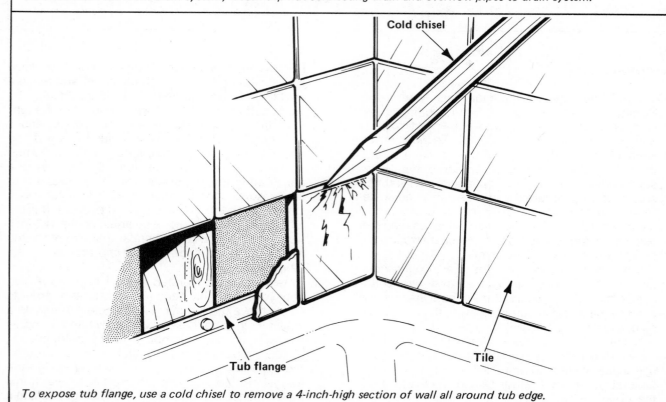

To expose tub flange, use a cold chisel to remove a 4-inch-high section of wall all around tub edge.

skirt. Continue to work the tub out of the recess until it can be lifted onto the dolly. You'll find it easier to lift the tub onto a dolly that's lying flat than it is to stand the tub on end and then get the foot of the dolly under the tub.

Installation

Unpack your new tub well in advance of the time when you'll want to install it. If installation instructions haven't been included, ask the dealer for a set. You'll need specific instructions, because there's not one standard installation method. And, since your dealer may have to order the instruction sheet from the tub manufacturer, you'll want to allow as much time as possible so that you'll have it when you're ready to begin work.

Some enameled steel and fiberglass tubs come with foam padding cemented to the bottom. This padding actually supports the tub. When the tub is properly leveled (with the help of a carpenter's level), the padding supports the tub at a height that leaves about a ⅛-inch gap between the floor and the bottom of the tub apron or skirt.

If one of these padded tubs can't be leveled, it might be necessary to remove a section of the floor under the tub, place shims on the joists, and then replace the flooring. Under no circumstances, however, should you attempt to put shims under the padding.

Some tubs are supported at the ends and along the back by wood supports nailed to the studs. These supports must be perfectly leveled and placed at the exact height required for the tub involved. Some plastic tubs have flange extensions that must be drilled at stud locations for nails or screws. Other tubs require special clips that fit over the tub flange and are nailed to the joists. And, some tubs with thick flanges make it necessary to nail shim strips to the stud faces so that there's a level base for the wallboard that has to extend down over the tub flange. Also, the width of the offset below the flange on some tubs dictates the thickness of wallboard that can be installed over the flange. So, you can see why you must have the manufacturer's instructions in order to install your new tub properly.

There are, however, some general rules to consider before attempting to install a recessed or corner tub.

1. Use a carpenter's level to be sure the tub and/or the tub flange supports are level. Do not rely on "eyeball" leveling.
2. Place a mineral fiber or glass fiber insulation blanket under steel or plastic tubs that do not come with padding. This insulation will reduce noise when the tub is filled. Use enough insulation to pack the space, but not enough to support the tub.
3. Wallboard must be installed over the tub flange, but it must not touch the tub rim. If it does touch the rim, it will soak up water, which will damage the board core. To avoid this problem, place ¼-inch wood strips around the rim to insure proper separation when you install the wallboard. When the wallboard is in place, pull out the strips and fill the gap with caulking or sealant material.

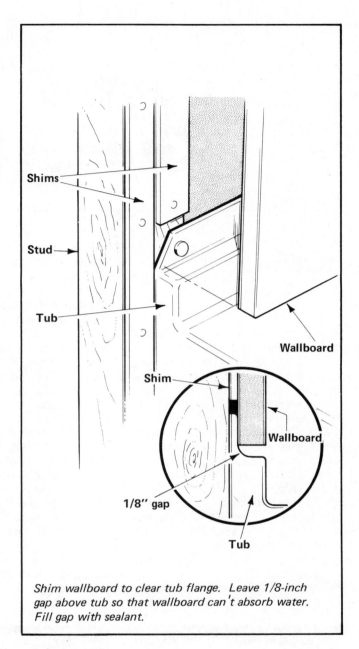

Shim wallboard to clear tub flange. Leave 1/8-inch gap above tub so that wallboard can't absorb water. Fill gap with sealant.

If your local building code requires special water-resistive wallboard for tub and shower enclosures, be sure to get the special sealant that goes with it. Whenever this type of wallboard is cut, the cut edge must be painted with the sealant to preserve the water-resistive properties of the core. Be aware that this type of gypsum board is intended for walls only, not for ceilings. On ceilings in high-humidity areas this board is less sag resistant than conventional wallboard.

4. You can replace the faucets and spout and connect the tub to the drain—in order to put the tub back into service—before you repair the wall area around the rim of the tub. However, because the rim of the tub won't yet be sealed, you must avoid splashing water into the wall cavity.

Buyers Guide: Fixtures

Toilets

Toilets are available in a variety of designs and in numerous styles and colors. But all conventionally designed toilets have one thing in common: they are made of vitreous china. Vitreous china is an excellent material for this purpose, because it is hygienic, easily cleaned, and highly stain resistant. But it is also relatively delicate and must be treated with reasonable care to avoid chipping or cracking.

The most obvious design distinction among toilets is the configuration of their bowls and tanks. The bowl and tank may be combined in a single molded unit, or they may be separate.

Two-piece toilets are less expensive than one-piece toilets and are available in either floor-mounted or wall-hung models. The advantage of a wall-hung toilet is that it leaves the floor below clear for easy cleaning. However, special wall reinforcement and plumbing hookups are required to install a wall-hung toilet. Special floor-mounted, two piece toilets with triangular tanks also are available for space-saving corner installation.

One-piece toilets for residential use are available only in floor-mounted models. The advantage of a one-piece toilet is that there is no possibility of a leak developing between the tank and the bowl. Also, one-piece toilets can be designed with lower tank heights than two-piece toilets; many people find the "low profile" design of some one-piece models more esthetically pleasing than the "high-on-the wall" design of two-piece toilets.

More important than whether the toilet is of one- or two-piece construction is the efficiency of its flushing action and the internal design of its bowl. A well-designed toilet should flush quietly and completely. The water in the bowl should be deep to keep the bowl surfaces clean. The water should also have a large exposed surface area to seal the bowl from the drain system. Each flushing should wash the entire inside surface of the bowl.

There are four distinct bowl designs: washdown, reverse trap, siphon jet, and siphon vortex.

The washdown toilet is the oldest and least desirable design. Water from the tank simply pushes waste out of the bowl, through the trap located in the front section of the bowl, and into the drain system. The washdown toilet is by far the noisiest type. It has the shallowest

Eljer Emblem. Approx. retail price: $83.35

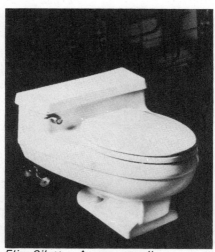

Eljer Silette. Approx. retail price: $288.20

Kohler Rochelle. Approx. retail price: $422.00 (white)

water seal and the smallest open water surface. Because of its inefficiency, the washdown toilet is not allowed by some plumbing codes. Its only advantage over the other three designs is that it is the least expensive.

The next step up in both efficiency and price is the reverse trap toilet. It is quieter than the washdown type, flushes more completely, has a deeper water seal, and its greater water surface makes it easier to keep clean. The reverse trap toilet works by siphon action, which pulls waste through the trap in the rear of the bowl. Reverse trap toilets are readily available in white and a few colors.

Although the siphon jet toilet is more expensive than the reverse trap toilet, it is quieter, more efficient, and it has a larger water surface and a deeper water seal to prevent the escape of sewer gases into the house. The flushing action is started by a jet of water.

The quietest and most efficient, as well as most expensive, toilet is the siphon vortex type. Flushing is initiated by a whirlpool action in the bowl, which leaves almost no dry interior surfaces.

Most toilets use 5 to 7 gallons of water for every flush. However, most of the major manufacturers either produce, or will soon produce, water-saver toilets. Artesian Industries, for instance, produces toilets of both siphon jet and reverse trap types that require only 3½ gallons per flush.

All the major manufacturers of bathroom fixtures, such as Kohler, American Standard, Crane, Universal-Rundle and Eljer, produce toilets of approximately equal excellence. Styles and colors, however, vary widely from manufacturer to manufacturer. For compatibility in styling and consistency of color tone, it's a good idea to buy all fixtures from one manufacturer. The major manufacturers produce one or more "high-style," "decorator," or "architectural" lines in which the various fixtures are style-coordinated. Introducing a fixture made by another manufacturer may cause a style mismatch. But the major manufacturers also produce fixtures that have no particular style and that usually are available only in white. These "standard" fixtures can be intermixed to no ill effect.

There are two standard bowl configurations—round and elongated. A variation is the sculptured or contour-styled bowl, which is an elongated bowl with a squared-off front. Usually, the seat of an elongated bowl is more comfortable than that of a round bowl. A round bowl, however, usually does not project from the wall as far as an elongated one and, therefore, should be considered when space is at a premium.

Toilets come as complete units ready for installation, including the seat. Inexpensive toilets often have seats made of pressed and molded wood fibers or chips. But such seats are not very durable. More expensive toilet models are fitted with sturdy plastic seats. But the seat design for either round or elongated bowls is more or less standard, and specialty or decorator toilet seats can readily be installed as replacements on all toilets.

Plumbing hookups for toilets are standardized, which means that toilets made by different manufacturers can be interchanged without altering your home's plumbing system. There are, however, certain restrictions. If you are purchasing a floor-mounted toilet, without the help of a plumber or designer, you must know the clearance between the center of the toilet drain pipe and the wall against which the toilet is to be placed. The standard clearance is 12 inches, although 10-inch and 14-inch clearances are common. A toilet that requires a clearance of 14 inches won't fit over a drain that is only 12 inches from the wall. Also, a toilet requiring a clearance of only 10 inches will leave an unsightly gap behind the tank if it is installed over a drain that is 14 inches from the wall.

There are no such restrictions on interchanging wall-hung toilets. The drain opening is standardized at 4 inches above the floor.

American Standard Lexington. Approx. retail price: $374.00 (color)

Universal-Rundle Delta. Approx. retail price: $154.47 (white)

Eljer Triangle. Approx. retail price: $103.95

Microphor Low Flush. Approx. retail price: $457.00

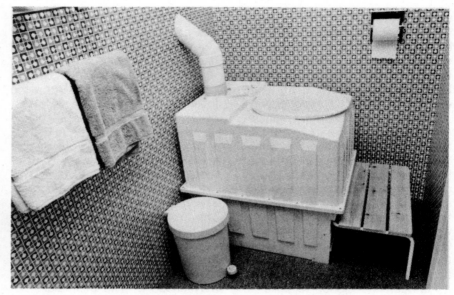

Mullbank Composting Toilet. Approx. retail price: $795.00

Toilets That Flush Upward

What if the existing drainpipe lies above the proposed toilet location? Yes, there are toilets made to flush upward. One such toilet is manufactured by McPherson, Inc., and is a self-contained unit with a specially designed double-acting flush valve that drives waste upward and into an overhead drainpipe.

Low-Flush Toilet

Even though water-saver toilets now are available from some manufacturers of standard toilets, the 3½ gallons they usually require per flush is still a lot of water—more, in fact, than is available at certain times of the year in some areas. A low-flush toilet is one answer to a water shortage problem. The Microphor toilet incorporates a special design that requires only 2 quarts of water per flush. It is similar in appearance to a conventional toilet, is made of vitreous china, and will directly replace a conventional toilet with either downward or rear discharge.

Composting Toilets

Perhaps the newest type of toilet, just now making an appearance in this country, is the composting type. A composting toilet works by reducing waste to a harmless residue through natural bacterial action. There are several different kinds and brands, and most are imported. No water whatsoever is needed, although in some cases a small amount of electricity may be needed for fans, heating elements, and other such components.

There are some definite drawbacks to composting toilets, such as the fact that they are unacceptable for use under many local plumbing codes. This usually has nothing to do with their efficacy, safety, or efficiency, but rather with the fact that such units were either nonexistant or never considered when the codes were written. Also, the prices of composting toilets are high.

Prices range from a minimum of $700 to as much as $3,000. "Decorator" styling is nonexistent; the units are starkly, simply functional, Installation of the large types is a major project that can include extensive remodeling or rebuilding. But, the important point is that they work exceptionally well, and that they do so at virtually no expense beyond the initial outlay, last indefinitely, and function in a far more environmentally sound fashion than do any other known waste disposal systems. A century from now, composting toilets may be the only allowable type.

Among the smaller composting units, which are self-contained and generally require only electrical hookup and forced-air venting, the Mullbank (Thornton Gore Enterprises) is a good example. Developed and made in Sweden, this is one of the most popular units in Europe. Another good one is the Bio-Toilet, made by Bio-Systems Toilets Corporation, Ltd. The Envirolet (Santerra Industries) is a sophisticated unit complete with electronic modules controlling its internal operations.

There are also large built-in composting toilet systems that require a large composting compartment to be installed in the basement or beneath the house. Such units are available for human waste composting only or to operate in conjunction with a waste-water disposal system. A special kitchen chute can even be incorporated to handle ordinary household garbage. Although installation is more difficult and much more space is needed than with the self-contained models, the large units are longer-lived, more effective and efficient, require less energy and maintenance, and have greater capabilities and capacity. Probably the best known of this group is the Clivus Multrum.

Lavatories

There are many different names for lavatories—lavatory basins, washbasins, sinks, washbowls—and they come in an awesome, if not confusing, array of styles, shapes, colors, designs, and sizes. Whatever the particular design requirement, somewhere there is a lavatory that will fill the bill. Color shades, tones and combinations are endless, as are the small design details. Common shapes include round, oval, square, rectangular and triangular, and there are others as well. But there are only three basic modes.

● The wall-hung basin is a complete unit, including provisions for faucets, designed to be mounted directly to a structural member embedded in the wall frame. Some of these hang free, while others have added front support legs.

● A pedestal basin consists of a washbowl and faucets mounted atop a freestanding column. It can also include a small countertop attached to, or integral with, the basin.

● Countertop basins consist of only the basin, with or without faucets, and sometimes a separate rim and special mounting hardware as well. They can be inset singly or multiply in countertops or cabinet tops of any appropriate width and length.

Countertop basins are offered in the greatest variety and are further broken down into four different types.

● The surface-mounted, or self-rimming, basin has an integral lip that overlaps the countertop when the basin is lowered into position from above. The integral rim provides the basin seal and bears the entire weight of the basin against the countertop.

● The flush-mounted basin is recessed into the countertop, and a separate metal rim is fitted around the basin and against the countertop. The rim provides the seal, and special hardware locks the basin and rim in place beneath the countertop for support.

● The recessed basin is installed from beneath the countertop, flush against the underside with the edge of the countertopping, overlapping the basin by a small amount.

● The integral basin is molded in one piece with a countertop, and is available in single- or double-basin styles in various countertop widths and lengths. The countertop may

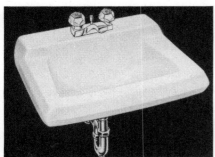
American Standard Comrade. Approx. retail price: $46.00

Eljer Owen. Approx. retail price: $57.00

American Standard Highlyn. Approx. retail price: $63.00

American Standard Tilche. Approx. retail price: $148.00

Kohler Lady Vanity. Approx. retail price: $159.00

be installed upon vanities, built-in cabinetry, or installed shelf-fashion.

The recessed basin is likely to be the most difficult to keep clean, while the self-rimming and flush-mounted basins are fairly easy to clean but are apt to accumulate dirt and residue around their rims. The integral kind is the most hygienic. With integral basins, faucets and controls usually are deck-mounted behind or beside the basins.

In most cases the plumbing is hidden in countertop basin installations, but is readily accessible.

Pedestal lavatories also hide the plumbing but the connections are much less accessible and trap removal is difficult. The plumbing is exposed to view in wall-hung lavatories and has to be kept clean and polished. Installation of countertop lavatories is not difficult, with the integral and self-rimming kinds being easiest. Pedestal basins are also relatively simple to install. Wall-hung basins are easy to put in if the wall support members exist but are problematical if new supports must be built into the wall.

Lavatories are manufactured in several different materials. Vitreous china is traditional and top-quality, and all the major fixture manufacturers offer a full line of countertop basins and wall-hung lavatories of vitreous china. In addition, wall-hung corner lavatories are available from Universal-Rundle, and special shampoo lavatories can be obtained from them and from Kohler. Unusual designer lines, like those from the Hastings Tile and Il Bagno Collection, are generally made of china.

Stainless steel is also sometimes used for countertop basins. This material is extremely durable, not subject to staining and cleans easily. However, it spots easily, especially with hard water, and requires constant polishing-up. Most stainless steel basins have a satiny, brushed finish that helps hide nicks and scratches. At least one manufacturer, however, makes a mirror-finish stainless steel basin. Such a basin is elegant, but it's not very practical if it's going to be used by kids, because scratches show up very clearly.

Enameled lavatories can be obtained in either cast iron or sheet steel. Of the two, cast iron is the more durable, has the thickest enameled surface and retains the heat of water for the longest time. Steel sinks are less durable but, nonetheless, long-lasting if properly cleaned and cared for. Lavatories made of these materials are now available only in a somewhat limited range of styles and colors, but continue to be fairly popular.

Countertop basins made of various plastics have become increasingly popular because of their durability, resistance to scratching and chipping, easy cleanability, interesting shapes and configurations, and attractive colors. A number of different plastics are used. One good material is Celcon acetal copolymer. This material was developed by Celanese Corporation, and is used in the Midcor Cameo line made by The Middlefield Corporation and in the Chi-Nelle basins by Arundale, Inc., as well as in several other lines by other manufacturers. American Standard pro-

American Standard Aladdin. Approx. retail price: $110.00

duces a fine line of Duramel plastic lavatory basins, and Crane offers a few models made of acrylic.

There is another general type of material that has gained great popularity in the past few years, a molded composition plastic that looks and feels like marble and is usually called cultured, synthetic or, imitation marble. This material is used to cast or mold one-piece lavatory units that consist of one or more basins and a countertop of variable dimensions, with or without backsplash or other features. This type of material is rather costly, but it does indeed have the sumptuous look of marble. It cleans easily, but requires some degree of special care and cannot be scoured. It is very heavy, but if properly installed with plenty of support, it is quite durable. Synthetic marble with a gel-coated surface may require some special maintenance to keep the appearance up.

DuPont Corian is probably the best known of synthetic marbles. This is a filled methyl methacrylate polymer that carries the color and

Crane Galaxy. Approx. retail price: $28.55

Arundale Chi-Nelle. Approx. retail price: $21.00

pattern all the way through the material, unlike many other types. Countertopping, lavatories, and other items made of, or surfaced with, Corian are very durable and easily cared for, and they can readily be repaired should minor accidental damage occur. Many other good brands of cultured marble lavatories are also available, however. The Commodore Vanity Company, for example, is a reputable manufacturer of cultured marble. And Pinta's Cultured Marble

Inc. manufactures countertopping, lavatories, and basins and also offers a custom service for designing and custom-molding cultured marble items of any sort.

There are other possibilities for lavatories, too. Both pewter and pottery basins are available from specialty shops. These also can be custom-made, as can molded fiberglass, cast concrete, beaten copper, spun pewter, mosaic tile, and turned or carved or steamed wood basins.

DuPont Corian vanity top (22" by 73"). Approx. retail price: $440.10

Bathtubs

Bathtubs are made in an extensive array of sizes, configurations, styles and colors. The major producers of bathroom fixtures offer a wide selection, of course, and others can be obtained through smaller companies and specialty houses. In addition, some bathtubs are custom-made, or else the overall bathtub installation is custom-designed to fit particular requirements. Truly, a bathtub can be purchased, or custom-built, to fulfill any need, desire, or whim.

Bathtubs usually are made of one of three materials: cast iron, stamped steel, or fiberglass reinforced plastic.

Cast iron and stamped steel tubs have enameled finishes. The enamel coating used on cast iron, however, is thicker than that used on steel. This, combined with the fact that cast iron is far more rigid than stamped steel, makes the finish on a cast iron tub more resistant to cracking and chipping. Cast iron also retains heat longer than steel does.

A cast iron tub will weigh between 300 and 500 pounds, while a steel tub usually will weigh between 125 and 250 pounds. A cast iron tub also will cost considerably more than a steel one. If you're remodeling on a tight budget, a steel tub is worth considering, both for its lower initial cost and because its lighter weight makes it more amenable to do-it-yourself installation.

Fiberglass tubs are lighter in weight than either cast iron or steel tubs, which can be a determining factor when choosing a tub for do-it-yourself installation. Fiberglass tubs are more expensive than steel tubs but they are not as costly as cast iron tubs. The major drawback to a fiberglass tub is that its surface is not as durable as the enamel finish of either a cast iron or steel tub; the surface scratches easily and, although a damaged enamel-coated tub can be reglazed, a damaged fiberglass tub cannot.

American Standard Fountaine. Approx. retail price: $1219.00

Kohler Steeping Bath. Approx. retail price: $628.00

The plastic used in fiberglass tubs can be either polyester or acrylic. The surface of acrylic tubs generally is a bit more scratch-resistant than that of polyester tubs.

Fiberglass tubs do not have the same "feel" as cast iron or steel tubs; they are somewhat flexible, or resilient. Some fiberglass tubs are less resilient than others, depending on the thickness of the plastic material and the type of reinforcing built into the tub. In general, the stiffer the tub, the higher the price. This does not mean, however, that a tub that is more resilient than others is of lower quality. In normal residential use, all fiberglass tubs manufactured in the United States are about equal in durability.

Almost all modern tubs are designed to be built in. Most are manufactured with a skirt along the long side that faces into the room. Tubs made for installation in a corner, however, are skirted both on a side and on one end. There are also many tub styles with no skirting whatsoever, which are designed to be set into a raised pedestal and skirted with, and supported by, ordinary building materials on all free sides, or recessed into the floor as a sunken tub installation.

Standard bathtub size is 29 to 32 inches wide, 5 feet long and 16 inches high. These rectangular tubs can be joined to the walls along one or two sides, or built entirely into an alcove. They are also available in 4-, 4½-, 5½- and 6-foot sizes.

Rectangular tubs are no longer as plain and simple as they once were, but include such safety and convenience features as built-in grab rails or handles, skid-free bottoms, headrests, integral "grooming seats" and assorted other fillips. Nor are the tub interiors necessarily rectangular, as witness American Standard's Oval Pool models available in both 6-foot and 7-foot lengths.

Besides the great variety of "standard" rectangular tubs, there are some other types as well. Oversize tubs, designed to hold at least two adults and maybe even a whole family, are being seen more and

American Standard 7' Oval Pool. Approx. retail price: $1297.00

Kohler's The Bath. Approx. retail price: $1100.00

more. Kohler's The Bath, a 5½- by-7-foot fiberglass model with dual faucet sets is an excellent example. At the opposite end of the size scale is the receptor tub. This is a small unit, generally about 3 feet long and 4 feet wide, that can be set in an alcove or installed in a corner. The low height of about 12 to 14 inches allows it to serve

particularly well for bathing children while at the same time doubling as a shower base.

There are also full-sized corner tubs, such as the Kohler Mayflower, and somewhat oversized and handsomely sculptured rectangular tubs such as the American Standard Gothic model (4½ feet wide, 6 feet long, and 20½ inches high).

Or, you can choose a square tub. Square tubs range in size from 4 by 4 feet to a bit over 5 by 5 feet. Square tubs can be hard to clean, however, and difficult to climb into and out of.

Another interesting type of tub is variously known as a soaking tub, Japanese tub, or furo. These tubs are round (although some have a squared top rim) and deep. Small sizes accommodate one soaker, large sizes can hold as many as three. Some are designed for sunken installations but most can be floor-mounted; some need decorative enclosures while others do not. Both fiberglass and wood models are available. American Standard's fiberglass soaking tub is a one-soaker size, with built-in seat.

And there is a relatively new material, now gaining greatly in popularity, that has changed the conventional look of bathtubs to an even greater degree. This is a solid composition plastic that molds easily and looks almost exactly like marble. This has given rise to several lines of bathtubs—such as those manufactured by the Molded Marble Division of Lippert Corporation—in unusual shapes and styles that can be fitted and arranged to suit many different bathroom designs and to give a luxurious custom look. The complete installation usually includes decking or steps, seats, and even planters made of the same material.

Should you be unable to locate a bathtub that completely fulfills your needs or desires, consider the possibility of designing and building one yourself, or having one made for you. A bathtub is essentially nothing more than a large watertight container. The key word is "watertight." The unit must be able to withstand a certain amount of hydrostatic pressure over an indefinite period of time, with no leaks or seepage—and once this hurdle has been overcome, the particular design, configuration, style, and color can be practically anything.

Custom bathtubs can be made from poured concrete overlaid with ceramic tile, just like a small bathing pool. Fiberglass cloth topped with layers of resin and molded upon a suitable framework is another possibility. Wood is also popular—redwood or cedar strips, marine plywood, ordinary Douglas fir plywood (exterior grade) or planking of practically any species will work fine, provided several coats of waterproof finish are applied and all joints are thoroughly glued and/or sealed. Or how about sheet copper, or polyurethaned brick laid inside a watertight container? The possibilities are endless; all you need is imagination.

The installation of a bathtub in new construction is not a terribly difficult job, particularly since arrangements will have been made during the construction to receive that particular tub. About all that is involved is setting the unit in place, making the necessary plumbing connections, and then continuing the construction, finish, and trim work around the tub site.

Replacing an old built-in tub with a new one, however, or installing a new tub in a different location during a remodeling job, is much more difficult work. Just removing an old tub is quite a chore, and involves a fair amount of demolition work and quite a bit of physical labor. Plumbing lines and fittings probably will have to be changed or shifted around. And if the piping is old, some of it might have to be replaced. Then, once the new tub is muscled into place and connections are made, there is a considerable amount of work left to do in making repairs to floor and walls and redoing the finish work. The do-it-yourselfer should recognize that not all of the installation can be made by one person alone. At least one helper is needed, more if the tub in question is a cast iron or synthetic marble unit. Unless you have had some experience with this type of work and also have a good selection of tools and equipment, tub installations are best left to the professionals.

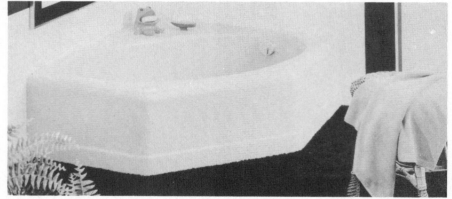

Kohler Mayflower. Approx. retail price: $610.00 w/o faucets

American Standard Restal. Approx. retail price: $396.00

American Standard Soaking Tub. Approx. retail price: $723.00

Tub/Showers

The tub/shower (Kohler calls it a bathing module) is exactly what the name implies—a bathtub arranged so that it can also be used for taking showers. The usual method is to provide an alcove tub with waterproof walls and to close off the open front of the alcove with a shower curtain or door, or to completely enclose an open bathtub with a shower curtain or with enclosure panels.

Freestanding island, pedestal, or sunken tubs can be fitted with rods set on extensions to support a shower curtain. They also can be semi-enclosed or surrounded with various kinds of clear, patterned, or colored self-supporting plastic partitions complete with doors; Tub-Master offers a custom line for such installations.

Existing alcove tubs have in the past commonly been fitted out with Melamine paneling (AFCO makes kits for this) or tile on the three walls to make a suitable waterproof enclosure. Now, however, one can also install a surround made of fiberglass or other plastics. Surround systems for alcove tubs generally come in three or five parts, consisting of two sides, one back and perhaps two corner sections.

The major fixture manufacturers all offer surround systems that can be used with their own bathtubs, and many such systems will fit other brands and older styles of tubs as well. Most of the systems come in three pieces that are quickly and easily installed. The Universal-Rundle and Aster Products systems are notable for the fact that they can be had with a top section so that the entire shower area is totally enclosed (except for the front) in molded fiberglass. Also noteworthy are the complete installation surround kits offered by Sears, Lyons Industries, Swan, and Novi American that are adjustable and trimmable to fit odd-sized tub alcoves and are easily installed by the do-it-yourselfer.

Masonite Tub Recess Kit. Approx. retail price: $149.95

Swan Tubwall. Approx retail price: $150.00.

Owens Corning 5' Time Control System. Approx. retail price: $288.33

New tub/shower installations can be made in the same way as those discussed above, of course, by simply fitting rods and curtains or surround systems to a new tub. However, there are other possibilities as well. Many major manufacturers, like Artesian Industries, can provide multipiece surround systems that are compatible with and particularly designed for their own lines of bathtubs, and which are installed at the same time as the tub to form a complete, totally watertight unit. Owens-Corning, for instance, produces an excellent sectional tub/shower unit complete with ceiling or "dome" with optional built-in vent. This unit has the advantages of being entirely self-supporting and readily assembled and installed by one person. Universal-Rundle also offers fiberglass multipiece tub/showers with optional ceiling section that, like most others, require structural support.

Kohler, American Standard, and some other manufacturers use a different approach. Their tub/shower units are supplied all in one piece, with the surrounds integral with the tub. They are made for a standard 5-foot alcove installation. Corl offers some unusual designs in this line, especially the Model 301. Waugh units feature an attractive exterior fascia surround and a durable acrylic finish, much tougher than the more common gel-coat finish.

Most bathtubs, except pedestal tubs and some soaking tubs, are installed during some stage of the construction or remodeling work and the trim and finish applied around them. However, the situation is different with one-piece or sectional tub/shower units. Here the room space must first be prepared in accordance with the specifications and requirements of the fixture being installed, and in most cases at least a good portion of the finish and trim work is completed. Depending upon the fixture, it may be slid into place as a unit, or assembled and installed in one operation, with the plumbing fittings being connected during the process. Only a minor amount of trim work, if any, is left to be done.

American Standard 5' Bath and Surround. Approx. retail price: $315.00.

Showers

A shower can be installed in a small bathroom in which there is insufficient space for a bathtub, in a bathroom in which a bathtub already exists, or instead of a bathtub, simply as a matter of preference. The smallest practical size for a shower is a cubicle measuring approximately 30 inches square, but 3 feet square is the smallest fully comfortable size. Beyond this point, showers can be installed in virtually any size and shape to accommodate one or several bathers. There are four basic types of shower installations: the ready-made freestanding cabinet, the molded one-piece alcove unit, the multi-sectional alcove kit, and the custom-built shower area.

The cabinet, or stall, shower is usually an open-topped freestanding unit made up of a shower base, three walls, sometimes a ceiling, and a door or curtain arrangement across the entry opening. Cabinet showers can be installed at any convenient spot against a wall, in a corner or even out in open floor area. Most cabinet showers must be located directly over a suitable 2-inch drainpipe fitted with a trap. However, some units, such as the stall shower made by Plaskolite, are designed for above-floor drainage connections. Numerous kinds of controls and shower heads can be used; they may or may not be supplied with the unit.

Cabinet showers are made in two prevalent standard sizes: 32 inches square and 36 inches square. Other sizes and shapes are available, too; for example, Kinkead offers both rounded and angled corner showers, and Swan makes a freestanding round model. Doors or curtain arrangements are often optional extras, and some models cannot be fitted with shower doors. Most units come unassembled but are easily put together.

Several different materials are used for construction of standard cabinet shower models. The cheapest and least satisfactory, because it is noisy and subject to rust, is the all-steel variety with a baked-on enamel finish. A better, although somewhat more expensive, cabinet is made with polyolefin plastic walls supported by a polypropylene framework and base. A cabinet made entirely of high-impact polypropylene is better yet. A cabinet with fiberglass walls that are supported by anodized aluminum framework, or an enclosure of molded ABS plastic that is attached to a heavy cast or molded base of cultured marble or similar material makes the best all-around cabinet shower.

Another possibility for a shower installation is to use a molded one-piece alcove unit, designed to be slid into and supported by a prepared alcove of appropriate size. Several different types and colors are available, made of fiberglass and other plastic materials. Some come in standard sizes,

Plaskolite shower stall. Approx. retail price: $129.00

Kinkead shower stall. Approx. retail price: $550.00

151

with 32 and 36 inches square being the most common sizes. Other units are nonstandard and must be placed in alcoves dimensioned for the particular units. The Waugh or Corl units are excellent products, as are those from Universal-Rundle and Kohler. Check to make sure that one-piece units can be wriggled through narrow hallways or doorways to reach the bathroom.

Sectional shower surround kits are also available to be installed in a constructed alcove. They come in numerous styles and colors, and they may be obtained with or without base (receptor) in either three-piece or five-piece kits. Surround systems are made in sizes that conform to standard receptors, but many can be adjusted over a several-inch span in both width and depth to fit odd-size alcoves and/or custom-fabricated receptors or shower floors. The panels are also trimmable for a precise fit where walls or floors are slightly out of plumb or off square. Many of these units feature molded-in soap holders, shampoo caddies, ledges, and the like. Universal-Rundle's Combo Shower, a three-piece unit with base, features an optional top. Five-piece systems, such as Versa-Wall by Artesian Industries, are somewhat easier to install in some situations because they have a greater degree of adjustability than do many three-piece models.

The fourth possibility for a shower unit is to custom build one in whatever size and configuration desired. Any kind of space can be used, from a small alcove or cubicle to a room of considerable size, and one or several sets of controls and shower heads might be installed. A standard receptor of molded or cast composition plastic might be used as a base; the floor itself, with a built-in drain, can also serve. Shower floors can be made of ceramic tile set in mortar, poured and properly finished concrete, terrazzo, or certain types of poured plastics. Shower walls traditionally are most often covered with ceramic tile set in either mastic or mortar, but can also be made of planed wood (laid on a waterproof backing and sealed with several coats of polyurethane), Melamine or plastic panels, or DuPont Corian.

The design of a custom shower must be carefully considered and well done; the materials must be of high quality, and the workmanship must be top-caliber for a successful installation. In addition, all facets of the shower must comply with local building and plumbing codes. But, as with any custom-built project, the results are handsome, unique, and often worth the extra effort and expense.

Kohler Trinidad. Approx. retail price: $328.00

Universal-Rundle Comboshower. Approx. retail price: $267.00

Bidets

The bidet is a bathroom fixture that affords the ultimate in personal hygiene. Although it is relatively new to the American bathroom scene, this fixture is widely used in most other parts of the western world. Its principal purpose is for washing the genital and anal (perineal) areas, an idea that originated with Napolean's cavalry men in France. Since that time, the concept has been further developed and popularized, resulting in today's modern bidet.

The bidet also is helpful in minimizing hemorrhoidal problems and permits beneficial cleansing of a perineal area afflicted with other types of medical problems. Bidets can be extremely helpful to infirm, handicapped, or elderly people who have difficulty with the normal anal cleaning procedure. The bidet makes an excellent addition to any fully-equipped bathroom.

Installing a bidet requires a drain outlet and both hot and cold water supply lines. In new construction this poses no difficulty, because the installation can be planned ahead of time. Installation in a remodeling job is more difficult because new plumbing must be installed and attached to the existing system. Since portions of the floor and walls must be opened up, the job should be tackled only by an experienced do-it-yourselfer or left to a professional plumber.

Bidets available today, all made of easily cleaned and maintained china, are produced by major plumbing fixture manufacturers and designed to coordinate in color and design with other top-of-the-line fixtures. Although bidets look similar to each other, there are some differences in plumbing arrangements. Those made by Crane and Universal-Rundle, for instance, have the controls located on the back of the fixture, and a large part of the piping and mechanics are open to view. Even though the exposed piping is chrome-plated, this arrangement is not particularly pleasing; frequent polishing is required to keep the chrome bright and shiny. The Kohler Caravelle Bidet, on the other hand, has attractive controls at the rear of the fixture and the plumbing and mechanics are enclosed in the fixture base. American Standard uses functional-looking—but attractive—wall-mounted fittings, although this approach makes installation a bit more complex.

When a separate bidet fixture cannot be installed, there is an alternative. Rusco American Bidet Corporation makes a simple unit that is designed to replace the seat assembly on any existing conventional toilet. The water supply is taken directly from the toilet's tank; the only additional requirement is a nearby electrical outlet. The entire installation, except perhaps for a new electrical outlet, can be made by the homeowner. This unit is even more versatile than a standard bidet fixture, since optional extras are available so that the bidet provides warm water from the rear or from the front, warm air from the rear, water pressure regulation, and a deodorant dispenser.

Crane Hygiene bidet. Approx. retail price: $356.00 w/fittings

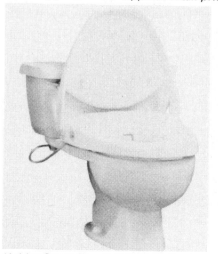

Kohler Caravelle. Approx. retail price: $136.00 w/o fittings

Rusco American bidet. Approx. retail price: $400.00 w/fittings

Faucets And Controls

Lavatory faucet sets are available in a profusion of decorator styles and designs. There are two basic arrangements: two valves and separate spout, all individually mounted; or the three elements as a single-piece unit. In either case the pop-up drain control is located at the back of the spout.

Mounting arrangements follow standard dimensions, so that most faucet assemblies will fit most lavatories. The assembly can be mounted directly upon the fixture in holes provided or deck-mounted upon the countertop; a few special models are designed for mounting on the wall behind the basin.

Faucet assemblies are made of several materials, but principally of a metal alloy. Of the metals, solid brass is best because it is the most durable and the least subject to corrosion. All the major fixture manufacturers offer lines of quality brass faucet assemblies, as do such individual manufacturers as U.S. Brass, Delta, and Moen.

Handsome lavatory faucet sets also come in vitreous china. These are available in single-unit or separated assemblies, with 24-carat gold trim or hand-painted floral designs as common decorative motifs. The Bradley Corporation, offers china fixtures, as do numerous specialty manufacturers. Although vitreous china faucets are elegant and easy to keep clean, they are relatively delicate, subject to cracking and chipping, and not impact-resistant; they must be treated gently.

As in most other areas, plastics have invaded the faucet field—and with good reason, because plastic faucets are absolutely noncorrodible, tough and durable, easily cleaned, can be made in a large number of styles, colors and finishes, and present a fine appearance. Lifetime Faucets uses a combination of CPVC and ABS plastics

U.S. Brass Aqua-Line Single Control. Approx. retail price: $50.00

Bradley Harmony Crystal-Glo. Approx. retail price: $30.00

Bradley Parisian china. Approx. retail price: $100.00

in manufacturing their fine line. Larden Plastics Co. makes their faucet underbodies of molded Celcon plastic. For a variety of reasons, both technical and practical, plastic faucet assemblies deliver excellent value and deserve serious consideration.

The inner workings of a faucet—the valve assembly, itself—can be either of two types: compression or noncompression.

Compression faucets are mounted in pairs—one faucet for the hot water and another for the cold. When you turn down the handle of a compression faucet, a shaft in the faucet housing presses a washer over the water inlet, thereby cutting off the water supply. Turning the faucet in the other direction lifts the washer and allows water to pass through the valve and to flow on to the spout.

The trouble with compression-type faucets is that they don't remain drip-free for very long. The washer wears out, or else the seat upon which the washer presses becomes worn, which allows water to seep between the washer and the seat. The result is a dripping faucet. Although replacing a washer is neither complicated nor difficult, it is a nuisance to be expected with a compression-type faucet.

In a noncompression faucet—also called a washerless, mixer, or single-handle faucet—the water flow is controlled by a sliding gate-like mechanism inside the faucet housing. This is a much more reliable valve design than that of the compression valve.

There are several ways in which noncompression valve assemblies are made, but the type in which the valve is enclosed in a replaceable cartridge is the most trouble-free. In fact, the cartridges in the faucets made by Lifetime are unconditionally guaranteed for life.

There are so many different brands of faucet assemblies that styles, colors, and finishes can be found to suit virtually any decor. Among the more popular finishes are brushed chrome, bright chrome, brushed or bright brass, gold or silver plate, plain or deco-rated porcelain, and pewter. Knobs can be had in still more finishes and materials, including synthetic marble and clear acrylic. Finish longevity is good (with proper care) for all types.

Much of the foregoing information also applies to bath and shower faucets, although the physical layout is a bit different. A bathtub can be fitted with two individual faucets and a spout, all three elements mounted either on the tub or on the wall above. Or, a spout can be used with a single mixing valve instead of two faucets. When a shower is added to the bathtub, a diverter control must be added to direct the water to the shower head instead of to the spout. The diverter can be part of the tub spout, in which case it is controlled by a lever, or it can be a separate control mounted on the wall. Most manufacturers of faucet assemblies make tub and shower faucet combinations to match their lavatory faucet assemblies. However, in many instances it is either necessary or desirable to use different brands of faucets and fittings for the various fixture installations. In this case, just as with lavatory units, you should look for top-name products, quality materials and finish, and a good warranty.

Stanadyne single-handle valve. Approx. retail price: $22.95

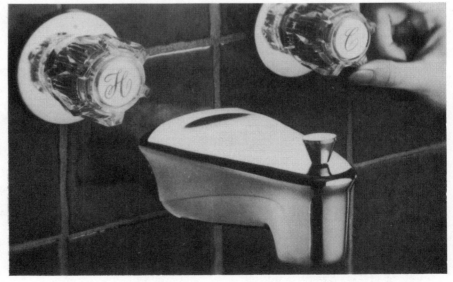

Stanadyne two-handle, shower head, tub spout. Approx. retail price: $34.95

Shower Heads

Shower heads are fully interchangeable on any shower arm or gooseneck, and there are many styles of shower heads to be considered. Most of the major plumbing fixture manufacturers supply a variety of shower heads, and so do a good many plumbing specialty manufacturers. Some heads are immovable, but a ball-joint head is more versatile and utilitarian. The spray pattern is fixed on some heads, but an adjustable pattern is more satisfactory. An adjustment to control the water droplet size and intensity (apart from adjusting water flow at the faucet) is also a plus, so that the spray can be adjusted to a flood rinse, gentle rinse, needle spray, mist, or anything in between.

In areas where water is in short supply, special water-saving shower heads, such as those made by Pryde, Inc., are well worth considering. Massage shower heads that can be adjusted for either pulsating or regular spray are available in numerous models from several manufacturers. The Touch Control heads made by Stanadyne and the Great Day massage shower heads made by Flo Products are excellent products of this type.

Personal or "telephone" showers are eminently practical and useful devices for showering. These consist of a small shower head attached to a handle and connected to the water supply by a flexible hose. The unit may be hand-held, clipped to a fixed wall bracket or to a height-adjustable slide bar, or attached directly to the shower arm. The flexible hose can be connected directly to the shower arm, to a tub spout, or to a special fitting placed between the standard shower head and the shower arm.

Personal showers are extremely versatile in both use and installation, and are available in a wide variety of styles, designs, and colors. A leader in the field, Teledyne

Water Pik, offers both wall-mount and hand-held models of The Shower Massage. Ondine's Daisy unit (by Interbath, Inc.) comes in several decorative colors and can be set for massage shower, aerated spray, or regular shower spray. Alsons' Personal Shower models are available in several styles, and there are systems and accessories for many different kinds of installations.

Stanadyne pulsating shower head. Approx. retail price: $24.95

Flo Products Div. Great Day shower head. Approx. retail price: $10.90

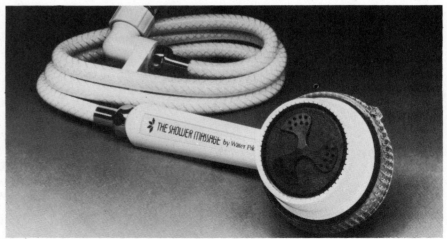

Water Pik hand-held Shower Massage. Approx. retail price: $39.95

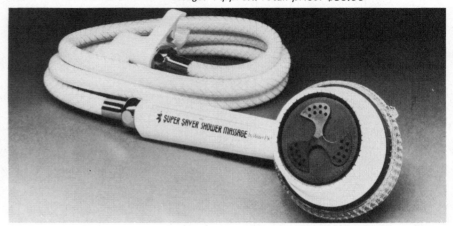

Water Pik Super Saver Shower Massage. Approx. retail price: $41.95

Whirlpool Baths

Hydrotherapy covers the entire range of bathing activities from quiet soaking to vigorous physical therapy. Hydromassage is now catching the public's fancy, due to the advent of whirlpool baths designed for installation in the home. After their initial introduction, home whirlpool baths were considered luxury items; this is no longer the case. If you are preparing to replace an existing bathtub or are building a new bathroom, you should investigate the possibility of installing a whirlpool bath instead of a standard bathtub.

In a whirlpool, hydromassage is accomplished by combining air and water in a stream under pressure. The air and water is mixed in a specific proportion and injected into the full tub. This creates a swirling pattern of constantly moving air bubbles and forceful water currents that bombard the skin of the bather. The benefits of hydromassage are widely recognized but difficult to fully appreciate until you have experienced them.

A modern whirlpool bath designed for residential installation may look like an ordinary bathtub or may take on the designs of large, ornate, and luxurious specialty tub units. They can also be obtained in hot-tub styles. Most whirlpool baths are available as packaged units, all put together and ready to be slid into place and connected. They require the same plumbing connections as a bathtub, plus an electrical supply. The tubs are fitted with one or more whirlpool outlets which are generally adjustable to control the velocity and the angle of the aerated water being injected into the tub. A suction fitting is built-in for continuous recirculation, and the pump, motor, and other controls and fittings are included.

Whirlpool baths do have some drawbacks. They are considerably more expensive than a standard

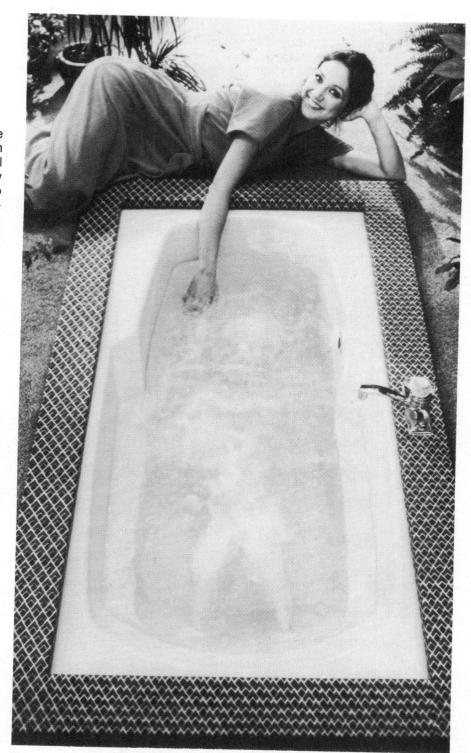

ThermaSol hydro-massage whirlpool tub. Approx. retail price: $1225.00 (5'x30")

bathtub. They also require a large amount of water—anywhere from 50 to 200 or more gallons. This means a tremendous amount of weight bearing upon the bathroom floor frame over a relatively small area; some added structural support may be necessary. When empty, a small, lightweight model can weigh as little as 125 pounds, but a large unit can weigh up to 700 pounds. When full, a big whirlpool bath might tip the scales at close to a ton of dead weight. The cost of operation must also be considered, since large quantities of hot water are required, and a certain amount of electricity is needed to operate the pump. Installation costs are also likely to run substantially more than for a bathtub or tub/shower of comparable size.

Kohler is one of the few manufacturers of standard bathroom fixture lines that offers whirlpool bathtubs. Their king-sized fiberglass tub, The Bath, is available with six adjustable whirlpool jets and all the attendant controls and equipment. Its Steeping Bath and Caribbean models—both made of enameled cast iron—cam be obtained fitted with four adjustable whirlpool jets. All of these tubs are quality deck-mounted units that can be installed in numerous ways. ThermaSol produces a fine lightweight fiberglass whirlpool tub with matching surround system.

Probably the best-known name in whirlpool baths, and also the commercial originator of them, is Jacuzzi Whirlpool Bath, Inc. Jacuzzi's line of products is extensive, handsome, and of high quality. Some models are made of fiberglass, and others are formed from a special molded marble-like material. One model, the Executive, measures only 53 inches long and 30 inches wide, which allows it to be built into a space smaller than an ordinary bathtub. The Cara V is designed to directly replace a conventional 5-foot bathtub. The Omni V will directly replace an existing 5-foot alcove tub and is complete with a surround system so that it is actually a bathtub, shower, and whirlpool all in one unit. Other models in both one- and two-person sizes designed for deck or other built-in modes are also offered.

Lifestyle uses a somewhat different approach with their Riviera Tiger Tub. This is a completely self-contained and portable unit, light and small enough in size so that it will go through most ordinary household doorways. This means it can be used indoors or out at any convenient location. Despite the

portability feature, it is large enough to hold two adults.

For those who like the idea of a hydromassage but don't wish to install a full-sized whirlpool tub, there is an alternative. The Dazey Cordless Whirlpool is a device that can be attached to the edge of a standard bathtub. It is small and

lightweight enough to be stored in a closet or in a vanity cabinet when not in use. The unit is completely portable, self-contained, and can be used in the home and taken along with you when you move or vacation. It is operated by a rechargeable battery, so there is no electrical danger.

Jacuzzi Executive. Approx. retail price: $1330.00

Riviera Tiger Tub. Approx. retail price: $2835.00 (67"x34")

158

Steam Baths

Steam baths have long been popular as a healthful and relaxing way of bathing. Rather than water immersion, a steam bath involves remaining for a period of time in an enclosed area filled with steam at a relatively low temperature—about 100°F. This induces perspiring and opens skin pores, which causes superficial impurities to be sloughed off. It also causes certain beneficial physiological effects upon the body, such as increased blood flow and oxygen supply. A steam bath is soothing and relaxing, and can be helpful for sufferers of arthritis, bursitis, backache, and similar ailments. Since a steam bath is basically a giant vaporizer, this kind of bathing can provide relief to those who suffer from colds, asthma, bronchitis, sinus problems, and certain allergies. Please note that steam bathing for medical reasons should only be done under the direction or consent of your physician.

One easy method of installing a steam bath in your bathroom, or anywhere that space permits, is to purchase a portable cabinet-type vapor steam bath, such as the VitaMaster Steam Sauna. These compact cabinets can be set anywhere and require only the presence of a standard 110-volt receptacle. They are self-contained units in which the user sits with only his or her head exposed. Some models can be used for either steam bathing or as a sauna (which produces only dry heat). Although confining, they work effectively in either mode.

Another possibility is to convert an existing bathtub, tub/shower, or shower stall into a steam bath. In order to make a suitable enclosure, a certain amount of simple remodeling must be done. First, any exposed wall or ceiling areas must be thoroughly waterproofed. This can be done by the addition of ceramic tile, by putting up melamine panels, or by a thorough coating with a polyurethane sealer. An existing bathtub might be fitted with a tub surround system that includes a ceiling panel.

In the case of a new installation, any one-piece molded fiberglass tub/shower, cabinet shower, multisectioned tub/shower, or shower surround system with a ceiling panel can be installed and quickly adapted for steam-bath use. In any of these arrangements the last step is to entirely enclose the front opening so that steam cannot escape from the fixture cubicle.

All that remains is to install a steam generator. ThermaSol manufactures such a device, which can be easily installed anywhere in the house within 50 feet of the bathroom. The attic or a closet are possible locations. The unit requires a 220-volt electrical line, a cold water supply, and a new ½-inch copper or brass steam line running to a steam outlet head located adjacent to the standard faucet assembly at the tub or shower. A timer switch, mounted on the wall outside the steam-bath enclosure, automatically turns off the generator after a preset amount of time (up to 30 minutes). If the water pressure in your household supply system is greater than 50 pounds per square inch, you'll also have to install a pressure regulator valve.

Viking Sauna Company manufactures small steam generators for easy shower and bathtub adaptations. Viking also makes a series of larger generators specifically for installation in steam-bath rooms of anywhere from 500 to 4500 cubic feet. This means that the home owner can construct or modify a separate small room or perhaps a glassed-in enclosure within a large bathroom, to serve the specific purpose of steam bathing. Such a steam room can be equipped with comfortable seating facilities, piped-in music, and other amenities and can serve the steam-bathing needs of several people simultaneously.

Those who don't want to go to the trouble or expense of installing a full-fledged steam bathing system might consider a device called Instant Spa by B & M Manufacturing Company. This accessory item requires no electrical or plumbing work, is inexpensive, and quickly connects between the shower outlet pipe and the shower head itself. It can be used in any enclosed tub or shower area. Steam is generated from hot water running into a special free-hanging head. The steam is directed downward so that it will billow up.

B&M Instant Spa. Approx. retail price: $49.95

VitaMaster Steam Sauna. Approx. retail price: $685.00

Saunas

The sauna is another type of health and hygiene aid that has gained popularity in home-use over the past decade. The ideal spot for a sauna is within or adjacent to a bathroom, although one can be installed at any convenient place in the house or even outside. The fact that a sauna can be readily built practically anywhere is one of the factors that has led to its popularity.

A sauna bath is both healthful and enjoyable. Unlike a steam bath that utilizes a steam-filled atmosphere at a temperature of about 100°F and a relative humidity of 100 percent, a sauna depends upon temperatures of as high as 200°F and a relative humidity hovering between 10 and 20 percent. Very little water is used, and in fact too much water vapor in a sauna environment, especially if produced suddenly, can cause an unhealthy physical shock. Because of the high heat and low humidity combination, persons using a sauna should be in good health. If you are unsure of how the sauna environment might affect you, check with your doctor. For most people a sauna bath is beneficial in that it relaxes and soothes muscular aches and pains, and it cleanses the skin by induced perspiration.

A sauna bath is a special installation, self-contained and fully enclosed. The entire interior, including all benches, backrests and other furnishings, are made of redwood which has the physical property of remaining relatively cool to the touch even at high sauna temperatures. The exception is the flooring which may be of concrete, ceramic tile, or vinyl—carpet or wood is not recommended—and is often overlaid at least in part with wooden deckboards. There should be no exposed metal, including nail heads, that might be inadvertently touched causing painful burns. Plastic should not be used in a sauna since it may become deformed.

Sauna baths can be custom-built

Metos sauna room kits are available in either precut or modular form. Every Metos kit includes the lumber, heater, controls, and accessories needed for constructing and using a sauna room. In the precut kits, all the necessary lumber is precut to size. In the modular kits, the walls and ceiling are partially preassembled in 24-inch-wide sections, with insulation already attached. Both precut and modular kits are available for constructing sauna rooms that range in size from 4 by 4 feet to 8 by 12 feet. Prices for precut kits range, according to the size of the room, from about $1100 to about $2800. For the modular kits, prices range from about $1600 to about $4100.

by constructing a fully or partially freestanding insulated cubicle or other redwood enclosure. The exterior can be faced and trimmed with any materials to suit the prevailing decor. The enclosure is fitted with wood furnishings, a special sauna heater of appropriate capacity for the volume of the room is installed, the necessary controls are mounted on the exterior of the enclosure, and the electrical connections made.

Sauna heaters are available in either gas or electric models from several companies, such as Crown Health Equipment Company or Viking Sauna Company. Gas types can be obtained for either natural or bottled gas. Most electric heaters are designed to operate on either 240 or 208 volts. Crown offers small units that will run on 110 volts, as well as a couple of wood-burning models. Certain accessories are also usually added, particularly a timing device, a hygrometer, and a thermometer.

Sauna baths are also available as complete units. Metos Sauna (Amerec Corporation) provides kit-form modules, complete with precut wood pieces and all necessary equipment and desired accessories, that can be put together by one man in a matter of hours. Several sizes are offered from 4 feet square to approximately 8½ by 12 feet. The module heights vary between 6½ and 7 feet, so the unit can be assembled in an existing room without running into ceiling difficulties. Helo-Crown Sauna Rooms are available from Crown Health Equipment Company in a wide range of sizes.

Sauna kits can also be obtained for custom installation into particular existing spaces. For instance, Viking Sauna offers a special service for this purpose. The homeowner provides the company with a certain series of dimensions along with any constrictions and restrictions, and it designs a sauna room to suit. When the design is approved, the company makes up a custom precut sauna-room package for installation by a capable homeowner or his contractor. Such installations can be fitted in almost anywhere.

One alternative to installing a complete sauna is to use Viking's Solo Door. This special door includes a built-in light fixture, vent window, heater controls and sauna heater all in one unit. This door can be hung in the existing door frame of any closet as small as 34½ by 31½ by 84 inches, or as large as 36 by 48 by 84 inches. The closet needs to be insulated, lined with redwood, equipped with a seat—and the sauna is done. Various other custom arrangements are available through Viking, Metos Sauna, and Crown Health Equipment Company.

Although even small saunas are expensive, they can be installed with relative ease. They not only pay great dividends in enjoyment but also add appreciably to the value of the property. Operation is simple, operating costs are low, and the benefits are substantial.

Metos sauna room kit doorway.

Hot Tubs

Despite all the recent interest in hot tubs, the idea is actually an ancient one. Many of today's hot tubs are almost identical to the traditional Japanese furo or soaking tub that has been in use for centuries. A hot tub is neither faddist nor far-out; it is a healthful, enjoyable bathing facility that also rates high in therapeutic value.

Hot tubs have been upgraded to suit modern living styles and tastes; many accessories and options are made for them. Most hot tubs are round, ranging from approximately 4 feet to about 8 feet in diameter, and about 4 feet deep; a few square models are also available. Most are built of redwood and the best, such as those manufactured by California Cooperage, are constructed of all heartwood. A few, such as The Paragon made by Jacuzzi Whirlpool Baths, or Viking Sauna's Spa, are molded of fiberglass. Most are freestanding, but they can also be partially or wholly sunken, decked around, or set into a pedestal or raised-deck arrangement.

Jacuzzi's Selva models, which are constructed with natural redwood, are fitted with whirlpool equipment. Similar whirlpool systems are either standard or optional with other makes of tubs. Most tubs have built-in seating, and are provided with integral water and heating units that run on either electricity or natural or bottled gas. The numerous accessories include covers, insulating blankets, shelves, thermometers, and steps. Since hot tubs, like pools, are designed to remain full with the water being kept warm and filtered, a quality heating and filtration system, along with the proper support controls and equipment, is essential. Outdoor hot tubs can be easily drained off, but indoor installations are usually fitted with a floor drain arrangement for connection to an existing drainpipe.

Wooden hot tubs are usually shipped unassembled as kits, and some include a do-it-yourself plumbing package. Others, especially those made for localized markets, are sold as complete prebuilt units; fiberglass hot tubs are also one-piece. Although most installations are relatively permanent, apartment dwellers can set up smaller models to be semipermanent and easily disconnected for moving.

Hot-tub assembly from a kit is not difficult and can be handled by a do-it-yourselfer, as can a large share of the installation and the addition of decking or other trim work. Even though plumbing and electrical hookups are simple, these jobs might have to be done by professionals; check local codes. Be sure that a hot-tub installation is allowable where you live, and that the particular hot-tub unit is an approved model. The most important approval is that given by the International Association of Plumbing and Mechanical Officials (IAPMO). Unapproved hot tubs could be unsafe, poorly constructed, or might not meet local approval required for an installation permit.

There are two other critical points to consider for hot-tub installation. One is size; even a small hot tub is bulky, and a fair amount of free surrounding space must be allowed for full enjoyment of the tub, as well as the building of decks, steps, and planters. More space is needed for the heater, filtration unit, assorted controls, and plumbing. The second consideration lies in the tremendous weight of a hot tub. A

California Cooperage hot tub. Approx. retail price (5 ft., elect.): $2205.00

large tub, complete with all equipment, can weigh over 1000 pounds empty. Add 1000 gallons of water to this, and you have a tremendous dead weight bearing upon a small area. This means that a hot tub must be carefully and sturdily set upon a solid foundation for best results; it cannot be parked upon the average wood-frame residence floor without plenty of additional structural support.

Another factor worth investigating is the cost of operating various models of hot tubs. Even small units require a fair amount of electricity or gas. Specific cost data depend entirely on the particular tub size, usage factors, presence of adequate thermal insulation, and the environment in which it is installed. In Denver, a study showed that a hot tub installed outdoors and used year round added an average of $17 a month to home energy costs. When considering a hot tub, be sure to ask the dealer for the full delivered price. Although a basic hot tub kit can range in price from about $1300 to $2300, shipping can boost the cost significantly if you live a long distance from the manufacturer.

Viking Sauna's The Spa. Approx. retail price (4'dia., 3'deep, heater, pump, instal.): $1999.00

Ambience Chamber

One the newest ideas in the field of health and personal care fixtures is the ambience chamber. Although best installed either within or as an adjunct to a master bathroom, an ambience chamber can actually be built in any convenient location. This is a self-contained and fully enclosed cubicle that can be installed in a floor-to-ceiling mode in which the cubicle is recessed into a wall or, like a sauna, it can be placed as an essentially freestanding module. The purpose of the chamber is to afford one or two users pleasure, relaxation, body cleansing, and a certain amount of mild physical and psychological therapy. This is accomplished through a controlled and programmable series of environmental, or "weather," phenomena within the chamber. The possibilities include simulated sunshine, gentle rain, warm fog or steam, and a light breeze in changeable sequence or in sequential combinations.

Ambience chambers come knocked-down in sections to be assembled and either built into a prepared space or converted to a freestanding module by encasing the unit. Water and drainpipe connections are required, along with an electrical supply of either 120 volts or 220 volts, depending upon the model. The chamber is fitted with sliding glass doors, and contains both ultraviolet and infrared lamps, spray nozzles, heater/blower unit and controls for the various functions. Built-in loudspeakers are provided for attachment to an outside sound source. Several options are also available, such as AM/FM stereo radio with eight-track tape player, comfort pads, special exterior front fascia panels, and bronze-tinted glass doors.

The Kohler Environment is a handsome, well-built unit measuring almost 9 feet long, over 3½ feet deep, and approximately ceiling height. The interior is crafted in teak wood with a cypress deck and contains a small storage cabinet, two shelves, a porthole window, and a lighted translucent panel in the rear wall. The functions are selected by a control panel mounted on the exterior of the unit cycling at up to 29 minutes per function. The four modes are also controllable to a certain degree as to intensity. Warmth is provided by infrared heat lamps and sun effect is by ultraviolet sun lamps. Either rain or showers emanate from spray heads, and steam comes from an integral steam generator. Wind is provided by two warm air circulating systems. A personal shower unit is also included.

Kohler's Habitat unit is somewhat smaller than the Environment and lacks some of the features but is an effective ambience chamber. The cubicle measures a bit over 7 feet long and 4 feet deep, and it stands a little over 5 feet high. It is designed to be inserted into a wall panel about 16 inches above floor level. The functions are fewer and the cycles somewhat shorter, but the experience of using a Habitat is no less pleasurable than using the Environment.

There are two major drawbacks to an ambience chamber. First is the matter of space. Even the smaller of the Kohler units is about a foot longer and 2 feet wider (front to back) than a standard bathtub and is about 5 feet high. The larger unit is designed to fill the entire height and length of a 9-foot-long wall to a depth of about 4 feet. So, unless you have a very large bathroom, you can count on extensive remodeling to incorporate either of these fixtures. And, even if space is not a problem, price can be; the smaller unit, Habitat, costs about $5000, not including freight and installation, and you can expect the cost of the larger unit, Environment, to be about twice that.

Kohler Habitat. Approx. retail price: $4700.00

Aids For The Handicapped

It is often necessary to equip a bathroom to meet the needs of handicapped, elderly, or infirm occupants of the household. Much of this equipment is highly specialized and directed toward particular handicaps or ailments. Such items are not generally found through retail outlets but rather through manufacturers or companies dealing with hospital, sickroom, and institutional equipment. Metropolitan areas usually have at least one supply outlet for this kind of equipment. Your doctor can furnish details for you, and you can also check the Yellow Pages under the headings, "Hospital Equipment & Supplies," "Orthopedic Appliances" and "Sickroom Supplies."

There are, however, a few items readily available from the major manufacturers of bathroom fixtures, as well as from a few specialty manufacturers of bath accessories and equipment, through local supply houses and dealers. The bidet is an excellent example; this bathroom fixture is widely recommended for people who have certain types of infirmities, handicaps, or medical problems. Whirlpool and steam baths may also be required as health aids, and so might a foot bath unit such as one of those made by Pollenex.

Universal-Rundle is a good source for some equipment. They offer a special wheelchair shower stall, the Liberte, complete with fold-down seat, safety and grab bars, wheelchair ramp, and special dimensions to accommodate a wheelchair. Certain of their bathtub and shower models are available with special nonskid bottoms and integral grab and safety bars that meet all current official standards. One of Universal-Rundle's standard toilets, Mercury III, is available with a bowl rim height of 18 inches instead of the standard 14 to 15 inches; this company also offers a wheelchair toilet.

Speciality houses offer a variety of products for the handicapped. The problem of getting in and out of a bathtub can be solved by using the Non-Electric Bath Lift made by Grant Water-X Corporation. This device can be arranged to suit nearly any bathtub, and easily lifts the bather in and out of the tub in a water-operated bucket seat. Frohock Stewart, Inc. manufactures a line of safety and security items, such as bathtub security rails to fit nearly all models of tubs, shower safety seats, and toilet guard rails.

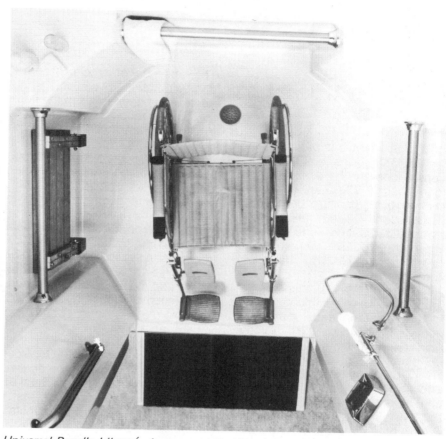

Universal-Rundle Liberté. Approx. retail price: $1818.00

(left) Universal-Rundle Mercury Toilet. Approx. retail price: $133.00
(above) Universal-Rundle Wheelchair Lavatory. Approx. retail price: $87.28

Buyers Guide: Materials

Flooring

All the generic types of finish flooring available for general residential applications can be used for bathroom flooring. There are numerous choices but some are better than others. Color, pattern, texture, and overall decorative effect apart, there are a number of points to consider in selecting bathroom flooring.

Durability. Most bathrooms get heavy use on a continuous basis. Flooring material must be sturdy enough to stand up for a reasonable length of time.

Cleanability. Frequent bathroom cleaning is both necessary and desirable. A flooring material that can be easily, quickly, and thoroughly cleaned makes good sense.

Moisture resistance. The bathroom floor is likely to be subjected not only to frequent cleaning, but also to repeated spillage of water and other liquids. This can have serious effects upon some floorings, while others are completely impervious.

Stain resistance. Many lotions and medications used in bathrooms can cause stains or can even remove applied finishes if spilled. Some floorings are more problematic than others, and all react in different ways.

Health factors. Bathroom hygienics are extremely important to the health and welfare of the users. The bathroom is highly susceptible to the presence and growth of harmful bacteria, mildew, fungus, and other undesirable organisms. The absence of cracks, fissures, porous materials or sealants, sharp angles, and open joints in the flooring greatly reduce the opportunity for such organisms to grow.

Resiliency. The resiliency of a flooring has a marked effect upon the comfort factor, especially when going barefoot. The softer the flooring, the more comfortable it is to walk on.

Thermal conductivity. At room temperature, materials with low thermal conductivity (such as wood) feel relatively warm to the touch and those with high conductivity (such as concrete) feel cold. Flooring materials of low conductivity are more pleasant to walk barefooted upon.

Installation factors. Consider whether the flooring can be applied on a do-it-yourself basis or must be laid by a professional. The easier the installation, the lower the installation cost. Check on the type of underlayment (if any) required and whether the flooring can be laid over an old floor. Give thought to how easily the flooring can be replaced or covered with another flooring during a future remodeling.

Unfortunately there is no such thing as an ideal bathroom flooring; one must pick, choose, and compromise to the best effect and live with the shortcomings. Here are some possibilities.

Wood

Wood makes a fine bathroom flooring, particularly in light of modern wood processing, finishes, and installation techniques. Ordinary nominal 1-inch softwood or hardwood boards of many species can be used—white, yellow, or red pine; spruces and firs; cedar; redwood; maple; oak; birch; teak; and walnut. Square-edged boards will do, but edge-matched, and preferably end-matched, stock is better. The boards can be laid in mastic and/or blind-nailed, or secured with countersunk screws capped with wood plugs. The flooring can be finished (and periodically refinished) with linseed oil, tung oil, Watco floor finish or a similar product, or several layers of a tough, waterproof finish such as Komac Gymseal or Poly-7, DuPont Polyurethane Wood Finish (low luster), or Nasco Clear Urethane Wood Finish (glossy).

Prefinished wood flooring is available in a number of different hardwoods; this saves time and trouble in the installation and affords an excellent, durable finish. The Memphis Hardwood Flooring Company, for instance, produces plank-type prefinished (and unfinished) flooring. PermaGrain Products, Inc., and Bangkok Industries both offer prefinished plank, strip, and parquet tile flooring. The Hartco Flooring System, by Tibbals Flooring Company, is comprised of parquet tiles of numerous woods and patterns, that are particularly good for do-it-yourself installation. The tiles are made of a wood veneer bonded to a resilient foam backing with a self-sticking bottom surface, which makes them very easy to install. Self-stick tiles will not adhere to certain types of underlayment or old floor coverings; check this detail before purchasing. One of the toughest and sturdiest finishes offered on plank or parquet wood flooring is produced by PermaGrain Products, Inc., in the Genuwood II line. This consists of a 20-mil vinyl sheeting bonded to a 12-mil hardwood veneer which, in turn, is laminated to a special composition base; this makes a superlative flooring material.

Vinyl

Sheet vinyl floor coverings are popular and sensible in bathroom applications because they are relatively easy to install, hygienic, and easy to clean and maintain. They are waterproof, relatively stain resistant, and durable. A tremendous array of colors, patterns, and textures is readily available in two principal forms: tiles and sheets. Tiles, usually 12 inches square, are the most easily applied. A special adhesive mastic is usually used to apply them. Some tiles are self-sticking, although they will not adhere to particle board underlayment and to some kinds of old flooring. Sheet vinyls come in large rolls and are bought by the running yard in various standard widths, then trimmed to fit. Most are laid with adhesive mastic, but some can be stapled down, which is good for the do-it-yourselfer. Installation of sheet vinyls is considerably more difficult than with tiles.

Both types of vinyl flooring are available in either resilient (cushioned) or solid form. The former is more comfortable and feels warmer, but the latter is less subject to mechanical damage and is apt to last longer. Better grades of vinyl flooring have a "no-wax" finish that is more durable and easier to maintain than other surfaces. Sheet vinyl is better than vinyl tiles because it can be laid in one or two large pieces, which makes the floor essentially free of germ-breeding cracks and seams.

When buying vinyl flooring, stay with the top name brands. Choose a color, pattern, and texture that you can live with for a long time. And check the warranty carefully. There are several major manufacturers that you can trust; Armstrong, for instance, has an extensive quality line. Congoleum, GAF, and Amtico also are good

names. The Nafco line by National Floor Products contains some handsome and unusual designs and Flintkote has an excellent tile line. Product quality is pretty much uniform among these manufacturers.

Ceramic Tile

Ceramic tile can be obtained in many sizes, patterns, shapes, colors and tones, and makes an excellent bathroom flooring. In many areas, ceramic tile is required by local building codes, even if only as an underlayment for other kinds of finish flooring. Ceramic tile, if properly laid, is durable, exceptionally long-lived, practically impervious to staining, waterproof, and easily maintained. It has the disadvantages of being relatively costly (especially when professionally installed), very hard, and cold to the touch.

Ceramic tile is available in many types that are suitable for flooring.

The two most appropriate classes of density are impervious and vitreous. Unglazed types work fine but if glazed tile is desired, matte finish is best, although semimatte can also be used. Some of the suitable categories are: glazed interior, faience or faience mosaic, ceramic mosaic, paver, porcelain, natural clay ceramic mosaic (paver tile), and quarry (packinghouse) tile.

For best results, ceramic floor tile should be laid in mortar on a concrete base and grouted with a resin or epoxy grout. It is best to leave this job to professionals. However, tile can be installed with an organic adhesive on concrete or other flooring bases. This can be done either professionally or by a competent do-it-yourselfer.

There is an amazing array of ceramic tile offered by numerous manufacturers throughout the country, often on a regional or even local basis; the consumer has a tremendous range of choices if he

Armstrong Solarian Premier Sundial. Approx. retail price: $14.00/sq. yd.

or she cares to search a bit. American Olean is one of the largest tile manufacturers, and offers an excellent line. Interpace has a particularly nice selection of floor tile, and Hastings Tile offers unusual bath-oriented tile that coordinates with their designer-line bathroom fixtures.

Carpeting

Bathroom carpeting has a luxurious look and is warm and comfortable to walk upon. It is relatively inexpensive and easily replaceable. Although carpeting would seem to be a natural for bathroom flooring, it has numerous drawbacks. It is neither overly hygienic nor easily cleaned, although some types are machine washable; it is also susceptible to water-soaking and staining. For best visual effects, carpeting should be fitted to the room and fixtures, but it should also be left loose so that it can easily be taken up for cleaning or washing; this means that some kinds of carpeting can never be made to lie flat. Some carpeting also has a tendency to shrink or curl. The floor beneath the carpet must be fully waterproof, and wet carpeting should always be immediately taken up and dried. Some carpet materials also have a propensity for retaining or generating odors; others do not and are also nonallergenic.

Neither ordinary room carpeting nor indoor/outdoor carpet is recommended for bathroom installations. Certain kinds of kitchen carpeting can be successfully used, and these are produced by numerous manufacturers. Celanese makes a few products that are suitable, and Borg produces a carpeting specifically for bathroom installation. This is a Dacron polyester fiber carpet that is mildew-resistant, nonallergenic, nonskid, machine-washable, and is designed for do-it-yourself installation and in-home cleaning.

Whatever the specific product, the disadvantages of carpeting should be carefully weighed against the advantages in each particular case. If you choose to have carpeting, you should search for the best possible quality of

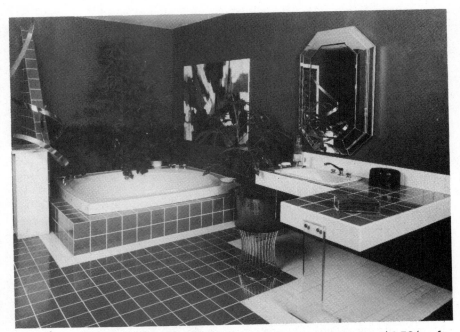

Interpace Franciscan Terra Grande (light tile). Approx. retail price: $4.50/sq. ft.

carpeting. With carpeting, cost should not be the deciding factor.

Other Possibilities

There are many other possibilities for flooring materials that lend themselves to satisfactory installation in a bathroom, particularly when two or more flooring materials are installed with one somewhat away from the centers of heavy usage. Stone has been successfully used, especially slate flags, marble tiles, or semipolished granite plate. Brick works well if laid in a mortar bed and heavily treated with a urethane sealer. Plain or painted concrete has been used many times. Cork sheet or tile makes an attractive and comfortable, although dark, flooring material but must be treated with an applied finish; it is prone to collecting dirt. One excellent alternative is rubber floor covering, either in tile or sheet form. the Flexco line by Textile Rubber is a good example.

Borg carpeting. Approx. retail price: $7.20--$15.00/sq. yd.

Wall Coverings

There are several materials that can successfully be used on bathroom walls with an incredible array of choices of colors, patterns, textures, and finishes. Two or more different materials can be used in combination, especially in larger bathrooms.

Walls in tub alcoves, tub/shower units, and showers must be completely waterproof for a substantial distance up the wall; they must also be easy to clean and maintain. Ceramic or plastic wall tile, melamine or similar paneling, plastic surround systems or plastic sheets like DuPont's Corian or laminates are good here. Other bathroom wall areas are best made water-resistant, though in large bathrooms this is less of a consideration for walls away from the fixtures. Ease of cleaning and hygienic qualities are factors to consider, and so is the overall color and decorative effect upon the room itself. Local building codes sometimes specify what can and cannot be used for bathroom wall coverings; be sure to check this.

Ceramic Tile

Ceramic tile has long been a favorite bathroom wall covering, and practically all types are serviceable. Impervious, vitreous, and semivitreous tiles can be used in bright, semimatte, matte, or unglazed finishes. The tile can be set with adhesive mastic on a firm, clean, water-resistant backing. Many tiles now come in pregrouted sheets; ungrouted tile is best grouted with resin, epoxy, or semiflexible polyurethane grout. Purchase ceramic tile all at one time from the same manufacturer's product run for color and pattern continuity; buy extras for later repair work. (See "Flooring" for suggested manufacturers).

Planks And Panels

Paneling is another wall-covering possibility; there are many varieties that are appropriate for bathroom installations. Stock planking, of either hardwood or softwood, works well if properly finished and sealed. Some prefinished wood flooring materials can also be applied to walls, including parquet tile. The Townsend line from Potlatch Corporation features solid hardwood planks that are sealed, finished, and made for wall installation. Wood veneer panels, preferably prefinished, can also be used. Most, like those offered by Georgia-Pacific, are ¼-inch-thick veneered plywood panels, but Bangkok also offers structural panels in ¾-inch thickness. You might consider Panelstrips by H.G.E., Inc., which are thin flexible wood strips that can

be easily and permanently applied to a sound backing in whichever decorative pattern is desired by the do-it-yourselfer. Strip-Panel by Real Wood Products is a similar material of great versatility and easy application. It is available in western red cedar or pine.

Paneling also comes in materials other than wood. For instance, Gold Bond manufactures an attractive and relatively inexpensive line of vinyl-surfaced gypsum decorator panels in simulated woodgrain, textiles, and various textures and patterns. AFCO panels are made of hardboard with a baked-on melamine finish that is waterproof, easily cleaned, and resistant to dirt and stain. Marlite offers both decorative paneling and textured planks that are excellent for bathroom wall coverings. Sheets of vertical-grade laminated plastic, such as those

American Olean Redi-Set ceramic tile. Approx. retail price: $2.89/sq. ft.

made by Formica or Micarta, might also be used. DuPont's Corian in ¼-inch-thick sheets can also be used as a wall covering, although it is most often applied over relatively small areas or as accents. One of the more unusual wall coverings suitable for bathroom purposes is the line of bright and colorful Homapal metallic laminates from the Diller Corporation. Although all of these materials vary considerably in cost, ease of installation, decorative effects, and appearance, they all are moisture-resistant and are easy to clean and maintain. Most can also be easily removed or recovered during a later remodeling.

Wallpaper

One of the most popular bathroom wall coverings is wallpaper. Ordinary paper wallpaper is unsatisfactory, since it is neither moisture-resistant nor easily cleanable. Practically any of the vinyl-laminated or plastic-coated papers or fabrics will work well as long as they are warranted to be scrubbable and humidity-proof. Lighter weights are somewhat easier to apply, but heavier ones are more likely to have better durability. Those with deep, well-defined patterns or textures are apt to be more difficult to clean. The new strippable wall coverings remove easily and simplify later redecorating. Prepasted coverings do not always adhere well, and many paperhangers prefer to apply additional paste for extra insurance. The paste, too, should be moisture-proof.

Hundreds of different patterns, colors, and designs of wallpapers suitable for bathroom application are available wherever interior decorating supplies are sold. Many large manufacturers offer them; those produced by Imperial, Columbus Coated Fabrics, Sherwin Williams, and Thomas Strahan, for instance, are excellent products. The easiest for do-it-yourself application are papers like Decro-wall's prepasted Wallpaper In Squares, matched 15¾-inch squares that are available in vinyl-coated and Mylar-faced types. There are also many regional manufacturers that produce goods of equal quality. Choose a reputable and well-known dealer or supplier, and be guided by his or her recommendations.

Miscellaneous

Bathroom walls can also be decorated with materials not normally associated with bathrooms (or interior walls); this is especially true for walls of large bathrooms that are remote from water-usage locations. For instance, a wall done in hand-cut cedar shakes, or even ordinary cedar shingles, provides a handsome focal point. Various other kinds of exterior siding might also be used. Brick, either old or new, can be used as a wall covering, and so can simulated brick or stone, such as that made by Z-Brick. Stucco is another possibility, and so is mirror tile or sheet. For an unusual decorative approach you might consider graphics, murals, or wall-sized color photographs of outdoor scenes—all of which are available for use as wall coverings.

Hoyne Panelstrips. Approx. retail price: $9.98/package (covers 32 sq. ft.)

Decro-wall Wallpaper In Squares. Approx. retail price: $6.98/package (covers 31 sq. ft.)

Ceilings

A bathroom ceiling should have a moisture-proof finish and not be susceptible to the effects of high humidity; this is especially true if the room is small or if quantities of steam are expected in normal daily bathroom use. A smooth and scrubbable surface is best, not only for ease of cleaning but also in order to reduce the need for cleaning in the first place. Rough-surfaced ceilings, such as those with heavy texturing or deep stippling, tend to accumulate peculiar-looking markings and residue from moisture that rises, often carrying grime particles to ceiling level, and then dries.

Any number of materials can be used to finish a ceiling. Old bathrooms frequently have lath-and-plaster ceilings, and newer ones usually have ceilings made of wallboard; if in sound condition, either will serve as a good backer for other ceiling materials or applied finishes. Many materials commonly employed for floors and walls can be installed with equal success on ceilings. Sealed and finished planking, paneling, or thin wood veneer can be arranged to give a handsome effect. Gypsum decorator panels work well and vinyl-coated wallpapers or fabrics are widely used as ceiling coverings. Other materials, such as ceramic tile, laminated plastic sheet, or metallic laminates, can be applied to bathroom ceilings, but they generally are not because of the difficulties involved in the installation.

Ceiling Tile

Another way to cover a ceiling is to install ceiling tiles. Commonly referred to as acoustical tiles, most of them actually are not "acoustical." The nonacoustical types actually are better because they often have smooth, washable surfaces. Ceiling tile is commonly available in 12-inch squares with interlocking edges; some tiles are designed to have their tiny joints hidden by the overall pattern, while others reveal the joints. For bathroom application, the tile finish should be washable. Although many are not particularly moisture-resistant, they do stand up fairly well and can be sealed and refinished as desired. Made of a fibrous composition material, tiles can be glued to a firm existing ceiling surface or backing, or stapled to a wood-strapping ceiling framework. Although they are easy to install and comparatively inexpensive, the most serious drawback to ceiling tile is that even the washable kinds are not particularly easy to clean.

Suspended Ceiling

An alternative method of installing a tile ceiling is to put up a suspended-grid system. This type of ceiling makes use of a gridwork of interlocking metal angles secured to the perimeter walls and suspended at midpoints by wires. The tile, which varies in size up to 4-feet square, is simply dropped into place in the framework. Tiles are available in numerous colors, styles, patterns, and finishes, some of them are extra-thick with high insulating value. In a flush system the tile faces lie flush with the framework faces; in the reveal system the tile faces protrude down below the gridwork.

There are several advantages to this kind of ceiling. An old and shabby ceiling in poor condition can be hidden from sight. In new construction, no ceiling or ceiling backing is necessary; the gridwork can be suspended directly from the joists and other structural members. A high ceiling can be lowered without building a new ceiling framework. Individual tiles can be quickly replaced, or taken down for cleaning or refinishing. The gridwork itself is also easy to clean. In addition, special fluorescent lighting fixtures, called troffers, can be installed directly in the ceiling grid. Part or all of the ceiling can be fitted with any of several different kinds of translucent plastic panels with strip-lighting fixtures mounted separately above the ceiling to make what is called a luminous ceiling—the whole ceiling lights up and glows softly.

Waterproof Ceilings

Ceilings located above tub/showers, separate shower installations, and steam baths require special consideration. In many cases the fixture will be installed in a complete enclosure with a plastic ceiling cap; virtually any kind of sub-ceiling covering—or none at all—is all right here. Some steam baths, saunas, and ambience chambers are also modular and have their own ceilings. Otherwise, open ceiling areas must be covered with a waterproof material, such as melamine or sheet plastic which must be well-fitted and sealed, or coated with a waterproof applied finish that will hold up under high-moisture conditions.

Armstrong Bennington. Approx. retail price: $0.70/sq. ft.

Cabinetry

Cabinetry is an essential facet of every complete bathroom. The cabinetry might consist of built-ins, custom-built cabinets fabricated either at the job site or in a custom cabinet shop, antique or new furniture that either serves as is or has been adapted for particular bathroom use, or certain kinds of commercially-made bathroom cabinets and accessory furnishings. Such cabinetry takes several particular forms, the most common of which are the medicine cabinet and the vanity cabinet. Other cabinetry might include linen and towel storage cabinets, base cabinets not used as vanities, general storage cabinets, cupboards or shelving sections, and hampers.

Some bathrooms, especially those of relatively large size and complex design, contain built-in or custom-made cabinetry intended to fulfill certain particular functions and occupy certain areas of the bathroom. In many cases, though, outfitting the bathroom with commercially-made stock cabinetry is the easier and less costly course, with equally satisfactory results.

Medicine Cabinets

Medicine cabinets come in two basic types; surface-mounted directly upon the wall, or recessed into the wall. Most are made of steel with a baked-on white enamel finish on the interior and a variety of exterior finishes. Some, such as Chemcraft's 1400 Series Wall Cabinets, are molded of high-impact white polystyrene. Doors may be solid decorative cabinet-style, or faced with a plain-framed or a decoratively-framed mirror. Some cabinets have two or even three door sections, independently operable. Medicine cabinets are available in a great range of sizes, shapes and decorative styles, though most recessed types are sized to fit into a standard wall-stud bay of 14½ inches. Large sizes are almost always surface-mounted.

All of the major manufacturers of bathroom furnishings and accessories offer fine lines of medicine cabinets. General Bathroom Products has an excellent selection that is coordinated with their other products—one, the Kenilworth Tilt-A-Mirror, features a three-section mirrored door with a center panel that tilts. Many cabinets, such as those from Perma-Bilt, Val-U-Bath (Williams) and General Bathroom

Products, feature light caps mounted on the cabinet top, or integral lighting fixtures at top or sides. Some manufacturers—Perma-Bilt, for instance—also offer a surface-mounted mirror, lighting, and medicine cabinet combination; instead of a full-sized medicine cabinet, a smaller, horizontally-placed, sliding-door cabinet is located below the mirror.

Vanity Cabinets

Vanity bases, the cabinets without tops or lavatory basins, come in a number of standard sizes from about 20 inches to as much as 5 feet wide. Cabinet depth is usually about 21 inches, and the standard height varies from around 29½ to 31 inches. Some companies offer space-saver models that are only 16 inches deep. A considerable array of styles is available—Early American, French Provincial, Mediterranean, Caribbean, Victorian, Western, "Modern," Country, Colonial, and so on. Natural wood is popular, with hickory, pine, oak, pecan and other hardwoods available; Portrait Kitchen has one model series done in Australian mallee burl wood. Simulated wood grains in vinyl cladding on plywood or hardboard are also plentiful.

General Marble linen topper.
Approx. retail price: $129.00

Manhattan recessed cabinet.
Approx. retail price: $49.00

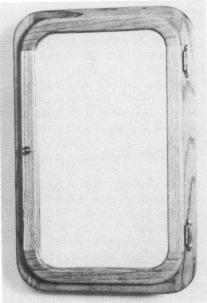

Heads Up Concord. Approx.
retail price: $158.00

Paint finish, often with gold or other contrasting painted trimwork, is also popular. Various vanity configurations are obtainable with doors, drawers, or combinations of both.

Large manufacturers with extensive lines of bathroom cabinetry, such as General Bathroom Products, Williams, Chemcraft, and Heads Up, match their assorted vanity cabinets with coordinated base and wall cabinets for other purposes such as hampers or linens, and also surface-mount or recessed medicine cabinets, framed mirrors, lighting fixtures, vanity tops, faucet assemblies, and accessory items. General Bathroom Products even offers matching toilet seats. Other manufacturers produce vanity bases alone, or combinations of bases and vanity tops along with one or two other items such as wall storage units or medicine cabinets. If you have no need for matching additional cabinetry, vanities made by Boro, Commodore Vanity, Ampco, General Marble, or Belwood are well worth investigating. Some of the lines produced by major kitchen cabinet manufacturers, such as Connor Forest Industries or Riviera Kitchens, offer kitchen cabinets that serve equally well in bathrooms.

Buying Cabinetry

With cabinetry you get what you pay for. Top-grade cabinetry is very expensive and medium-grade cabinetry is a bit less. Cheap cabinetry is cheap in quality and, in the long run, not a good buy. By comparison, custom cabinetry fabricated and installed on the job site is extremely expensive. A well-skilled do-it-yourselfer who is an amateur cabinetmaker can indeed build his own and save hundreds of dollars; but, factory-made cabinetry, on the average, is likely to be generally more satisfactory.

When purchasing commercially-made cabinetry and furnishings for the bath, there are several points to consider. Cabinetry made of solid wood, or with solid wood face frame and trimwork applied to hardwood veneer plywood, is the best. Thin plywood, hardboard, particle board, pressed wood or heavy cardboard do not hold up well and are unsatisfactory from a number of standpoints. Look for a tough, durable, well-applied finish; most of them are plasticized for longevity and easy cleaning. Styles with few cracks, indentations, joint lines, or deep patterns in the design are easiest to clean. Construction should be sturdy and solid, with

moisture-proof glue, screws, and glue blocks at stress points used throughout; units slapped together with a daub of glue and a handful of staples are not sturdy enough for use in the bathroom. Hardware should be well machined or cast, nicely finished, properly aligned, and solidly anchored. Mounting strips for cabinets that are wall-hung or base cabinets that will be secured to the house structure should be rugged and solidly attached to the cabinet body.

Most factory-made cabinetry is delivered in unit form, all put together and ready to install; provided they were well-made in the first place, these units will be the sturdiest and most solid. Some cabinetry, especially vanity bases, are available in knocked-down form to be assembled at home by the purchaser. There is a certain amount of convenience and some small savings—though perhaps more for the manufacturer than the purchaser—in this arrangement, and cabinet assembly is not at all difficult. If the cabinet is well-designed, the sections well-built, and the fastening arrangement a good one, the cabinetry will be relatively sturdy and long-lived. Knock-down cabinetry of poor quality is a waste of money.

General Bathroom Traditional vanity base TOB-3019-D and marble top MIB-3119. Approx. retail price: $185.00 (base), $111.00 (top)

Heads Up Harvest vanity and bowl (30" wide). Approx. retail price: top and bowl, $462--$845 (19"--48"); cabinet, $232--$632 (19"--48")

173

Countertops

Countertopping is not much of a concern in small bathrooms where little or no counterspace is a part of the overall design. In larger bathrooms, however, ample counterspace is a valuable asset. Countertopping, while fulfilling its practical function, can also play a large part in the decor of the bathroom. Countertopping materials can be used for vanity tops, to surface built-in base cabinetry, and to cover wall-hung ledge-type counters. In addition, these materials can be used for backsplashes, window sills, shelving, planters, bathtub edging, and seating ledges.

Laminates

One popular bathroom countertopping material is laminated plastic, which is also used for kitchen countertops. There are several national brands—such as Formica, Wilsonart, Textolite and Micarta—and laminated plastic can be obtained in a tremendous range of colors, textures, and patterns from any well-stocked lumberyard or building supply house. Laminated plastic can be applied to many horizontal or vertical surface—there are different grades for each. It is attached to plywood, particle board, hardboard, and a few other backing materials by gluing it down with a special adhesive called contact bond cement; do-it-yourselfers should use only the nonflammable kind of bond cement. Custom installations of any sort can be made either by a professional or by a do-it-yourselfer with a little experience. The job is not terribly difficult but special tools are needed. Various kinds of angled counter edges are easily made, but curved or rolled edges, or coves are quite tricky and must be done with a special postforming grade of laminate.

This material can also be obtained already bonded to a heavy countertop backing with factory-formed edges and with or without an integral backsplash. The countertop comes in standard widths and lengths which must be cut to fit a solid, secure base such as a vanity or other base cabinetry. Washbasins, faucets, or other items can be installed in the countertop after it has been set by carefully cutting or drilling openings of appropriate size.

Whether prebonded or custom-installed, plastic laminates make durable and easily-cleaned countertops. With proper care they will remain attractive indefinitely, but they are somewhat susceptible to scratching, gouging, abrasion, some staining, and extreme localized heat.

Ceramic Tile

Ceramic tile is another very popular kind of countertopping material. All of the different kinds of tile that can be used for flooring or wall covering are suitable for countertop application. There are dozens of regionally or locally made tiles that are suitable for the purpose in unusual or highly decorative colors, designs, and patterns. Many of these are hand-made and hand-decorated. Provided that they are glazed or are at least semi-vitreous, this kind of tile will serve well and make for a unique decorative scheme.

Ceramic tile makes a handsome countertop that is easily installed by the do-it-yourselfer and will last

Wilsonart Calabria marble pattern plastic laminate. Approx. retail price: $0.80--0.90/ft.

DuPont Corian top and bowl. Approx. retail price: $350.00

Interpace Franciscan Sierra tile. Approx. retail price: $3.00/sq. ft.

Diller cloth laminates with melamine. Approx. retail price: $2.00/sq. ft.

practically forever. There are, however, a few drawbacks to ceramic tile used as countertopping. The grouted joints between the tile pieces have a tendency to collect dirt, grime, and soap film, and the cementitious grouts can be difficult to keep clean and are apt to stain easily. Resin and epoxy grouts overcome this problem to some degree, but polyurethane grouts are the best bet. Ceramic tile is extremely hard, and glass objects dropped upon it will probably break. Heavy objects dropped upon the tile can crack or break the tile itself. Glazed tile in a bright finish is preferable, but highly reflective of light; matte finish is comfortable on the eyes, but a bit more difficult to clean. A semi-matte finish is a good compromise.

Cultured Marble

Cultured or synthetic marble is a new material commonly used as countertopping. There are several different methods of manufacture—finely-ground marble or onyx mixed in a resin matrix is one method—but all make satisfactory countertops. Cultured marble is widely used for vanity tops with an integral washbasin molded in. These are available in single- or double-basin units of standard dimensions from about 20 inches to 5 feet long and in slightly varying depths. Cultured marble tops can be applied to cabinets of any kind that are of appropriate size. Some manufacturers also offer matching blank sheets of cultured marble for plain countertopping.

Although cultured marble is easily cleaned, it is susceptible to scratches and abrasion and must be well cared for. Gel-coated surfaces are less durable than acrylic finishes.

DuPont Corian synthetic marble, available in several sheet sizes and thicknesses, makes an excellent countertopping. Since the color and pattern goes entirely through the sheet, scratches or abrasions can be easily repolished. The material can also be custom-cut, routed, edge-molded, or even carved to whatever design is desired.

Miscellaneous

There are several other possibilities for countertops. Wood, such as veneer plywood, glued-up solid planks, or butcher blocks, is one alternative. Wood countertops should have smooth surfaces with no open cracks or joints and should be finished with several coats of a tough, waterproof finish such as polyurethane. Another possibility, using wood or other material as a base, is to pour a thick surface layer of casting resin. This material is hard, glossy, practically indestructible. It can be used to cover decoupage and collage materials, or to embed seashells, wildflowers, leaves, or anything else that might provide a decorative design. Sheet vinyl flooring also makes a good countertopping material. It is easily cut, fitted, and glued down with mastic adhesive, and the counter edges can be trimmed off with special metal edging strips, wood strips, or ceramic bullnose tile. The surface is tough, durable, easily cleaned, inexpensive, and readily replaceable. For unusual treatments, genuine marble, soapstone, polished granite or slate, plate glass over a shadow or diorama box-shelf, or a glass-topped aquarium or terrarium arrangement are further possibilities.

Mirrors

At least one mirror is an essential accessory in any bathroom. Often, this is in the form of a mirrored medicine cabinet door. There are several other approaches to mirror installation, however, and literally hundreds of different mirror styles and designs. Often, several are used in combination.

One possibility is to mount a sheet of plate glass mirror directly upon the wall. Stock mirror glass is available in numerous standard sizes at all glass stores and many hardware stores, and it can be cut to custom sizes and shapes. The mirror can be mounted with metal or plastic mirror-mounting clips, or glued to the wall surface with special mastic adhesive.

The standard sheets of plate glass mirror handled by dealers measure 72 inches by 100 inches. You can have a sheet cut and finished to any size within those dimensions. Figure about $4 per square foot. However, if one of the dimensions is less than an even foot, you might have to pay for the next full foot. That is, if you want a mirror that is 2½ by 4 feet, the dealer will cut the mirror to that size, but you might have to pay the same price as for a mirror that measures 3 by 4 feet. Check with the dealer about this before you have the glass cut.

Surface-mounted framed mirrors are also very popular. Any type can be used, but those with cardboard or thin wood backings do not hold up well in the humidity of a bathroom. Also, in time, the silvering on some older mirrors can be adversely affected by dampness, although this is not a problem with modern electrolytically-protected mirror glass.

Many styles of mirrors made specifically for bathroom use can be obtained from manufacturers of bathroom accessories. Perma-Bilt offers plate glass mirrors decoratively framed, plain stainless-steel framed, framed with a small shelf below, and unframed. General Bathroom Products also makes a variety of framed mirrors in several styles—Contemporary, Baroque, Traditional, and so on.

For an unusual approach that can be varied according to the whims and imagination of the homeowner, tiles of plain or decorative mirror glass can be mounted upon any flat (and some curved) bathroom surfaces, including ceilings, shower walls or cabinet doors. They can be cut like ordinary glass and are easily mounted. Hoyne Industries, Inc. makes clear, smoked, and marble-patterned tiles, as well as tiles in a variety of wallpaper-like patterns. The tiles are mounted with a special double-face tape provided by the manufacturer.

One of the most interesting possibilities, both practical and decorative, is the installation of full-size door mirrors. One method is to install a sliding bypass tub enclosure door. Diston Industries, besides making mirrored tub enclosure doors, also makes full-height mirrored wardrobe doors in either bi-fold or sliding style.

Hoyne Fern Mirror Tile. Approx. retail price: $7.99/package of six

Shower Curtains And Doors

In order to convert an existing bathtub to a tub/shower unit, some arrangement must be made to enclose the open portion around the tub to prevent water from spraying out onto the floor. The same is true when a new tub/shower unit is not supplied with a closure, or when a separate bathtub and tub-surround system is installed, or when a shower cabinet or custom-built shower stall lacks a closure. There are two possibilities: install a rod and shower curtain, or put in a shower door.

Shower curtain rod assemblies are made in numerous configurations: they usually are chrome-plated and come complete with all hardware. They can be obtained in straight sections of various lengths (many are adjustable), right-angle models to enclose a bathtub side and end, and in rail-and-stanchion models for island bathtubs or showers. They are widely distributed through plumbing and bath supply dealers.

Shower curtains are likewise available nearly anywhere, and are made in a vast array of patterns, and colors. Vinyl has become the standard curtain material, because it is easy to clean and is mildew-proof. When shopping for a curtain, look for a fairly heavy gauge of vinyl for durability.

So-called decorator shower curtains are made up of two parts: a fabric drape or pair of drapes, with or without a valance, that mounts outside the bathtub or shower alcove and covers the entire installation, plus a vinyl liner that mounts inside the enclosure. You can buy drapes and liners in matched sets or individually. Drapes that are made especially for bathing enclosures should be mildew resistant. Although drapes can be custom

Kinkead Shower Stall 2036. Approx. retail price: $470.00

made from nearly any fabric, synthetic fibers are best, because they are not as susceptible to mildew damage as natural fibers. Shower curtains of all sorts are easily found in bath shops, hardware stores, houseware supply outlets and the like. J.C. Penney, Sears, and Montgomery Ward are excellent sources.

Tub and shower doors come in three general types: folding or collapsible, hinged, and bypass sliding. In custom installations, a full-

American Shower Door 503. Approx. retail price: $150.00

American Shower Door 503 and mirror. Approx. retail price: $300.00

sliding pocket door might also be arranged. This type of door slides completely into a slot, or pocket, constructed in the wall.

Most door assemblies are built with anodized and/or decorated aluminum frames for strength and rigidity, as well as for ease of installation. Higher-quality hinged or sliding doors are glazed with tempered or safety glass, either clear, tinted, patterned, or decorated. Less expensive ones are often glazed with shatter-resistant plastic (usually polyethylene or styrene) panels. Plastic panels are lighter and less costly than glass ones and do their job well, but they do not clean as easily and are far more susceptible to scratching than are glass panels. Collapsible or folding doors usually are made of flexible plastic (usually polyethylene or vinyl); although these doors are shatterproof and crackproof, and therefore safe and reasonably durable, they are more difficult to clean than hinged and sliding doors with fixed rigid panels.

Kinkead's Showerfold line is a leader in the collapsible door field, while Tubmaster offers a broad range of tub and shower doors of all kinds and also has a custom service for building both doors and enclosures for tubs and showers. American Shower Door markets an adjustable shower door, and Academy Manufacturing Co., Inc. makes sliding doors with attractive gold-finish frames, as well as handsome and utilitarian mirror-door models.

When selecting tub or shower door assemblies, look for firm glazing that is watertight and shatterproof; tracks that are quiet-running, are easy to clean, and that work freely; an even finish; a certain amount of adjustability to fit slightly off-line enclosure openings; solid and conveniently located grab bars, handles or other hardware; and a finish that will be easy to keep clean. Avoid doors that have plastic hinges, which do not stand up well even in normal use; a door that comes off its hinge as you step from the shower can cause a serious accident. And, above all, check the warranty.

Lights, Vents, Heaters

In every modern bathroom there is a considerable amount of electrical equipment. Every bathroom also has large quantities of water being used, several water-containing fixtures, and at least a few metallic, conductive objects. Water and electricity do not mix; the juxtaposition of the two in the bathroom constitutes a hazardous situation for the users. Making the bathroom as free as possible from all potential dangers of electrical shock and possible electrocution is absolutely imperative. There are several things you can do to increase the electrical safety and convenience levels of your bathroom, whether it is an existing one or a new installation.

Make sure that the electrical design and layout for your new bathroom is properly and conveniently arranged and fulfills all local and national code requirements. In the case of an existing bathroom, whether being redecorated or remodeled, investigate updating or rewiring the bathroom area for greater safety, even if you originally had no plans to touch the wiring.

When buying electrical apparatus, check the product to make sure it is approved and carries a seal such as the UL (Underwriters Laboratories). Some electrical gear may have other seals; check with your local building official to make sure that the items are approved for local installation. Stay with top name-brand products for all electrical equipment. High cost does not necessarily mean high quality, but a cut-rate price often means junk. Purchase only the best electrical equipment; if you are unsure about a particular item, get the opinion of an electrician or your local building code official. Make sure that all electrical equipment is properly installed.

Lighting Fixtures

All lighting fixtures installed in a bathroom must be of an approved make and properly installed. All exposed conductive parts must be grounded to the equipment grounding circuit unless the fixture is mounted on a nonconductive surface at least 8 feet vertically or 5 feet horizontally from a conducting and grounding surface. In a bathroom installation, thorough grounding of all fixtures under all circumstances is best. Ordinary lighting fixtures can be installed in most areas of the bathroom. However, any fixtures mounted within a tub/shower unit, shower stall, or steam room must be specifically approved for damp or wet locations. Recessed lighting fixtures must have a

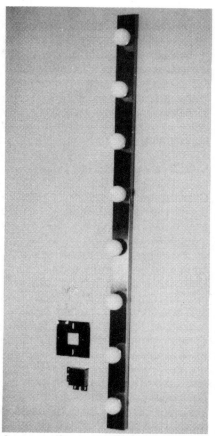

Sears metallic vanity fixture 87441. Approx. retail price: $19.99

Sears recessed lighting 89602. Approx. retail price: $8.50

minimum ½-inch clearance from any combustible materials, and have a 3-inch side clearance and 2-foot top clearance from thermal insulation, unless it is a special, approved type.

Many top-line name brands of lighting fixtures are available that are suitable for bathroom applications. Makers of general lighting fixture lines, such as Thomas Industries, Lightolier, Prestigeline, and Geringer, provide an ample selection from which to choose. You can also buy them from mail-order houses such as J.C. Penney, Montgomery Ward, and Sears. Many manufacturers of bathroom cabinetry or accessory items, such as Miami-Carey or General Bathroom Products, offer lighting fixtures that are coordinated in style, design, and finish with their other bathroom products. Monarch Metal Products produces a series of lighting fixtures that coordinate with matching medicine cabinets and mirrors, and are made especially for bathroom applications.

Vent Fans

Vent fans are frequently used, and often required, in bathrooms. They may be wired to a separate switch, to a timer, or to operate in conjunction with the principal bathroom lighting fixture. Bathroom exhaust fans are usually ceiling-mounted at a central location in the room; they should be equipped with an automatic damper that closes when the unit is not in operation. A vent fan can be installed alone, but several kinds of combination units can be obtained. These units combine a fan with one or more infrared or ultraviolet lamps, a lighting fixture, a radiant or forced-air heating unit, or some combination of these. Suitable control units are included as necessary; heatlamps and sunlamps, for example, generally are activated by a timer switch. There are many different models available, and most of them can be installed with relative ease. NuTone is a leader in the field and Fasco has an excellent line.

Exhaust fans are rated in two respects—the amount of air they can remove in a minute and the amount of noise they make in doing it.

For a 5-by-8-foot bathroom, a fan rated at 50 or 60 cubic feet per minute (CFM) is quite adequate. Whatever the size of your bathroom, the exhaust fan should be capable of completely changing the air approximately eight times every hour. To figure the CFM rating you need, determine the volume of air in your bathroom by multiplying together the length, width, and height of the bathroom. Then multiply the result by 8. This gives you the total volume of air that must be moved every 60 minutes. Divide by 60 to determine the amount of air that must be exchanged each minute. You should get a fan with a CFM rating of at least that number. Standard fans range from 50 to 100 CFM.

The amount of noise a fan makes while operating depends on the mechanical design of the unit and on the materials from which its components are made. The loudness is rated in sones. A fan rated at 2.5 sones is very quiet; a light hum is all you'll hear. One rated at 6.5 sones is relatively noisy; in fact, many people find 6.5 sones uncomfortable. You can expect to pay more for an exhaust fan with a low sone rating.

Comfort Heaters

Comfort heaters generally are installed in a bathroom either to provide immediate and temporary local heat for comfort while bathing or dressing, or for thermostatically controlled permanent area heating. Unit heaters are readily available for both purposes. Fasco and NuTone make ceiling-mounted radiant or forced-air units for temporary heating. Units are also made for wall installations; most of these are the low-volume forced-air type, and care should be taken with the positioning of the units so that they are clear from all combustibles and there is no danger of people being burned. Also, Emerson-Chromalox manufactures a line of electric

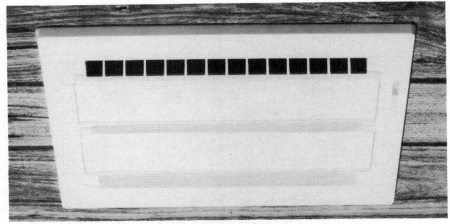

NuTone Quiettest fan. Approx. retail price: $68.00

NuTone Heat-A-Ventlite. Approx. retail price: $119.00

baseboard heating units for permanent area heating, as well as other types suitable for bathroom applications.

Skylights

Skylights and similar kinds of roof glazing are problematic from several standpoints—leakage, heat loss, excessive heat gain, fading from direct sunlight, inconvenient cleaning and maintenance, and installation difficulties that may include structural problems in large units. However, skylights and roof glazing make exciting and dramatic additions to overall bathroom decor, and if properly chosen, and correctly positioned, and installed, they can be trouble-free and enjoyable.

Skylights are obtainable in a variety of sizes, shapes, and styles from many manufacturers. They may be flat or domed, fixed or openable, and glazed with either glass or various sorts of clear, reflective, or tinted plastic. Plastic is the more commonly-used material because it is less subject to breakage, but it is also more susceptible to clouding and scratching over a period of time. Domed skylights are partially self-cleaning on the outside from the effects of rain and are somewhat easier to maintain than the flat style. Double glazing is offered for heat-loss problems and also to reduce the possibility of condensation. For soft lighting, a translucent plastic panel can be fitted below the skylight, with light-ing fixtures between. The effect is a luminous panel installation by day or by night. Ventarama Skylight produces a full line of weathertight skylights, and Wasco's new Sky-window units are designed for do-it-yourself installation.

Velux-America takes a somewhat different approach with their Roof Windows, which are designed to be installed directly in a pitched roof. As opposed to operable skylights, Roof Windows are actually specially-designed openable windows that rotate 180 degrees for easy cleaning on either side. Special ventilation flaps and a series of accessories including awnings, screens, venetian blinds, and remote control opening operators are available for them.

Wasco Model GA Skywindow. Approx. retail price: $240.00

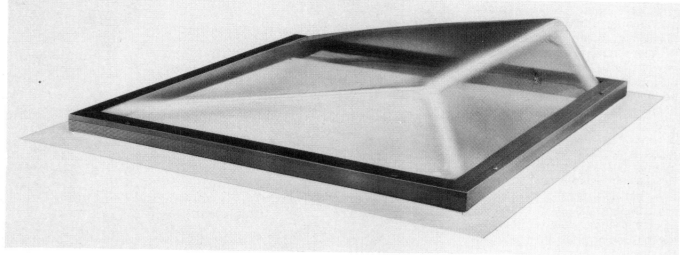

Wasco Model DA Skywindow. Approx. retail price: $200.00

Maintenance And Repair

A certain amount of repair work in any bathroom is inevitable, and refinishing or refurbishing is often desirable in an older bathroom, either piecemeal upon need or as part of a rejuvenation program. In fact, judicious repair and refinishing often can obviate the need for buying new equipment and thereby save you a considerable amount of money.

Nearly all tired mechanical apparatus that is found in a bathroom can be repaired by the replacement of minor operating parts, provided that the fixture or equipment is not too far gone to salvage. Faucet assemblies are a good case in point. Several manufacturers make complete lines of faucet stems or cartridges that are easily installed and will quickly bring an old faucet ensemble back to like-new operation. Stem Search, for instance, offers a complete line for do-it-yourself repair work, and Wrightway Manufacturing makes a vast assortment of stems and also a large selection of faucet seats, washers, O-rings, and even a line of replacement faucet handles. The faucet bodies themselves can be refinished at local metal-plating firms.

Various parts also are widely available for reworking old or malfunctioning toilets. Provided that the china bowl is intact, practically anything else can be fixed or replaced. New china water tanks can be obtained, and Universal-Rundle offers a plastic replacement tank that eliminates condensation on the outside. New hardware of various types is available, and so are the internal flushing mechanisms. Fillpro (JH Industries) is a leader in this field and, among other items, the company makes valve assemblies that completely replace troublesome old float ball and rod mechanisms. For those who are interested in conserving water, the

Conservation Products Multi-Flush flapper tank ball. Approx. retail price: $3.49

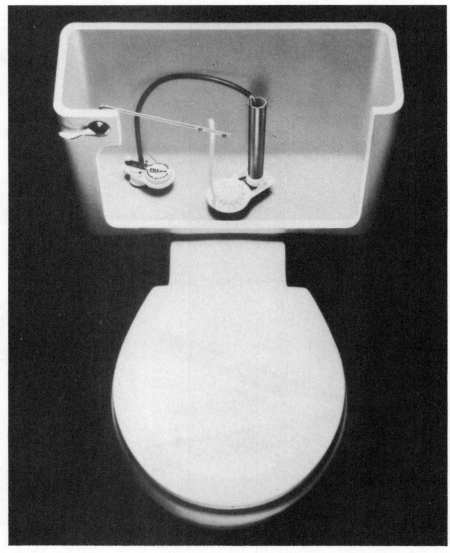

Fillpro Flap Jack Flapper. Approx. retail price: $1.59 (tank ball), $5.89 (valve)

Klenk's tub and tile epoxy.
Approx. retail price: $6.99/pint

Model 1000 Multi-Flush flapper tank ball by Conservation Products is an excellent choice.

Refinishing by means of an applied liquid finish is commonplace; we do this all the time by painting woodwork or walls, redoing ceilings or perhaps spray-painting tired lighting fixtures. New products now make it possible to extend this concept to bathroom fixtures and even ceramic tile. For example, Klenk's Epoxy Enamel Tub & Tile Finish can be applied to lavatory basins, tubs, toilets and also to ceramic tile, walls, woodwork, appliances and practically anything else. The enamel can be rolled, brushed or sprayed on, and the result is a tough, durable porcelain-like finish. The surface is not, however, as hard or long-lasting as an original vitreous china or ceramic glaze finish.

Another possibility along these lines is the Renew-A-Tub kit offered by Spectrodyne Industries. The kit, available with or without a spray gun, includes all necessary equipment and supplies to recoat a conventional bathtub, and the resulting hard, glossy surface is quite satisfactory. Keeping these finishes in prime condition requires that the fixture be correctly cleaned on a weekly basis and otherwise handled and used properly to prevent damage. Minor nicks and scratches in porcelain finishes on fixtures in otherwise good condition can easily be fixed with the aid of an inexpensive porcelain-enamel touch-up kit, such as one of those available from K.I.T. Industries.

The best approach to resurfacing a bathroom fixture, which includes repairing nicks, scratches, and chips, is to have a professional reglazing job done. This is by far the best way to restore an antique bathtub or basin, and is also an excellent way to avoid shelling out a substantial sum to have an existing alcove bathtub replaced. Lectroglaz is one company that does this kind of work; they have a network of dealers all over the country. Check the Yellow Pages under "Porcelain Enamel Repairing & Refinishing" or Bathtubs—Refinishing."

The reglazing process is a matter of applying a new glaze to the old surface by using special materials and techniques. This can be done to bathtubs, lavatory basins, toilets, or ceramic tile. While tubs, lavatories, and tile are done in the home, toilets must be done in-shop where the necessary facilities are located.

Tub and lavatory refinished with Spectrodyne Renew-A-Tub kit. Approx. retail price: $70.00 (materials only)

The process works well for all fixtures, but it is most economically feasible for tubs and tile, and less so for lavatories and toilets unless there is a particular reason for keeping the original fixture. You can probably buy a new lavatory or toilet, including installation, for what it would cost to have the fixture reglazed; an additional drawback to reglazing a toilet is that the fixture must afterwards be kept exceptionally clean at all times to avoid eventual deterioration of the finish. Lectroglaz guarantees its glazing work for one year, and the cost is reasonable. Reglazing a tub runs less than $300, as opposed to a tab of $2000 to $3000 for a complete new professionally-done tub installation. Other companies, such as Kott Koatings, offer similar services. In most cases, custom colors can be made up to specifications, and color-matching to other fixtures or finishes can also be accomplished.

Another area that sometimes needs attention, either in repair work or when replacing fixtures, lies with the drains, traps and necessary connection fittings and pipes. Except in unusual circumstances, this material all falls into several common categories of sizes, configurations and dimensions, and the parts for readily obtainable practically anywhere. Larden Plastics, for instance, produces the Grabber line of lavatory hook-up kits that features special fittings and polybutylene tubing to make do-it-yourself lavatory connections a snap. Genova offers a line of polybutylene lavatory riser kits, as well as a full line of virtually indestructable polypropylene traps. These and Genova's other home plumbing products are specifically geared to the do-it-yourselfer and come complete with detailed instructions to cover numerous installation situations. Qest Products also has an excellent line of polybutylene tubing and Celcon plastic fittings and adapters for fast, easy, foolproof plumbing hook-ups of all kinds. Chrome-plated brass traps, bends, tailpieces and associated hardware, as well as PVC and ABS plastic items, are available from

Town & Country Products. Chicago Specialty offers brass tubular drain system parts and hardware, as well as other plumbing repair parts, of high quality and sufficient range to cover just about any repair or replacement job. This line is aimed particularly at the do-it-yourselfer, and the company also has helpful how-to books on various aspects of plumbing repair and installation.

Paint And Varnish

Applied finishes are liquids that are used to coat a surface in order to provide a decorative effect, and to seal and protect that surface. They include primers, sealers, paints, oils, stains, varnishes, and other assorted synthetic finishes. The type of applied finish that you choose depends upon the conditions to which the finish will be subjected, and the kind of surface to which the finish will be applied. Applied finishes should be carefully chosen for bathrooms so that the resulting surface will be durable, mildew-resistant, easy to clean, and either moisture-resistant or moisture-proof. There are several applied finishes that will do a good job.

Paint is perhaps the most popular and commonly used finish in bathrooms because it is easy to apply, inexpensive, the job can be done by the homeowner, and redecorating at a later date is simple. There are several good choices for bathroom walls and ceilings of plaster and wallboard. Alkyd enamel (oil-based) is an excellent choice and will give best results. Interior latex or rubber-base paint, both of which are thinned and cleaned up with water, also work well. These paints can be applied over the old finishes or other surfaces, such as wallpaper or paneling. Be sure to check specific manufacturers' recommendations and application procedures and always use the proper primer or undercoat. Other possibilities for bathroom walls and ceilings include polyurethane enamels and epoxy paints. These paints afford an excellent finish if properly applied, but they must be used with compatible primers and cannot be

applied to all kinds of surfaces; check the manufacturer's recommendations for the specific paint and application in question.

All of these paints can also be applied on wood surfaces, including walls and trimwork, but should not be used upon wood flooring. There are other possibilities for woodwork, too. Transparent, semitransparent, or solid-body stains of oil, alcohol, or water base can be used, but should be covered with one or two coats of a clear hard finish. Natural wood should also be coated with a clear finish. Interior varnish, polyurethane varnish, and clear urethane make good topcoats.

Wood floors should be painted with porch/deck/floor enamel or a polyurethane enamel; note that the latter might not be compatible with some old finishes. Several kinds of stains and oil finishes can be applied, and in most cases these should be covered with a clear top coat of exterior spar varnish, polyurethane varnish, or clear urethane. Natural floors can be finished with the same materials.

Bathroom finishes can be high-gloss, which is easiest to clean but also very reflective and tends to chip easily. A semigloss finish, is probably the best all-around compromise. Flat finishes are unsatisfactory because they mark easily and will not withstand scrubbing. Floor finishes should not be slippery, especially when wet. Colors, shades, and tones can all be custom-mixed at any good paint store. Always check the manufacturers' recommendations for application. Purchase only top name-brand applied finishes from reputable dealers who will stand behind their products and who are willing to give you help and advice in their use. There are many major manufacturers of complete paint lines whose recommendations and products you can trust; Benjamin Moore, Martin Senour, Devoe, Pittsburgh, Komac, DuPont, Sherwin Williams and Glidden are just a few of these. Watco, DuPont, and Nasco make excellent floor-finishing products and Olympic and Cabot are good names in stains.

Directory Of Manufacturers

A

A&L Fabricating Co.
Hwy. M-26
Dollar Bay, MI 49922

Abitibi Corp.
Building Products Div.
3250 Big Beaver Rd.
Troy, MI 48084

Academy Manufacturing Co., Inc.
1519 W. 132nd St.
Gardena, CA 90249

AFCO Industries, Inc.
9999 Richmond Ave., Suite 150
Houston, TX 77042

Alsons Corp.
see Flo Products Division

American Biltrite, Inc.
see Amtico Flooring Division

American Olean Tile Co.
Executive Offices
Lansdale, PA 19446

American Shower Door Co., Inc.
3401 Exposition Blvd.
Santa Monica, CA 90406

American Standard Inc.
U.S. Plumbing Products
P.O. Box 2003
New Brunswick, NJ 08903

Ampco Products, Inc.
7797 W. 20th Ave.
Hialeah, FL 33014

Amtico Flooring Division
American Biltrite, Inc.
Amtico Square
Trenton, NJ 08607

Aqua Stream
Div. of Scott & Fetzer Co.
821 Sharon Dr.
Westlake, OH 44145

The Aqua-Tainer Co.
320 Railroad St.
Joliet, IL 60436

Armstrong Cork Co.
Consumer Services
Lancaster, PA 17604

Artesian Industries
Plumbing Products Div.
Mansfield, OH 44901

Arundale, Inc.
1173 Reco Ave.
St. Louis, MO 63126

Associated Mills Inc.
209 S. Jefferson
Chicago, IL 60606

Aster Products
1400 Willow Ave.
Melrose Park, PA 19126

Azrock Floor Products
P.O. Box 531
San Antonio, TX 78292

B

B&M Manufacturing Co.
1801 2nd St. Pike
Richboro, PA 18954

Bangkok Industries
1900 S. 20th St.
Philadelphia, PA 19145

Bathroom Jewelry Inc.
1888 S. Sepulveda Blvd.
Los Angeles, CA 90025

Belwood Vanities
P.O. Drawer A
Ackerman, MS 39735

Bio-Systems Toilets
  Corp., Ltd.
Box 539
Hawkesbury, Ont.
Canada K6A 2GB

Wayne Boren Corp.
4960 Cranswick
Houston, TX 77040

Borg Textiles
Suite 1900
233 N. Michigan Ave.
Chicago, IL 60601

Boro Industries, Inc.
2901 Stanley
Fort Worth, TX 76110

Bowles Fluidics Corp.
9347 Fraser Ave.
Silver Spring, MD 20910

Bradley Corp.
Faucet & Special Products Div.
P.O. Box 348
Menomonee Falls, WI 53051

The Brearley Co.
2107 Kishwaukee St.
Rockford, IL 61101

Bufalini Marble Corp.
4 West 56th St.
New York, NY 10019

C

California Cooperage
850 Capitolio Way
Suite E
San Luis Obispo, CA 93401

Celanese Corp.
1211-T Avenue of the Americas
New York, NY 10036

Chemcraft, Inc.
1520 Adams St.
Elkhart, IN 56514

Chicago Specialty
  Manufacturing Co.
7500 N. Linder
Skokie, IL 60076

Chromalloy, Ampco Div.
P.O. Box 608
Rosedale, MS 38769

Clivus Multrum USA, Inc.
14A Eliot St.
Cambridge, MA 02138

The Commodore Vanity Co.
7735 Kester Ave.
Van Nuys, CA 91405

Congoleum
195 Belgrove Dr.
Kearny, NJ 07032

Connor Forest Ind.
P.O. Box 847
Wausau, WI 54401

Conservation Products Corp.
435 Crossen Ave.
Elk Grove Village, IL 60007

Corl Corp.
500 Commerce Bldg.
Fort Wayne, IN 46802

Crane Co.
300 Park Ave.
New York, NY 10022

D

Dallas Ceramic Co.
7834 C.F. Hawn Frwy.
Dallas, TX 75217

Dal-Tile
see Dallas Ceramic Co.

Dazey Products Co.
One Dazey Circle
Johnson County Ind. Airport
Industrial Airport, KS 66031

The Decro-Wall Corp.
375 Executive Blvd.
Elmsford, NY 10523

Delta Faucet Co.
931 E. 86th St.
Indianapolis, IN 46240

Diller Corp.
6126-T Madison Ct.
Morton Grove, IL 60053

Diston Industries, Inc.
3293 E. 11th Ave.
Hialeah, FL 33013

E.I. DuPont de Nemours
   & Co., Inc.
"Corian" Products
Wilmington, DE 19898

E

Eljer Plumbingware
3 Gateway Ctr.
Pittsburgh, PA 15222

Elmer's Product Information
   Center (Borden)
P.O. Box 157
Hilliard, OH 43026

Emerso Chromalox Div.
Emerson Electric Co.
8106 Florissant St.
St. Louis, MO 63136

F

Fasco Industries, Inc.
P.O. Box 150
Fayetteville, NC 28302

Fillpro Div.
JH Industries
1712-F Newport Circle
Santa Ana, CA 92705

Flexco
see Textile Rubber Co.

Flintkote
see National Floor Products

Flo Products Division
Alsons Corp.
P.O. Box 311
Covina, CA 91723

Formica Corp.
120 E. Fourth St.
Cincinnati, OH 45232

Franciscan Tile
see Interpace Corp.

Frohock Stewart, Inc.
455 Whitney Ave.
Northboro, MA 01532

G

GAF Building Materials Group,
   Floor Products
140 N. 51st St.
New York, NY 10020

General Bathroom Products Corp.
2201 Touhy Ave.
Elk Grove Village, IL 60007

General Electric Co.
Laminated & Insulating
   Materials
Business Dept.
10 Plastics Ave.
Coshocton, OH 43812

General Marble Corp.
9146 E. 9th St.
Cucamonga, CA 91730

Genova
7034 E. Court St.
Davison, MI 48423

Georgia Pacific
900 SW Fifth Ave.
Portland, OR 97204

Geringer & Sons Mfg. Co.
A Lightron Co.
Peekskill, NY 10566

Gold Bond Building Products
Div. of National Gypsum Co.
325 Delaware Ave.
Buffalo, NY 14202

Grant Water-X Corp.
1010 Washington Blvd.
Stanford, CT 06904

H

Hartco
see Tibbals Flooring Co.

Hastings Tile
410 Lakeville Rd.
Lake Success, NY 11040

Heads Up, Inc.
3201 W. MacArthur Blvd.
Santa Ana, CA 92704

H.G.E., Inc.
7626 Varna Ave.
North Hollywood, CA 91605

Hoyne Industries, Inc.
East Tower
Suite 825
Rolling Meadows, IL 60008

I

Il Bagno Collection
see Hastings Tile

Interbath, Inc.
427 N. Baldwin Park Blvd.
City of Industry, CA 91746

Interpace Corp.
2901 Los Feliz Blvd.
Los Angeles, CA 90039

J

Jacuzzi Whirlpool Bath, Inc.
298 N. Wiget Lane
P.O. Drawer J
Walnut Creek, CA 94596

K

Kinkead
U.S. Gypsum
101 S. Wacker Dr.
Chicago, IL 60606

K.I.T. Industries
Burlington Ave. & Cooper St.
Delanco, NJ 08075

Klenk's
Zynolite Products
15700 So. Avalon Blvd.
Compton, CA 90224

Kohler Co.
Kohler, WI 53044

Kohler McLister Paint Co.
Box 546
Denver, CO 80236

Komac
see Kohler McLister Paint Co.

Kott Koatings
Paralta Drive
Suite K-12
Laguna Hills, CA 92653

L

Larden Plastics Co.
Div. of Bristol Products, Inc.
Davisburg, MI 48019

Lectroglaz
4022 W. Armitage Ave.
Chicago, IL 60639

Lifestyle of California
2260 Sheridan Rd.
Zion, IL 60099

Lifetime Faucets, Inc.
Box 171231
Memphis, TN 38117

Lightolier, Inc.
346 Claremont Ave.
Jersey City, NJ 07305

Lippert Corp.
Molded Marble Div.
W142 N8999 Fountain Blvd.
Menomonee Falls, WI 53051

Lyons Industries, Inc.
107 Beeson St.
Dowagiac, MI 49047

M

Marlite
Masonite Corp.
Home Improvement Div.
29 N. Wacker Dr.
Chicago, IL 60606

McPherson, Inc.
P.O. Box 15133
Tampa, FL 33614

Memphis Hardwood Flooring Co.
1551 Thomas
Memphis, TN 38107

Metos Sauna, Inc.
Amerec Corp.
P.O. Box 3825
Bellevue, WA 98005

Miami Carey
203 Garver Rd.
Monroe, OH 45050

Micarta
see Westinghouse Electric Corp.

Microphor, Inc.
P.O. Box 490
Willits, CA 95490

Middlefield Corp.
P.O. Box 795
Middlefield, OH 44062

Moen
Div. of Stanadyne
377 Woodland Ave.
Elyria, OH 44035

Monarch Metal Products Corp.
1901 Estes Ave.
Elk Grove Village, IL 60007

Montgomery Ward & Co., Inc.
618 W. Chicago Ave.
Chicago, IL 60607

Mullbank
see Thornton Gore Ent.

N

Nafco
see National Floor Products

Nasco
National Solvent Co.
955 W. Smith Rd.
Medina, OH 44256

National Floor Products
P.O. Box 354-A
Florence, AL 35630

Novi American Inc.
40200 Grand River Rd.
Novi, MI 48050

NuTone
Div. of Scovill
Madison & Red Bank Rds.
Cincinnati, OH 45227

O

Owens Corning Fiberglas
Fiberglas Tower
Toledo, OH 43659

P

Perma-Bilt Ind.
19306 S. Normandie Ave.
Torrance, CA 90502

Permagrain Products, Inc.
22 W. State St.
Media, PA 19063

Pinta's Cultured Marble Inc.
5859 W. 117th Pl.
Worth, IL 60482

Plaskolite, Inc.
1770 Joyce Ave.
Columbus, OH 43216

Portrait Kitchens, Inc.
185 Norman St.
Rochester, NY 14613

Potlatch Corp.
Wood Products Div.
P.O. Box 916
Stuttgart, AR 72160

Prestigeline Inc.
P.O. Box 417
5 Inez Dr.
Brentwood, NY 11717

Pryde, Inc.
3517 Cardiff Ave.
Cincinnati, OH 45209

Q

Qest Products, Inc.
P.O. Box 1746
Elkhart, IN 46515

R

Real Wood Products
3240 Olympic
Springfield, OR 97477

Riviera Spa Corp.
11735 Sheldon St.
Sun Valley, CA 91352

Rusco American Bidet Corp.
3000 N. San Fernando Blvd.
Burbank, CA 91504

S

Santerra Industries Ltd.
1018 Alness St.
Downsview, Ont.
Canada M3J 2J1

Sears, Roebuck and Co.
Sears Tower
Chicago, IL 60684

Sherwin Williams
101 Prospect Ave., NW
Cleveland, OH 44101

Spectrodyne Industries
2005 N. Keystone Ave.
Chicago, IL 60641

Stanadyne, Inc.
Consumer Product Div.
377 Woodland Ave.
Elyria, OH 44035

Stem Search, Inc.
1603 W. 135th St.
Gardena, CA 90249

The Swan Corp.
408 Olive St.
St. Louis, MO 63102

T

Teledyne Water Pik
1730 E. Prospect St.
Fort Collins, CO 80521

Textile Rubber Co.
P.O. Box 553
Tuscumbia, AL 35674

Textolite
see General Electric Co.

Thomas Industries, Inc.
207 E. Broadway
Louisville, KY 40202

Thornton Gore Ent.
Box HED
Compton, NH 03223

Tibbals Flooring Co.
P.O. Drawer A
Oneida, TN 37841

Tile Council of America, Inc.
P.O. Box 2222
Princeton, NJ 08540

Town & Country Plumbing
   Products
A Division of Dearborn Brass
Box 1388
Cedar Rapids, IA 52406

Tub-Master Corp.
413 Virginia Dr.
Orlando, FL 32803

U

U.S. Brass
Wallace Murray Corp.
901 10th St.
Plano, TX 75074

U.S. Plywood
Champion Building Products
P.O. Box 61
New York, NY 10046

Universal-Rundle Corp.
217 No. Mill St.
New Castle, PA 16103

V

Val-U-Bath
see Williams Division of Leigh
   Products

Velux-America
78 Cummings Park
Woburn, MA 01801

Ventarama Skylight Corp.
40 Haven Ave.
Port Washington, NY 11050

Viking Sauna Co.
909 Park Ave.
San Jose, CA 95150

VitaMaster Industries, Inc.
455 Smith St.
Brooklyn, NY 11231

W

Wards
see Montgomery Ward & Co., Inc.

Wasco Products, Inc.
P.O. Box 351
Sanford, ME 04073

Watco-Dennis Corp.
1756 22nd St.
Santa Monica, CA 90404

Waugh
4130 N. Canal
Jacksonville, FL 32209

Westinghouse Electric Corp.
Industrial Plastics Div.
1585 Lebanon School Rd.
West Miflin, PA 15122

Williams Division
   of Leigh Products
1536 Grant St.
Elkhart, IN 46515

Wilsonart Laminated Plastic
Ralph Wilson Plastics Co.
600 General Bruce Dr.
Temple, TX 76501

Wrightway Manufacturing Co.
1050 Central Ave.
Park Forest South, IL 60466

Z

Z-Brick
UMC Corp.
P.O. Box 628
Woodinville, WA 98072

Index